PAST, PRESENT, AND FUTURE

IRWIN C. LIEB

PAST, PRESENT, AND FUTURE

A PHILOSOPHICAL ESSAY ABOUT TIME

UNIVERSITY OF ILLINOIS PRESS

URBANA AND CHICAGO

Library of Congress Cataloging-in-Publication Data

Lieb, Irwin C.
    Past, present, and future : a philosophical essay about time /
Irwin C. Lieb.
        p.   cm.
    Includes index.
    ISBN 0-252-01804-4 (cloth : alk. paper).—ISBN 0-252-06182-9 (paper : alk. paper)
    1. Time.   I. Title.
BD638 L48 1991
115—dc20   90-20259

For Michael and Gordon Lieb

who often wondered why it was taking me
so long to think about time

CONTENTS

CHAPTER ONE

INTRODUCTION

THIS ESSAY is about time: the past, the present, and the future. It is also about the things that are in time. Its main ideas are that time is fundamentally real and that it passes not, as Newton said, "of itself, and from its own nature" but because of the things that are in time. Time and the things that are in time cannot be separated from one another. Because they are uneasily inside of one another the future becomes present, the present is the time of action, and things come finally to be past. In this essay, the things that are in time are called *individuals*. They cause the division into past, present, and future time. In turn, the time that is inside individuals in the present provokes, dimensions, and closes their activity.

The most helpful introduction I can give to these ideas is to say what led me to think of the need for them, to describe how they were constructed, and to explain what I have tried to do with them.

What occurred to me first—though the impression grew over a long period of time—was that ideas about time have dominated our thought in the last hundred years or so. I saw them in relativity theory; in biological and geological theories of evolution, in history, in psychiatry, and in research on human development and learning; and in modal logic, in linguistic studies of tense, and in hermeneutics. I came to see time's prominence in new ideas in business, industry, and politics: work by the hour; the speed of communications; concerns for the birth, growth, and aging of cities; the development of economies and nations; and the tides of revolution and the ending of empires. Time is also prominent in our concern for an aging population; for retirement and leisure; for arts and films; for changes of fashion, sports and transportation; and, of course, for calendars, clocks, alarms, and schedules. It seemed to me that time was everywhere. I saw it all the time, heard about it all the time and, like everyone else, when I talked about it, I fell into puns and paradoxes. This, too, seemed to me significant.

I came to realize, however, that even though time has been prominent in our recent thought, not all our ideas about it, perhaps not even the most important of them, are recent or new. Through the ages, there have been fine philosophical and scientific conceptions of time. Many of our deepest feelings have been about it, about the transience of life; about foolishness and wisdom; tradition and hope; creation and redemption; and eternity, heaven, and hell.

I wondered how our thoughts and our feelings, both recent and inherited, could be ordered and arranged. I thought that if they were ordered we would understand them better and that our feelings might be made finer and more informed. Many of our ideas are obviously related, but some of them are not compatible with others; some are isolated, and some have seemed to me wrong, though almost never simply so.

The issue was not to place all ideas, all formulations, in a neat array. I was not concerned to set them into columns under general and specific themes or to find some other formal arrangement for them. There would, no doubt, be some good in that, but there would not be much understanding. I wanted what is called a philosophical understanding of time. I hoped that, because of its basic questions, such a philosophy would widen or deepen our other understandings. So I thought of developing a philosophy that takes account of what has been thought and felt about time, but I wanted it to be more than a genial review of what we already know, even in philosophy.

What more should it be? Not, I thought, a generalization of the ideas in one or several of the sciences, nor a general formulation of even the most profound of our feelings and attitudes. Philosophy has its own questions. As leading questions do, these order what we know. The most basic questions in philosophy are about the reality of things, so the leading question for me became the reality of time. What kind of reality is time? What kind of reality does it have? In addition, it seemed to me equally important to ask about the reality of individuals, for time and individuals, I came to think, are inseparable. The two have to be understood together; neither can be understood alone.

What are the relevant questions about the reality of time and individuals? Everything is real: persons, animals, and things are real; minds, ideas, dreams, and shadows are real; even appearances are real. Individuals and time are also real. Because everything is real, being real is not a distinctive mark of anything, so how does knowing that time is real help us understand it and order and understand more of what we already know about it? The answer is that the distinction we need is not between what is and is not real but between kinds of reality. *Everything* is real, but things are real in different ways; there are different kinds of realities or differences between the kinds of reality. The questions for this essay, then, are what kinds of realities are time and individuals or what kinds of reality do they have?

The most revealing grand division among realities is between those that are fundamental and those that are derived from the fundamental ones. Appearances, dreams, and shadows are derivative realities. They are appearances, dreams, and shadows *of* something. They can not exist by themselves; what they really are cannot be understood without referring to something else. There may also be realities derived from the (first) derivative realities. Plato, for example, says that a picture of a bed is at a third remove from reality: there is the picture, the bed itself, and the even more real idea of bed. There may be many forms of derivation. Whatever they are—creation, causation, appearance, imitation, participation, or prehension—a derivative reality owes its reality to one or more realities that are as basic or more basic than itself. A fundamental reality, however, does not derive from other realities. It can be by itself and be understood in itself. If there is more than one underived reality, if there must be more than one, the several realities will exist together; they must be together in some way. They must also derive some of their features from one another, which is a reason for thinking that there is more than one of them. Still, if each is a fundamental reality, it is not itself derived from something else.

What is the reality of time? The major opinion in the history of both Western and Eastern thought is that time, or the time that measures change, is a derivative reality: it is an image or appearance of something that does not change. It is an aspect of things, a measure of their motions or other changes, a form for our experience, or a set of distinctive relations that hold between the objects we experience.

There have been a few exceptions to the tradition. Those who preceded it had a different view, of course. Heraclitus, for example, says that the whole of things is like an ever-living fire. The most notable exception in the modern period is Newton. He claims that time and space are fundamentally real and that, because they are, there are temporal and spatial relations between the things that are in space and time. More recently, Bergson, some of the pragmatists, and those who think that process is fundamental have been exceptions. They, too, think that time, or something like it, is either fundamental or at least more real than most philosophers have supposed.

In this essay I claim that time is a fundamental reality. Time is not derived from anything else and its reality is most evident in the continuous passing in everything that moves, changes, lasts, or even remains the same. The claim, however, is not simply that individuals move and change and last but that the passing that occurs in individuals is time itself. Time is a part of the things that are in time, and its passing inside them continually provokes them to act. Time must, of course, be shown to have this reality. It also must be shown—this will be a part of the argument for time's reality—that notions of time as a derived reality are either not sound or not complete. In my opinion, the so-called derivations suffer from one or the other of these two defects: either the derivations cannot be explained at all, or those that can be explained and can be thought to have to do with time derive their most important character from time itself, so that time is presupposed in showing that it is derived.

For example, think of Plato's idea that time is the moving image of eternity or of the idea that time is in some other way the appearance of some unchanging thing. These ideas characterize time as real only in the way that an image or an appearance is real, as revealing something more real than itself. The final rationale for these ideas is that there is one fundamental reality and that everything else owes its own reality to it. Everything else is connected with it as an instance, image, or appearance of it. Time, on this account, is the changing appearance of a reality that does not change. This probably should be interpreted to mean not that time is itself an instance of the first reality but that it is a motion common to all the images and appearances and that, in connection with them, it is also significant, perhaps of an order that the images must have. Time would then be not a changing image but a certain changing of the images or the appearances of the preeminent reality.

The obvious question about this theme is what makes the images or the appearances move. Plato's answer is that the motion is not caused by the preeminent reality. It is caused by something *entirely* different, something he calls *the flux,* which is constantly moving and in which the images or appearances are embedded. Plato says that the flux is not real, but he means only that the flux is not an instance of the preeminent reality; it does not share its nature. He does not mean that the flux has no existence or being or that, in connection with images, it cannot be significant. There is an uncertain distinction in Plato between what is real and what otherwise *is*. The real, Plato thinks, *is*—and is without change; other realities merely participate in it. The flux, however, is a different kind of *is,* and it causes the motion of the things that are embedded in it. The flux, therefore, has some substantiality. It is the same as a moving but ever-present time, or it is like such a time, and that time is not derived from another being or even, on Plato's account, from a preeminent reality. Such significance as it has may be derived—so one can think of it partly as a moving image—but its significance is not the whole of it. It has an underlying being of its own. The claim, then, that time is through and through a version of something else has not been proved. There is no thorough derivation of passing time, even in Plato's profound view.

There is a variant of Plato's view, explicit in Aristotle, that has often been urged in recent times. Aristotle says that time is motion, without saying what motion it is, or that time is a measure of motion, and that is what most moderns seem to think. They suppose that time is or has to do with certain relations between the motions and changes of things, with "before" and "after" and with duration. Substances are the prominent realities. They move and change, and we develop clocks to measure these motions and changes. Perhaps not all our requirements for clocks can be met or be known to have been met—the motion of good clocks should be continuous, steady, and independent of all other motions or at least the ones they are to measure—still, on this view, time has to do with clocks. There is nothing true of time apart from the motions and changes of things and the clocks that measure them. There is nothing above or beneath them that might be called time itself.

Though there have been many elaborations in this view, it is probably the simplest view that one can have of time, and it is not wrong. It is, however, incomplete. There is a motion that it neglects, that cannot be measured, and this motion gives the distinctive temporal meaning to the terms "before" and "after." This is the *motion* in which things are continuously contemporaneous. You and I continue to be contemporaries no matter how quickly or slowly either of us moves or changes. Clocks measure only comparative motions, motions that are at the same rate or faster or slower than one another. They do not measure the time in which we continue to exist, whatever the rate at which we move or change, and it is that time to which we refer when we think of things occurring before and after one another. It may be true that when things go quickly or slowly the rates of certain other motions are themselves changed. There will seem to be puzzles about this point if it seems that the rates do not change but that time is distended with different rates of speed—but, no matter how quickly or slowly they move, contemporaries remain contemporaries if they continue to exist, and we have to wonder why this is so.

The answer is that the things that continue to be contemporaries when they move or change are in the same time and that time is also in them. If there were a separate time for each thing and for each of its motions, it would either be a coincidence that things are contemporary or there would be no way of knowing when they are. Having things be continually contemporary is too invariable a fact of our experience to be a coincidence. There must therefore be something that makes for these coordinations, something continuous, steady, and independent of other motions, and this can be called time itself. Something has been left out, then, in saying that time is only a measure of motions, that it is nothing more than what good clocks say. What is left out is the condition for there being measurable motions, and that condition is underived; it is time itself. If time were only a measure and a set of relations, it would be a derivative reality, yet its derivation would depend on a time that is not derived or on something like a time. And what should be said about that time? We should say, as Newton does, that things are *in* time. We should, however, also say that time is *in* the things themselves and *in* their relations to one another. We should say both, and we will see why later on.

There are comparable issues for the other, perhaps for all other, accounts of time as a derivative reality. The derivation cannot be set out, or it may take a kind of time, or it presupposes a kind of time on which the derivative is imposed. In all such cases, we must appeal to a time that is not derived to explain how another kind of time comes to be derived—but then we have not given an account of the more basic reality of time.

Most of the problems in the derivations stem from issues about the distinction and the connection between time and the things that are in time. To eliminate the difficulties and to develop a notion of time's fundamental reality, it seems to me that, from the start and throughout, time and the things in time should be considered together. If time is a fundamental reality, individuals are also a fundamental reality. Neither time nor individuals are derived from anything else, but each of them affects the other. Their affecting each other explains why time passes in the present but not in the future and the past, why individuals come to be present, why they must change and act, and why they become past. My general notion is that we can not understand very much about time and the things in time if we suppose that either of them is a derivative reality. On the other hand, if we think of them both as fundamental and as affecting each other we can set out all their general characters. This is my aim in this essay.

The construction of its concepts and arguments verges now and then toward very austere abstractions. Sometimes the abstractions are so barely accessible that they must be understood through metaphors. This happens in all philosophies, but it happens often in philosophies about time. This is because notions about time are very deep in our thought and language—there is, for example, the idea that everything is somehow in time—and when we try to formulate different ideas about time, our language and the images it suggests cast onto the new ideas the meanings of the older ones, and we fumble into unintended pun and paradox.

Can we, for example, make coherent an idea of time's passing if we also suppose that whatever passes takes time to pass, so that time takes time to pass, and its passage is measured by a further time that does not pass? Can we consider that there is a past or future if we also imagine that they exist *now* and are parts of an eternal present that is not contrasted with a past or future time?

There is no ready answer to such questions; there is perhaps no final coherence for philosophic thought. New ideas are constructed through the ideas we already have. If the old ideas are very deep, as our ideas of time are, we cannot avoid feeling their effects, even though we think there may be something wrong in them. Metaphors are emphatic devices that we use on behalf of the new ideas against the effects of the older ones. They are not arguments, but by their emphasis on parts of the new ideas they weigh against the deep, persuasive images. They accompany the abstract ideas in this essay, supporting their construction and making their meanings more accessible. The austerity of the abstractions is the counterpart to the depth of our older notions. We must go far away from them; we must become abstract to loosen their hold on us. Then metaphors help to bring us back, showing how the abstractions can be applied. Even then, perhaps, there will still be shadows of the first forms in which our thoughts and language began to grow. Philosophy's poignant incoherence is owed not to a careless compilation of incompatible claims but to the ground and the growth of philosophy itself.

To stay this incoherence, to hedge the ground for it, I start this essay from two very vague commonsense ideas. They are too vague to be wrong but not so vague that they cannot serve as a start. My aim is to make the intuitions clear and to argue for them or to make them clearer by arguments. I think the little that is definite in them can be made more definite without contradicting the vaguer notions from which the clearer notions take their start.

This is a version of the principle that a philosophy should begin either with no suppositions or with only a small number of them, and then only with those that are certain. My version of the principle is that, because we cannot begin without suppositions, we should begin with suppositions that are certain, not by being self-evident but by being too vague to be wrong. The danger for a philosophy that begins this way need not be incompatibility. It will be whether meanings are well developed, whether vaguenesses remain, or, what would be worse, whether other important meanings are made obscure.

The two intuitions from which this essay starts are that each present moment is new and that there must always be new present moments; the world must go on. These are notions about novelty and necessity, the novelty of presents and the necessity for there continuing to be new ones. They are gray in imprecision. They have to be made more clear and definite. How can that be done? What methods are there for making notions clear? How will we know when they are clear enough or altogether clear?

There is no one settled or even widely approved way of making notions clear. Different methods suit different issues; one is better than another for us depending on our purposes. For the purposes of this essay, it is best simply to start discussion—to ask questions about the intuitions and to make the intuitions clearer by answering them and by giving reasons for thinking that the answers are correct. There will be more questions, and then more. Our intuitions will be made clearer by their fitting in with the many other things we think to ask and say about time and by their distinguishing and ordering our ideas and taking them further. The intuitions will have been made clear enough if we can answer every question we can think to ask about time. If even more clarity is wanted, it will not be because we have not become clear but because we sense that discussion has not yet gone far enough.

To begin, then: each and every present moment is new. There must always be new moments.

What are present moments? Are there moments that are not present? What are the differences between them? Are present moments experienced and other moments only remembered, anticipated, or imagined? Are there many present moments "now," or is there only one present at a time? Given that a present moment must be a time, is it a part of time or is it all the time there is, and must it be the time at which or in which something is? How closely connected, then, is a present moment with the thing or the things in it? Does each thing have its own present, so that there cannot be many things at the same present time? Or can there be a common present for things even though each of them is bound so closely to the present that it will not be exactly the same when it is in another time? Or are both of these somehow true?

How do new presents come about? Why do they come about? Why do they come about continually? Why do they have to come about? Why does not the world just stop? If it cannot, why not?

What happens to the old moments and what was in them when new moments come about? Do they become past? Do they pass away and cease to be? Or do they crowd into the new moments without taking up their time? Does what was in an old moment desert that moment as it passes and get itself into a new moment? Or does it have new moments come into it?

How and when do new moments come to be present? Can it take a moment for a new moment to come about? Or must a new moment become present in a present passing time, replacing the present, part by part, as it passes? Where does a new moment and what is or will be in it come from? Is a new present and what is in it just the lasting of what already was, so that nothing really new occurs? Could we get older if that were true? Could we even know that all we had done is lost if we did not have the later new thought that things are still the same as they were before?

Is it true, as it seems to be, that the things in time must always change or move? What kinds of things are they? Why, how, when, and in what ways do they change, and is their having to change connected with each moment's having to be new? How can there be any change in things if they are wholly in a present moment? Must they not have a past and a future, so that they are affected by what they were and face prospects they can bring about? Or does something else give them their possibilities? Might the things that must change not be wholly or merely in the present? Could they also somehow be ahead of the activity that occurs in the present and also beyond it, settled and past? Could they be partly future and partly past even while they are also present and active—and doesn't the necessity for their having to act and change have something to do with time's also being future and past and having implacably to pass?

More questions could easily be raised, but the ones that have been set out suggest the themes that will be prominent in this essay. They are about novelty and necessity in change. The deepest principle in the development of these themes is the classical one that it is impossible for something to arise from nothing: when something new occurs it is an extension, elaboration, creation, exfoliation, or other sort of trans-formation of something that is already real. What is new is newly transformed; its being is not new. This opaque and inescapable principle—about what can and cannot be thought and what can and cannot be—sets some of our first questions aside and cautions us about the sense of some of the others. It also tests the suggestions that arise when other questions are ordered and answered; in doing so, it is itself made more clear.

The two intuitions about the newness of moments lead to the view that individuals must reconstitute themselves in order to last. The con-ception of individuals is the most difficult notion in this essay. It is diffi-cult because it is so different from our familiar and seemingly obvious idea of "things." As the term is used here, individuals are a certain kind of *activity* in which there is always a going on. However, it is not simply that there are individuals and that they are always doing one thing or another. They are always active, they cause their own activity, but a part of their activity has not yet taken place and another part of it is already done. The part of the activity that is going on is present; the part that has not yet taken place is future; and the part that has taken place is past. This idea is expressed by saying that individuals are not wholly in the present. They are not wholly in the present because they are activities, and there could be no activity in them if their whole being were in a present time.

Many philosophers have, of course, seen that for things to change, and not just to change their positions, there must be some potentiality in them or some possibilities of change for them. They also must have definite features; these are the features that change. But then most philosophers think that potentialities are "buried inside" the things, or they think that possibilities are not in time but are "given" to things in the processes in which they change, and they think that the definite features of things are features they *have* in a present time. In my opinion, burying potentialities makes for an incoherent account of what things are when they are present. It also seems to me that the idea of giving possibilities cannot be explained and that it is a mistake to suppose that things have definite properties in the present. What we should say, I think, is that in the present things are coming to have definite properties but that when the properties become entirely definite they have already become past. Many philosophical accounts of change put too much into the present, or, seeing that something is needed to explain change and seeing that it cannot be in the present, they suppose that it is not in time at all. My opinion is that all that is needed to explain change is in time itself: some of it is in the present, the remainder in the future and the past.

As used in this essay, then, individuals, even while they are present, are also in the future and the past; they have their being in the three parts of time. What individuals make definite when they change is therefore not a possibility that has somehow been given to them; it is a part of their future being, and they make it definite partly through that part of themselves that is already definite and past. What many philosophers have either buried in a thing when it is present or conceived of as timeless possibilities are viewed in this essay as *spread out* in time. Individuals are conceived to extend from the present into the future and the past, and each state of them is different from the others.

One consequence of this conception is that individuals have no core, no form, no self that remains unchanged through different present times; there is no bottom to an individual's depth. Individuals are always changing, through and through. Their fundamental change is to reconstitute themselves. While they are present but also passing they use what is already past and definite in themselves to reconstitute themselves out of their future being. Not being confined wholly to a moment, individuals are spread through time. Time and individuals are inseparable. They are connected one to the other in different ways, making for the different parts of time. In their activity, individuals divide time into present, past, and future; time, in turn, causes, extends, and marks the close of their activity. Time and individuals cause these changes in each other. Understanding the changes will, I hope, enable us to understand many, perhaps most, of our other ideas about time and the things that are in it.

The place to begin is with the present: how we locate it, what is in it, and why and how new present moments ceaselessly occur. The present is nodal for the other parts of time. We locate the past and future by referring to it. Understanding the passage of time and the reconstitution of individuals in the present will help us see what the past and future are, how individuals become past and are, even now, extended in the future. It will also lead to our seeing that there must be a single past and a common future for the individuals that are at or in the present time.

The present provides the first focus for the questions and answers that are considered in the later chapters about the past and future. In the final section, I consider some important issues about time and value, and these lead me to talk about what is unchanging in the whole of things. I think our most general view must be that the whole of things is not a process to which there are new additions and increases at each moment. Rather, it seems to me that the passage of time and the activity of individuals are strands of process inside the unchanging totality of the real.

PART I

THE PRESENT

CHAPTER TWO

THE CONTEMPORARY WORLD

TIME IS NOT in itself divided into a past, a present, and a future. This division is owed to the things that are in time. In the present, as things change and last, they have an effect on time, and this causes time to act on them in turn. The final entities that are in time are *individuals*. We will have to understand their natures, their actions, and, especially, their effects on time. Toward understanding them it seems best to think of them first as they are when they are present. There are always many individuals in the present. They act and act on one another then; together, they are a world of contemporary entities.

What is the present? The most obvious answer is that the present is the time when things change, act, and persist, when there are events or occurrences, when causes cause, and when things have become what they are and have ceased to be what they were. The present is so different from the past and future—there are no occurrences in them—that it seems obviously to be the time of activity. It seems sophistry to argue that it is not.

There is, however, a very strong objection to the idea that things really occur in the present. The objection is that the present is too short for anything to happen in it. It is only a point, it has no length; it is not long enough for anything to occur in it. Should we say, then, as most philosophers do, that things are not really *in* time and that time is not a reality *in* which things can be? Should we say only that things are *at* different times and that the only consistent meaning we can give to "time" is that there are temporal relations between occurrences that occur *at* different times, like "before" and "after?" What would we make of the present, then? Could we define a contemporary world? Would there have to be many entities in it? Might there be only one or none? Even if there had to be many things, how should we think of their being together so as to constitute a single world? The ideas of *time* and *individuals* in this essay have been constructed to answer such arguments and questions. The answers, though at first abstract, will be an introduction to the ideas of time and individuals and to the uses that can be made of them.

Can Anything Happen in the Present?

The present is different from the past and the future; they seem to be long and it seems to be short, so short that many philosophers think of it as a point and therefore as something not quite real. They also note that if the present had a length it could be divided into parts, but the parts, or what is in them, could not all be present or all occur at once. One part would occur first, then another, and so on for the other parts; some parts would be past before the others had come about. These philosophers argue that a present must be without length, that is, without "past" or "future" parts in it. For them, the idea that something happens in the present seems an impossibility. There must be some successiveness in every occurrence, but the successive parts of an occurrence cannot occur at once. If nothing happens in the present, though, and if, as seems obvious, nothing happens in the past or the future, it follows that nothing really happens in any time. This consequence shows that there is something wrong with the idea that the present is a point *in* time.

What is wrong with it? Most philosophers think that it is simply wrong to think that time is something real and that things must be *in* it at one point or place or another. What is one to say instead? What is the right idea? For most philosophers, there has seemed only one alternative: time is not a fundamental reality; things are not *in* time; there are occurrences, but they are not *in* anything, and what we think of as points of time are only marks on a clock to which we refer when we measure the duration of occurrences.

The options, then, have seemed to be that (1) time is real and things are *in* it, but there are no real occurrences; or (2) there are occurrences, but time is not a fundamental reality. The second option is the vastly favored one. In a moment I will argue that it is not sound and that the first option, though also not sound, is not as wrong as it seems. There is something right in it, and if it were turned around it would become a third and acceptable option: that what is actual is or comes to be in a real and present time.

The first option—that the present is real, that there is something *in* it but that there is no successiveness in it—has been defended very insightfully. The defense is that, though presents are momentary, what is in them differs from present to present and that these different presents are really the successiveness in what seem to be occurrences. What is real are the slightly different contents of real and successive presents. The idea is simply that what the second option takes to be whole and unbroken occurrences are really the contents of momentary points, like the frames on a motion picture film.

The most dramatic version of this idea is that the world is created anew at each moment. This is what Descartes argues in the third of his *Meditations*. He is explicit that the present is a point and that existing things are at a point in time; he says that they are actually and wholly there. He means that actual things have no being in reserve. They have no power or capacity that might show itself at some later time. No part of them is not completely actual. There is nothing that they can become, and they cannot even maintain their own existence because that would require a power they do not have. How, then, do they continue to exist? The answer must be that they are continued by something else whose being is not confined within a present time, which is the answer Descartes gives. He thinks that things continue to exist because God creates them afresh at each moment. He completely creates them at each moment, they are completely actual, and his creation is itself complete. Descartes thinks that God not only created things initially—if they were completely actual when they were first created, they could not have lasted on their own—he creates them continually. "Creation" and "conservation," Descartes says, are names for the same fact. His view, then, is that nothing happens in any moment but that, as God creates or re-creates entities, there are changes from moment to moment, so there seem to be occurrences. The only real activity, however, is God's continually creating the world, and that does not take place in time.

The most important modern formulation of the idea that the actual is or becomes so in the present is in Whitehead's *Process and Reality*. For Whitehead, what come to be are *occasions,* not substances, and occasions are processes of actualization. They are not at all like those processes in which something already actual is said to undergo an incidental change. There is a sequence in such processes—an entity first has a certain property and then comes to have a different one. Whitehead says that there is no such sequence in the process of actualization. There is nothing actual in such a process until the process is complete, until the possibilities that had been given for actualization are made concrete. Because there is no *before* and *afterward* in a process of actualization, an occasion is present as a whole, though its presence has an extent because it is complex. Succession occurs as one occasion follows another, and occasions follow one another endlessly. The world goes on, Whitehead thinks, because possibilities are continually made available for actualization by an unusual occasion that Whitehead likens to the divine. For Whitehead, as for Descartes, what is not present, and perhaps not in time at all, is the cause of what is in the present time.

Though Descartes's and Whitehead's views seem plainly implausible, something in them is surely true. They see that something present is completely actual or is becoming so. It is or becomes so concrete and so full in detail that it cannot become anything more or anything else. They see that there is nothing virtual, potential, or even possible in what is actual, and then they have to think just what that is and how it has come about. There can be no doubt, I think, that what Descartes and Whitehead see is there to see. What is actual or is becoming so is present and nowhere else; either that, or nothing becomes actual at all. The question is what we should understand the actual to be.

Descartes and Whitehead think that the actual comprises substances and occasions and that these are momentary entities. They are not the completed parts of more extended entities. What succeeds them are not further parts of themselves but new entities that are actual or becoming so. What is actual is present, but the present is a point, and what is in it does not go beyond it. The actual is therefore complete and completely in a present time.

How do such actual entities come to be? As I mentioned, for Descartes and Whitehead, they are caused to exist, wholly or partly, by something else. The causes of their existence stand apart from the actualities and, perhaps, apart from time. How do they cause the existence of a present entity? God's creation is Descartes's answer. For Whitehead, the answer is that possibilities—he calls them "eternal objects"—are given for actualization by God; their being given is one of the conditions for there being new occasions.

Descartes and Whitehead had to give these sorts of answers. There are no other kinds of explanation for there being momentary substances or momentary processes of actualization. These actualities are or come to be present, and something apart from them must be their cause. Descartes's and Whitehead's theories elaborate something that is true about actualities. Why is it that most philosophers think that their theories are wrong? Why do most philosophers take the second option—that there are occurrences but that neither the present nor any other part of time is real?

The answer is that they think that there are real and whole occurrences and that there is something continuous in the occurrences that cannot be built of momentary points. They do not believe that God creates momentary entities. The real causes of occurrences, they think, are existing things. They act, change, and last for more than a moment. These occurrences are not *in* time; instead, they begin *at* one time and end *at* another. The philosophers who take this view therefore think that there are no real moments of time and that time itself is not something that things are *in*. All that we can really talk about, they think, are things that are what they are *at* different times. A thing is now this and later on that, and the states of things *at* different times are temporally related: one state is before another, one is after another; one is first or earlier, another is second or later. Their theory is that what we mean by "time" is that there are certain kinds of relations between the different states of things.

I now turn to this important and very strong theory. Later on, I will return to the first option and turn it around. That revision will show, I think—against the two options that have been mentioned—that one can, indeed, one must, hold that occurrences are continuous only because the present and time itself are real.

The Relational View of Time and the Real Present

If the present were real, most philosophers think, it would only be a moment long, and they think that nothing could occur in that moment. Things that are present cannot change while they are present—there is not time enough in a moment for them to change. Since it seems so clear that there are changes and other occurrences, it has also seemed clear that there is something wrong in the ideas that things are *in* the present, that the present is a part of time, and that time itself is real.

It has therefore seemed obvious to most philosophers that the right view is not that things are *in* the present but that they are *at* different times. Something starts to change *at* a certain time, and the change is complete *at* a later time; change is what goes on between the beginning and the end. These two times are merely notes or marks in the occurrence. They are made by us for the purpose of measuring its length; an "at" is not a place in a real time. An occurrence has a duration, and we establish how long it is by putting a mark on it and comparing it to other occurrences that we have also marked: it may, for example, take as long as another occurrence or half as long. Any other occurrence can be a clock, though the best clock is obviously a change that occurs at a constant rate and that can readily be divided into intervals. When we compare an occurrence to the constant change of the earth's rotation about its axis, we say, for example, that it began at nine or ten o'clock and that it went on for an hour or for some other length of time.

The notion that things begin to move or change at a certain time, that they are going on at another time, and that they end at a still later time is obviously very sensible. It may be the only notion we need for understanding how long things last or even for understanding *when* they occur: they occur before or after or at the same time as other occurrences. Still, the idea that time is only a name for certain kinds of relations and comparisons between occurrences—the relational theory of time—is not clear enough, full enough, or even true enough to be an acceptable general theory of time.

Its limitations are that (1) there is no clear idea of what the theory is about and especially of just what kind of thing it is that is *at* a time; (2) the idea that "occurrences" are at different times does not ensure that anything really does occur; and (3) it is also deeply uncertain whether all occurrences are or can be known to be in a single series, related as before and after one another. The series may seem different to different persons depending on their experience.

The main limitation in the relational theory is that it is not about the real occurrence of anything. It imagines that the world is like an endless diary in which there are already entries for every date. What is wrong about this picture is that one writes a diary page by page; writing entries is something that one does, and there are dates in an endless diary on which nothing has yet occurred. Still, there are some good uses for the relational view. It is useful for calendars or diaries. We can calculate with it; we can figure how long things have been going on and how long we will have to wait to reach a certain date. The critical point, however, is that though we may divide the *time* of occurrences into days, there still must be a real present when something really does occur, and if we are not to think of the real present as a point, we will have to think of it in another way.

What is this theory about, then? It is about occurrences, and on the relational view of time, occurrences are before and after one another, or they overlap. For what occurrences is this true? It seems true for events that have already occurred, or it was true of them when they occurred; they occurred after the events that preceded them. Historians are occupied with such orderings of past events. They establish chronologies, and they even imagine events intervening between those for which they have evidence.

On the relational theory, however, it is not only *past* events that are before and after one another; all events are related so. *Future* events, speaking loosely, are also said to be before and after one another: they come after all the events that have already occurred, and we can predict that some of them will occur before others; a lot will happen, for example, before Halley's comet returns. On the relational view, though it is loose to speak of them so, all events, past as well as future, *are* related as before and after. It is as if representations of them were spread before us and we could see, in their arrangement, how they are related to one another. All events have a place in a chronology. In the chronology itself they are not past, present, or future, though in relation to us that is how they seem.

What kinds of things are events that are ordered as before and after one another, apart from all issues about their occurring? What are events that have already or have not yet occurred? What should they be understood to be? What is the relational theory about? The events that the relational theory describes seem most like what past events would be if they were still real and discrete and lined up in the order in which they had occurred. The relational view, however, characterizes all events this way, whether or not they have (or seem to have) occurred. It sees the world as if the whole of it were there, all at once; everything is *there,* only there is the little oddity that to us things seem to be going on. Perhaps, then, there is not much *we* can say about the nature of the events in such a world. If we had the perspective of the divine we would, presumably, understand their nature, but our perspective, at least at first, is with how things seem to us. Were we to think beyond these appearances, we might come to *see* them differently.

"Idealist" philosophers—they are the ones who have most extensively elaborated and defended the relational view, though there is also a strong analogue of it in modern physics—think we should go beyond the idea that things have, do, and will occur; they think that this idea has to do only with the appearances of things and that we should think our way beyond appearances to uncover what is finally real. They think that there are contradictions in or among appearances and they want to resolve them in stages of reflection: appearances contain contradictions, which our first reflections about appearances may not totally eliminate; our second reflections may still contain some, so we must go on and on, until even the possibility of contradiction is removed. Only then will we understand what time has to do with reality. There is, therefore, not much that we can say about it now; we do not know—not even many idealists know—just what the relational view thinks is ultimately real.

Idealists start with an observation they think obvious—that there is something difficult, impenetrable, or even contradictory in the idea that what is fundamentally real changes into something else, that what *is* real can become less or more real or become another reality. Yet it is also obvious that things change. What is not obvious is just what changes. Is it the real that changes, or does it only appear to change? Or are the changes only changes in the appearances of things? What are we to make of happenings?

Something comes about. There is a difference between something's not having occurred and its having occurred, and the occurring takes place *now,* in a present time—and we are not deluded in seeing that it does. This is how things seem to us, and idealists do not deny that this is how things *seem.* What they deny is that this is true of what *is* real; it is not true of what *is* real that it ever became real or that it will ever cease to be real. They deny that what is ultimately real was once not quite real but only possible, that it came later on to be fully real and actual, and that it did this wonderful thing all by itself when it got to the magical moment of a *now.* Idealists think this is a contradictory idea—and it is; we all think so. All of us think that what is finally real does not change, though it can appear to change, and we come to understand that it does not really change by reflecting on the contradictions in what seemed to occur. No change involving ultimately real things is, through and through, a change. This is the idealist's view; their notion is also that what is finally real is unchanging. Events, then, *so far as they are real,* have no change in them; they do not pass; there is no *now* at which they occur. They just *are.* It is just that it seems to us that they occur.

The idealists' view, and the version of it in modern physics, is very strong, and not much can be said on behalf of the usual arguments devised for refuting it—kicking stones and being emphatic about being here and now and really seeing one's hand before one's face. The usual arguments no doubt show something, but we don't know what. The idealists' view, and the strength of it, is developed from a distinction we all make between reality and appearance. We all think that the real can be very different from appearance. Is the coin round and elliptical? Is the stick in the water both bent and straight? Can the same event be first future, then present, and then past? No. It would be contradictory to suppose so, yet coins, sticks, and events appear in different ways. This is the point of the distinction between appearance and reality: something occurs to us that cannot really be true of what caused it to occur—the one is the appearance, the other (relative to it) is the reality, and we must say either what the reality is or at least that it is not what it appears to be. We all know that we must think beyond appearances to find the real. We must think, for example, of what a thing's real color and real shape are. In the course of our thought, we may decide not that it is really red or round but that we have to become clearer about what "color" and "shape" are, and we also have to become clearer about how things really stand in relation to time.

Do we become clear about how things stand to time by supposing that an event was first future, then present, and then past? Do we become clear by supposing that this is how the event must be because we first anticipated it, then saw it occur, and then remembered it, so that there had to be some *occurring* for the event to move from being future to being present and to being past? Idealists would say that these are very confused notions, and the notions are confused, though not, I think, for the reasons that idealists have supposed.

For idealists, the core theme, the sure sense in all the seeming about past, present, and future, is that so far as they are real, events are before and after one another, and it is only because they appear to us in one way or another that it seems as if time were real. The idiosyncrasy of appearing seems all the more plain when we realize that what seems to us past or present can seem future to someone else; we may have already heard the thunder that people miles away have not yet heard.

Whether we should say that events appear past or future to us depending on where we are or whether the order of events itself can seem different (idealists and relativity theorists differ on this point), is, for idealists, a matter only of appearing. The real, whatever it is, is very different from what it appears to be. It appears as *now* this and *now* that, but to know it as it really is one would have to know it, as perhaps God would know it, all at once and not in appearances. Idealists do not claim that we can do this, or do it readily, but they think that we can recognize limits in our knowing and that we can imagine what knowledge that is not limited would be.

I mentioned previously that there are limitations in the view that things are not *in* time but are *at* different times, before and after one another: (1) we can't make out just what is *at* the different times, (2) there is no real *now* at which any one of them occurs, and (3) there may not be a single order in which things appear to be before and after one another. The idealists' very firm response is that these are not limitations at all; they are indications of contradictions among appearances, so that the only sense that we can find when we reflect on the contradictions is that there is a reality and that it is not distributed into past, present, and future times. For idealists, arguments repeatedly turn on a distinction between appearance and reality: the real appears, but it is not the same as its appearances; it could not be. To discover what it is, one must go not from one appearance to another but beyond all appearances, to think in a different way and to apprehend, if possible, the real itself.

Since so much in the idealists' view depends on their distinction between appearance and reality, the strongest and most fundamental objection to it is that idealists have not understood the distinction correctly. Ironically, the objection is that, for all their talk about contradiction, idealists virtually contradict themselves. They say that there are appearances and a reality, but what of the distinction itself? Is it a real distinction or only an apparent one? Are there really appearances or only apparent appearances? There are difficulties in either case. For appearances, real or apparent, occur somehow, and idealists cannot explain why there must be appearances, why anything can even seem to occur. Appearing should not be merely a possibility for a reality. A reality must be such that it can appear; indeed, it must appear somewhere at some time, but idealists cannot show why this must be so. They have distinguished appearance and reality so severely that they cannot explain why there is anything distinct from the appearing reality to which the reality itself appears.

What should one say instead? The great answer in modern philosophy has been that the real is not altogether separate from its appearances, that to know the real, so far as it can be known, is not therefore to go beyond all appearances but to go to further appearances and to search for order and regularity among them. The great answer has been that the appearances of a reality do not contradict one another, they are just different from one another; that there are fundamental regularities in the ways that things appear; and that when we discover them, we can understand why things appear to us as they do. The answer, then, is not that a reality is the same as its appearances but that what is real really appears and affects other realities. Because we do not need to suppose that appearances are contradictory and that the real is altogether different from *its* appearances, thinking about the real is not a dialectic whose stages are more and more removed from appearances, becoming more and more, like God's, pure thought. Our thinking about what is real starts in experience and concludes, if it ever does, in knowing what is true about what we will experience; it concerns what has, does, can, and will occur in our experience. It always carries, and never leaves behind, its notes about present, past, and future time.

The final limitation in the idealist view is in its conception of reality—though it is difficult to develop a different and a sounder one. My notion is that the real consists of at least two kinds of realities that are together and that are in each other in different ways. Idealists think that there is one reality that does not change in whole or in part. If appearances, experiences, and other occurrences are real, however, they have their explanation not in a single and unchanging reality but in at least two realities, one of which explains the duration or temporal extension of the other, whereas the second explains there having continually to be new moments of occurrence and transiency. These are the conceptions of time and individuals developed in this essay, and if they are sound, then the idealist's view of reality, though insightful, neglects or misinterprets part of it. It is true of only part of reality, the part that does not change and whose own parts are together all at once. Idealism is, I think, true of the past; it is almost entirely correct about it, as I hope will become clear later on, but by being true only of the past, the idealist view is not a sound account of the whole of reality.

It is led to its partiality by its notion that the real is not in time but only appears to be. Thus, it cannot explain something that clearly is in time—the fact of real and present appearances and occurrences. To reconcile what idealism sees and what it cannot explain, I suggest that the reality it understands is indeed not in time at the present; nevertheless, it is not altogether apart from time. Idealism's reality is the past. It tries to construe the whole of reality as if it were past, and as idealists see, if it were really past, there would be no contrast between it and the present and the future, and there would be no references to time. In addition to the real past, however, there is a present of real occurrences, at least of appearances, and idealism misinterprets it.

It does this not by inadvertence but by wanting the kind of understanding that resolves the seeming opposition in appearances by positing a reality that appears and construing conflicting appearances as different appearances of it. The sheer differences in there being different presents, however, need not be resolved. There is no logical opposition, no contradiction, between them. They are the differences in an individual's being really different now, and different now, and different now. There is something brute in the fact of an individual's being present. It is here and now. Where we have one kind of understanding, then, for the *what* that appeared to us, we should have another kind of understanding, a historical understanding, for the fact *that* something has occurred. In turn, these understandings lead to a different conception of reality.

The relational view of time is, though full of sight, not true of the whole of what is real. "Before" and "after" are not the only terms we need in talking about what is real, even in the occurrences of appearances. It may be that in the past there are only *befores* and *afters;* perhaps after they have occurred things are related only in this way. To acknowledge appearances and occurrences themselves, however, we have to acknowledge a real present and to think of a real future as well; we need a very different view of time.

What view should that be? At the start of this discussion there seemed to be only two options: (1) that time is real, or that the present is, and that things are *in* the present but do not change while they are in it or, indeed, do not change at any time; and (2) that there are events or the appearances of them, that they are related to one another but they are not *in* time, and that time itself is not a reality. The views of Descartes and Whitehead present the first option—and they are unsatisfactory; the idealist views present the second, and they are unsatisfactory, too. Is there a third option, beyond being or not being *in* time? It seems to me there is; it is the first option *turned around.*

Descartes and Whitehead both suppose that what is actual is present or becoming present, that the actual is present momentarily. Neither Descartes nor Whitehead, however, consider that time itself might be a reality and that it could be affected by something else. Given what they otherwise think, such an idea probably could not have occurred to them, but something like it did occur to Schopenhauer and to Bergson, and there are intimations of the unconsidered alternative in their thought. The alternative is to note that where Descartes and Whitehead think that what is actual is *thereby* present, simply by turning things around, we can think that it is in becoming present that something becomes actual.

The unconsidered alternative is that time is real and that individuals are actual not only when they are *in* time but when time, as it is when it becomes present, is also *in* them and *in* their activity; the unconsidered alternative is that as individuals become present, they also become actual. This turn preserves Descartes's and Whitehead's view that what is actual is present, but it also construes that which becomes actual and present as neither a substance (as Descartes thinks), a complete process (as Whitehead thinks), nor a mere phenomenon (as idealists think). It also requires that the present not be the whole of time. There is more to individuals and more in them than there is when they are simply actual at the present time. One has to say, of course, what more there is to the realities that become actual and to explain how the time that comes to be present comes into them. These explanations of how there come to be present actualities will be very different from those of Descartes and Whitehead. The explanations, like those of Descartes and Whitehead, will appeal to something apart from the present, but they will not appeal to anything apart from time.

The unconsidered alternative, then, is that becoming present is what makes for actuality. Critics are right: if the present were a point, nothing could happen in it. However, if the present is when individuals are in time and time is also in them, as it seems to me it is, there will be something happening in the present: individuals becoming singular and actual and becoming past. There is room enough in the present for these activities to occur.

Must There Be Many Individuals in the Present?

Suppose there is a real present—why must there be anything in it? Could it be empty? Or if there must be occurrences in it, could there be only one? Must there, in every present, be many occurrences, many individuals?

The present cannot be empty. Time could not have become present if there were nothing in a prior present to cause the new present to come about, and the individuals that were in that prior present could not have caused a new one to come about unless they also continued themselves in it. To continue themselves, however, individuals must interact with other individuals; they must separate themselves from the other individuals that are also continuing. In every present moment, then, there are and must be many individuals. They cannot continue themselves without acting, and they cannot act without separating themselves from one another. The present, as we will see, is the only time in which there are singular entities. There are none in the past and none in the future. There being a present depends on there being many individuals, and there being many singular individuals depends on there being a present time.

These answers must be explained and justified. What seems most implausible in them is the idea that, in any present, there *must be* many entities. It seems easy to imagine that there could be only one or, perhaps, none at all. Could the present not be like the sky at night, could the stars not disappear one by one, until there is only one, and could that one not disappear, so that only an empty blackness remained? It also seems possible that in the past there may have been more or fewer entities than there are now; that might be true of the future, too, and if fewer, why not one or even none? How can one rule against these possibilities when it seems that we can imagine them?

The difficulty in these possibilities is that we don't know what we are imagining. It is no easier to establish a possibility than to show that something must be so. Do we think that stars can literally cease to be, so that nothing of them remains? Do we really think that at one time there could have been nothing or only a single entity and that at a later time many entities of the same kind could have come to be? And do we really think that, following many entities, there could be only one? What do we think we are imagining? Creation? Destruction? Growth? Decay? The dissociation of time and the things in time? Kant said that we can not imagine things apart from time but that we can think of time without things in it. He did not mean, however, that we can think of an empty present time.

The thin truth in these unclear imaginings is that there seems to be no necessity for there being the number of things there are. The number seems a sheer fact, a contingent matter, and if there is no reason for the number, there might have been more or fewer entities. On the other hand, if there is a reason for things being as they are, but we don't know what the reason is, we can suppose that what exists came about by choice and that another choice was possible. This is near to Leibniz's supposition that, of the possible worlds that God might create, he chose only one.

The most intriguing issues in these reflections are about what must occur and what simply happens to occur; they are about what and where there are necessities and contingencies in things. In the early modern views the contingencies seem to be whether there must be a world at all and what it was in its first or an early state: it was thought that there might not have to be a world or that the world might have turned out differently because of its being different at the start. These were thought to be the only contingencies. All that had come about since the creation or since the early state of things was thought to have come about by necessity; things had to be what they turned out to be. There was thought to be no possibility that, after their start, things could have differed from what they had in fact become.

There are, however, or there seem to be, many more contingencies than these older views allow, and they seem to be in a different place as well, not just before the world began or in its first or an early state. In every moment, as things continue themselves, there seems to be a specialness in things, and it seems that there might have been a different specialness instead. It may even be that the contingencies that occur as things continue themselves are the only contingencies. Were this the case—were the only contingencies in how individuals continue themselves—we would have to rethink how and when causes are effective. Causes would have to allow for the contingencies—older notions of necessity in causality did not—and we would have to think of the realities on which the contingencies depend. It seems obvious that, if the contingencies are in the continuing of entities, the realities will concern how the entities are constituted and why they always act to continue themselves. That means that the realities will be "active" in constituting them. They will not be very far from the entities themselves, as a creator of entities was thought to be.

These last notions of the locale of contingencies and of their explanation are very different from the older views that there might not have been a world or that it might have been different at its start. They are the ideas that there always was and will always be a world, that there must be entities in it that continue themselves, and that exactly what the entities will become is contingent, too. These ideas allow for the massive bearing of the past on what occurs without supposing that the past wholly determines it; it seems obvious that a cause cannot be the cause of the whole being of its effect. In turn, this seems to mean that causes are effective not from the present to the future but from the past to a present in which there is always something new and in which the new is then formed on what has already occurred. Such causes allow for the development of variety and specialness and, perhaps, even for a change in the special laws according to which entities continue themselves and otherwise act. The general law that entities must always continue themselves, however, remains unchanged, and we need to see the necessity for its being so.

These seem to be the shapes of the understanding we should have of continuing entities and the contingencies that occur in every moment. From what conceptions are they to be constructed? None of those that have been criticized in this essay will do—forms, for example, or atoms, or substances, or monads, or occasions, or even what Paul Weiss calls actualities. The conceptions that I think most nearly provide for such an understanding are the conceptions of *time* and *individualness*. Time and individualness seem to be basic realities. As they are together, and together in different ways, they explain that there are singular entities in the present; they explain why and how entities must continue themselves and why and how the past bears on what they become. The world is as necessary as time and individuals are necessary, and it is because of them that contingencies must always occur. If this is true, the necessary and the contingent will not be separated so far from one another that their connection cannot be understood. The necessary realities on which the world depends are not apart from the world; they do not create it from afar. Their activity continually constitutes the world, or the present, and it also explains why there must be many individuals in every present time. The reason is that, as an individual continues itself, it must individuate itself anew, and it does this by distinguishing itself against other individuals. This action is what explains the close connection between there being many individuals and there being a present time.

There must be many individuals in the present, but only in the present. There were many individuals in presents that have now passed, but that does not mean that there are many singular individuals in the past. Similarly, there will be many individuals in the future, but only when the future becomes present. The present, then, is the only time in which there are many individuals, which is also, of course, what we would say if we think that the past and future are not real and that the present is the only time. If the past and future are real, however, our notion will be that in becoming past the singularity of individuals is lost and that in the future it has not yet been achieved. What is it about the present that makes it the time in which there must be many individuals? What is it about there being many individuals that makes for there being a present time?

Individuals are singular only when they act, and they act only in a present time; because individuals and time are bound together, their lasting causes time to be present and its becoming present causes them to act. There being many acting individuals is not incidental to there being a present time, and there being a present time is not incidental to there being many individuals and to their acting to continue themselves.

The specific idea that supports these claims is that the being of individuals is not wholly in the present. Individuals are like actions that cause their own activity, and their action in any moment is not the whole of them, just as one's life in a moment is not the whole of one's life. The completed part of an individual's activity is past, the part of it that is not yet complete is future, and the past and future parts are very different from the present part. The main difference is that only in the present do individuals act; nothing happens in the past or the future. It is also only in the present that individuals are discrete, or singular. In the past and future parts of them individuals are merged together. In the past there is no longer anything to separate them or to set and keep them apart, and in the future the kind of action that makes for single-ness and separation has not yet occurred. What makes for the singularity, then, occurs in the present, and it occurs as singular individuals con-tinue themselves: they individuate the future being they share with other individuals, and in doing that, they define themselves against one another, they oppose and resist one another, they interact with one another. That is why, in the present, there could never have been, nor can there ever come to be, only one of them.

There are two very strong arguments against the notion that, in the present, individuals affect one another, though each depends on its own distinct conception of singular entities. One of the arguments is that, at any time, entities are already so complete that they cannot interact; the other is that, in the present, entities are too incomplete to be able to affect one another. Leibniz formulated the first objection; Whitehead, the second. The difficulties in them are, as we will see, that Leibniz can give no account of entities' being present and that Whitehead cannot explain the necessity for there continuing to be singular entities. The conception of individuals just presented avoids both these consequences by characterizing a present, singular individual as neither complete nor wholly engaged in forming itself. When an individual continues itself it makes the incomplete part of itself more definite, but it also draws to itself a further indefinite part that it continues to complete. Singular individuals, in being singular, must be in the present; in the present, they must continue to make themselves singular, and in doing so, they separate themselves from other individuals in the present.

Leibniz thinks that singular or monadic entities do not interact in the present or at any other time because he supposes that the world is created, that the creation is complete, and that there could be nothing contingent in it. If contingencies could occur in the world, it would not have been completely created, and it would have been less good than God intended it to be. The natures and characters of all monads are therefore complete in their creation. If monads could be said to act at all, their actions would have to be exhibitions of their already completed natures. The unfolding of one of these natures would not affect what is unfolded in any of the others.

What seems most to show the unsoundness in Leibniz's view are its consequences for time and action. Because Leibniz thinks that every state of every monad has been created in full detail, there is no difference for him between a past, a present, and a future state of things. The differences between the different states have nothing to do with time. For Leibniz, monads are not in time. Their succeeding states are related to one another internally, like numbers in a sequence, not by being at succeeding places in a time that is outside of them. One state of a monad is not really earlier or later than another, and none of them is at the present point in time. We should therefore say that monads do not act at all.

These consequences would seem to Leibniz not awkward but true. The series of completed states of the monads is the way in which God sees the world; he created it as an array of completed states. There would not be much to object to in this, for us at least, if different states of monads appeared to occur at different times. Leibniz seemed to think that they do: we are in one state, and correlated states of other monads appear to us; we are in another state, and there are other appearances. For us, Leibniz thinks, there appear to be changes and different times.

Given what Leibniz thinks about monads, though, we are not saved even by appearances, because the consciousness in one state of a monad does not really occur later than the consciousness in another. Leibniz says that we are conscious in all the states of our monad and all of them are actual. We are, therefore, not first conscious of one thing and then conscious of another later on. There is no real temporal succession in the states of a monad, no succession in the consciousness that occurs in each of them. On Leibniz's view, my being conscious of things is like looking out a thousand windows at the same time; what I would be conscious of through each of the windows would be different, but I would not be conscious of a change, I would just be seeing lots of things. To be conscious of a change I must be conscious of different things at really different times, and since for Leibniz there are no really different times, we cannot say that things even appear to have changed. To be without even the appearances of change is too severe a consequence, even for Leibniz. Had he seen this consequence, I think that he also would have thought it too severe, and he would, perhaps, have revised his view.

The obvious revision is to suppose real activity in the states of a monad. Real activity requires a real distinction between earlier and later states or activities. This means, though, that adventitious features will surely occur. No state of a monad will be complete before or even as activity occurs, and no prior state could determine entirely what will occur in a later state; a later state starts its own activity. God's creation will not, then, have been complete; monads will not have been thoroughly harmonized; they will have to work things out for themselves, and the value of the world will have to be achieved without our being assured that it is as good as possible. This obvious revision makes the monad very like an *individual,* at least as an individual is singular and active, but we would also have to compare their past and future states. For the way in which they are in a present, though, the comparison is almost exact. When individuals act to become more self-contained, as monads do, they must affect one another; were monads really to act, at least in part, they would have to maintain their distinction from one another, which is what individuals also do.

The second objection to the idea that present individuals affect one another is that they are not complete enough to act on one another in the present. That is when they are forming themselves, but when they are completely formed they are no longer present but past. The occasions that form themselves later on take account of those that have just been formed; past entities affect present entities, but contemporaries have no effect on one another. This view, this conception of actual occasions, is Whitehead's in *Process and Reality.* Part of this idea was considered earlier in relation to the reality of time.

Whitehead's actual occasions are like stages in Leibniz's monads, except that something goes on in them even though they are atomic and only a moment long. They are present as they are becoming actual; they are self-creating and each of them is new. Each has a predecessor, each will have a successor, and occasions are otherwise coordinated, though they do not interact. The coordination is owed to a distinctive occasion that Whitehead thinks of as divine. Without creating the occasions themselves, God makes available to all of them the forms they incorporate as aims, and these ensure the coordination of the occasions and the bearing that past occasions have on the formation of the present ones.

A great deal is sound in Whitehead's view. One important difficulty in it, however, is that it characterizes actual occasions as either becoming or as already past, and no reason is to be found in them for thinking that the world must go on after they have been formed. In arguing that things must go on, the views to which Whitehead is most opposed suppose that the final entities of the world are material particles; they are made of a stuff that cannot naturally cease to be. For Whitehead, though, the basic entities are processes of actualization. They create themselves, and they cease to be present when they are complete. Why, then, must there continue to be new occasions? Nothing, no occasion, requires or explains this necessity, not even Whitehead's God. According to Whitehead, God acts to provide the forms for the definiteness of new occasions, not to create the occasions themselves. Nor is it enough to claim, as Whitehead does, that each occasion is "a potentiality for incorporation in subsequent occasions." This means only that if there are new occasions, they will form themselves by taking account of the occasions that preceded them, not that the past occasions cause the new ones to occur. Nothing causes them to occur. They are, Whitehead says, self-creating. There is no reason, then, in Whitehead's view, why there must or should continue to be new occasions, though it seems obvious that the world's persistence is not a contingency.

The least change to Whitehead's view that will ensure the necessity for there continuing to be singular occurrences is a revision in the conception of "actual occasions." It is to think that new occasions will continue to form and that occasions will be continuous because the process of forming is continuously fomented by a reality that cannot pass away. This change also requires a change in Whitehead's conception of "creativity." Instead of pulses of creativity, the passing that is the basis for whatever other changes occur in the coming to be and passing away of things must itself be continuous. The argument, then, that the formation of occasions is atomic and altogether self-enclosed is set aside. It is based on the notion that coming to be actual is present and all at once. The notion we should have instead is that the part of the being that is made to be present thereby becomes actual but that not all of it is present; some of it is no longer becoming actual and some of it is not yet present. With these changes, the conception of *actual occasions* becomes the conception of *individuals* and there is, as well, a reference to the reality of time.

The arguments by Leibniz and Whitehead are that singular entities cannot affect or separate themselves from one another either because they are already complete or because they are not as yet complete, respectively. The consequence of these arguments is that there is no necessity for there being either a present or a future time. If we make the simplest changes in them that will ensure these necessities the conceptions of the *monad* and the *actual occasion* become very like the conception of an *individual*. Individuals are singular in the present, where they are partly complete and partly not. This is true of them because their being is not wholly in the present, which is what Whitehead thinks about the being of actual entities. It extends beyond the present. The being of a monad also extends beyond a single state but, unlike a monad, an individual is not singular and definite as it extends into the future.

Individuals last by continuing to make themselves singular and definite; in doing so, they distinguish and separate themselves from one another. They do not first become singular and then oppose and resist one another. Their opposing and resisting one another is part of the process in which they continue to make themselves singular. Leibniz is right that if or after entities are concrete they do not interact. Whitehead is right that they do not interact before they come to be concrete. Leibniz, however, thinks that the definiteness of entities never really comes about, and Whitehead thinks that it comes about in a moment, all at once. Individuals, however, continue to make themselves singular while the part of them that is becoming definite is becoming past. There is both definiteness and indefiniteness in individuals in the present, and there is also time enough to have them interact.

Individuals interact because they share their future being; they contend with one another as they portion it among themselves. Their future being does not divide itself, part here, part there, as if the parts had been preassigned and made available to them. There is some struggle among them as they continue to exist, some pressing out and some drawing in. These are the marks of the present time and of the tensions in the space between newly singular individuals. Were there no opposition in the present, there would not be many individuals or many actions in it. The world, if continuing at all, would be a single event of variegated character. It would not consist of distinct individuals and actions. It would not be a world of contemporaries.

Still, having individuals oppose one another as they continue to make themselves singular is not enough to explain what the present is. It shows us each individual as opposed to other individuals, but we need to see further into the connection between individuals and time to see that all singular individuals are contemporary and are, together, a single world.

Individuals are inseparable from time, both when they are singular and when they are not. They are not what they are apart from time and then somehow set into it. There is no one place that they are in time. Individuals are past, present, and future, and the differences are in how they are together with time. They are together with it in one way in the past, in another way in the future, and in still another way in the present. I will soon consider in detail what these ways are and try to say why there are such different ways, but what should be noted first is that a present time is both *inside* and *outside* individuals. Inside, it is the passing, the transience in their action and ongoing; outside, it is the common time or the common space they share. As inside individuals, time shares in their activity; as outside them, it makes for their being together as a single world.

If time were not inside present individuals they would not differ from past individuals; the past and present would be indistinguishable. One obvious difference between them is that individuals act in the present, there is ongoing in the present, but there is no action or ongoing in the past. Even if it were true that the past is always becoming more past, that would not be because of anything that the past individuals do. The difference between the present and the past results partly from time, from its being in individuals in the present but not being in them in the past. If it were not in individuals in the present, all the ongoing, all the transience, the whole of their continuing, would be owed to the individuals alone. There would be no explanation of why individuals must act to continue to be singular, nor would there be an understanding of the duration of their actions or of the fact that, while they are acting, they are also becoming partly past, with the ongoing and the passing in different individuals occurring at the same rate, so that however much or little individuals may do there are and continue to be many individuals in each new present time.

If time were not also a space outside present individuals they would not differ from future individuals; the present and the future would be indistinguishable. There would be no space in which individuals could be related. There would be nothing in them owed to their opposing one another, marking out a place of their own. They would not be singular, and they would not be contemporaries. The difference between the present and the future is the difference in the ways in which individuals and time are together. In the future, time is not outside individuals; in the present, it is both inside and outside them.

How can time be both inside and outside individuals? How can singular individuals be temporal through and through but be in time as well? The answer, it seems, though now only in a preliminary form, must be that, as becoming present, time comes into individuals, that as they continue themselves they shear and stay a portion of it for themselves, but that time does not allow itself to be entirely contained within individuals and also passes over them. The uneasiness in the togetherness of time and individuals as they are present is that individuals provoke time to pass and that, as it passes over and into them, it makes them partly past and thereby provokes them to act to continue being singular. Time passes into individuals as they continue themselves—it is the duration of their activity of continuing—and they try to hold on to the time they have portioned for themselves. It is in constituting themselves and portioning the time and being that comes into them that they oppose one another. The time of a whole and common future faces all singular and present individuals; it passes into all of them. It is a whole reality, however, distinct from them, and they cannot destroy its wholeness by dividing it among themselves. As the present time, it is therefore outside them as well.

The present, then, is when time passes into and over individuals and the opposition between individuals takes place. For there to be a present there must be many individuals, and they oppose one another as they take time into themselves and succeed in making it part of their activity. Individuals cannot continue to be singular without affecting other individuals, without contending with them, without distinguishing themselves from their contemporaries. Individuals are contemporaries when time is in them and they are in time. It may sometimes be difficult to decide whether some individuals or their appearances are contemporary, but even if we are not sure of the full composition of the contemporary world, we can be sure that there must be many individuals in it, all in the present, and that new present moments must come about.

CHAPTER THREE

THE BECOMING OF THE PRESENT

EACH PRESENT moment is new. The time of each present is new, its presence is new, and part of what is in the present moment is also new. These two newnesses—a newness of time and of individuals—occur together. They occur because of the ways in which time and individuals affect each other.

How, why, and from what do these novelties of time and of individuals come about?

The time that becomes new as present was future before it became present. It is therefore new as being present but not as being time. What becomes new in an individual was part of the individual before it became present; it was part of the individual's being that was spread into the future. It is therefore new not as the being of an individual but in being singular and definite.

These two newnesses are transformations of part of time and part of the being of individuals. They come about, and they must come about, because of the ways in which individuals are in time and time is in individuals. Perhaps it will help explain these answers to sketch the larger picture of time and individuals in which the details of the answers will have their place.

The main lines of the picture are that individuals are not wholly in the present and that the present is not the whole of time. Individuals are present, but even while they are, part of them is past and part is future. This will seem false if we think that individuals are what they are, where they are, and when they are and that they cannot be in two or three different times at once. Many of us think that singular entities must be at a single place and at a single time. This would be right if individuals were always and only singular, if each of them were always completely definite and self-contained in the way that an atom or a stone is thought to be. Think of an entity as self-contained and it is foolish to think that it is in the past, the present, and the future *at the same time;* if individuals are not self-contained, however, if individuals are in action and if being singular is only one stage of their activity, then it is not false but sound to think that they are spread through time and have different forms in the different parts of time.

Why the unusual thought that individuals are spread through time? Because unless we think of them in this way we will not be able to understand how they persist and change and act to do other things. The traditional doctrines about such singulars as atoms admit that they cannot act—they cannot do anything. All that happens to them is that they are moved by something else. They are usually said to be moved by a force transmitted to them in an impact or to be carried along in a moving medium. They are like billiard balls or bottles in an ocean, and their inability to act is connected with their self-containment and their existence at a single place in time. Individuals, however, must act to continue to be singular; they initiate, direct, control, and affect changes from within themselves, and to understand that this is something that they can do we must understand them to have, as parts of themselves, the powers, tensions, and the very stuff of which actions are made. A thing whose whole being is in the present cannot do anything, not even move itself. An individual that is spread from past through future and is tensed into singularity in the present can persist and act in other ways as well.

In the picture to be detailed, then, individuals are spread through the past, the present, and the future, and their lasting is a transformation within them. When present, they are continuous with their own past and future being. They are affected by their past and they affect their future, but they are singular only in the present. In the past and future, individuals are merged together; there are no singulars. The past, present, and future differ; time and individuals constitute them in different ways. They are together in one way in the present and in different ways in the past and future. Time and individuals are never separate. There is no empty time and individuals are never apart from time. We are temporal, through and through. What is new in us in each new present comes to be in us because of time, and time comes to fresh presence partly through the actions of the individuals in it.

Three themes in this chapter help explain this picture and develop some of its details. The first is about the different ways in which time and individuals are together; the second is about how time and individuals jeopardize each other's being as they constitute the present; and the third describes how these jeopardies are reduced by individuals' persistence and time's passage, only to have the jeopardies reintroduced by the action and passage themselves. Finally, there is a critical summary of the notions that individuals persist, that time passes, and that, in becoming present, there is something new in both time and individuals.

How Time and Individuals Are Together

Time and individuals constitute the present by being together in a certain way. There are two other ways in which they are together; these constitute the future and the past. The easiest distinction between these ways of being together is based on whether time and individuals are *inside* or *outside* each other. In the future, time is inside individuals; in the past, individuals are inside time. In the present, time is inside individuals and individuals are inside time. There is contention between time and individuals in the present; it is unsettled which of them is dominant, and out of this contention individuals continue themselves and time continues to pass.

In the present, as present, individuals are singular and time is both inside and outside them. As inside them it is the duration, transience, and extension of their action; as outside them it is the space in which individuals are together. The time inside individuals is continuous with the time or space outside them. Individuals do not cut time apart—though their borders are where time or space is tensed—but they try to take and keep a portion of time inside themselves, and time resists their doing so.

The present is a passing time, but it is not the only time there is. Time is future as well as present, though the future has no extent: there is no sequence in it. It is also not a space; there is no space in the future, only in the present. Future time is whole and undivided, and so is the future being of individuals. Present individuals extend through the future. They are singular in the present but not in the future. Most Buddhists think that singular entities are only apparently discrete, that their singularity is not finally real. These Buddhists are not right about individuals as they are present, but they are right about them as they are in the future. The being of all individuals is merged in the future; there is no discreteness in it. There are no separate futures for present individuals. The seemingly separate futures that we think we will have—your future and mine—will be separate only when they become present; they are not already separate in the future, not even possibly separate. The future does not consist of definite possibilities. The being that is future can and will become singular, and the time that is future will surely pass, but there is no passing and no singularity in the future itself.

There is also a past. Time passes in the present and nothing escapes its passage, nothing eludes it to remain in a new present. Some of what passes from the present passes away and ceases to be, but what has become definite in individuals does not pass away; it becomes past. Those who think of the present as being the only time suppose that what is no longer present has ceased to be, preserved, perhaps, in memories. But the past is no less real than the present. It consists of time and of what was present in individuals, but it consists of them as they have been transformed. We overlook this important transformation because we are pragmatically concerned for what we can do and what will come about. When we act and something new occurs, however, the last part of what we already are does not fade away, it is transformed. It remains real but is becoming or has already become past. The major change in individuals when they are transformed thus is that their singularity is lost. As I have said, there is no singularity in individuals in the future, and they make themselves singular in the present. Then, though they retain the definiteness they have achieved, their singularity is overcome when an implacable passing time carries them into the past. In passing, time comes to dominate individuals; they are made to be inside it. Time thereby unifies the definite in the singular and separate present individuals. It is what accounts for there being a single and whole past, which is the past of and for the individuals that are present. The past has no space in it and no sequence. The way we know and describe it differs from the way we know and describe the present and the future.

This first theme, then, which is geometrical and partly metaphorical, is that time and individuals penetrate, suffuse, interleaf, and overlap each other. They are inseparable. The present, future, and past are the two of them as together: inside, outside, and both inside and outside each other. In the present, time is inside and outside individuals. As they act, individuals make themselves newly present, newly singular, and then they are made to be past. There is one past; it is the past consisting of all the individuals that were ever present and the past of all the individuals now present. It is a sheaf of definiteness dominated by time, and it is used by present individuals to make more definite the future being that is thrust on them. The being that individuals make newly singular in the present is their own future being, and, as future, it is not divided into separate futures, one for each of the present individuals. Nor are there even real, distinct possibilities—though, because time is inside individuals in the future and not readily seen, some philosophers think that what individuals will become is already definite. They are only partly right, however; they are right that the future being of individuals is real but not right that it consists of definite possibilities. How the future comes to presence, how individuals act to cause it to come about, is the subject of the second theme. It is about how new moments come to be.

The Occurrence of New Moments

Individuals act in every present, even when all they do is persist. There are no moments when they are paused and time is either stopped or the only thing that moves. Individuals and time suffuse one another, and neither can change without affecting the other.

As the future becomes present, time also acts. Its activity is called "passing." Time is made to pass partly because of what individuals do, and individuals are made to act partly because of passing time. The action of each calls for the action of the other; neither can act alone.

Present individuals take into themselves a portion of their future being and make it definite. Individuals persist by bringing their future being into themselves, or rather, by having it brought into them. Individuals must act to continue over a period of time. This would not be true if they were made of an indestructible matter and if their shapes were also indestructible, but all that such indestructible things could do is last, and that does not require any effort on their part; they could not otherwise act at all. If entities consisted partly of an indestructible matter, as Aristotle thinks, they might be able to act, but there would have to be a form in them to shape and direct their matter. Even if a substance were not otherwise acting, if it were resting, its form would always have to act on its matter to keep making it the matter of that very thing. In something capable of acting it is not the thing's matter that accounts for its lasting but some continuing inner action. This is also true of individuals, though they do not consist of an indestructible matter. Everything in individuals is changing in every present, and the basic activity of their lasting is their taking into themselves a portion of their own future being, making it present and definite. Individuals persist not as an atom or a substance does but as a continuing swell and heave into presence of their future being.

Time as well as their own being comes into individuals as they act to continue. Both are new in the present; together, they make the present new. The being that is new in individuals is brought into them by time as it passes, and time passes not of itself but because of what individuals do to it as they act to continue themselves. What they do is try to hold time in themselves, to keep it unchanging, unpassing in themselves. Because they cannot keep time from passing, the only way they can persist is by continuing themselves. Time is implacable in its passing. It passes continually to avoid the jeopardy individuals make for it.

The jeopardy is that individuals will divide the whole and undivided reality of time into separate times inside singular and separate individuals. To recover from this jeopardy, time passes from inside individuals to being altogether outside of them. Were individuals to succeed even for a moment in holding time within themselves, time would no longer be a single and whole reality. There would be as many times as there are separate individuals; there would be no common time; the separate times would be cut off from the time that is future, and the world would stop.

Time, however, prevents individuals from dividing it. The most that individuals can do is strain it some, thereby distinguishing between internal and external time. Though strained then, time is still undivided, but it responds to the strain by passing through individuals to remove the hold that they have on it. Passing is time's way of recovering from a jeopardy to its whole reality.

What may be especially troublesome in this idea is the Parmenidean notion that a fundamental reality does not move or change, it just is; it does not need to change itself to continue to exist. It is indeed difficult to understand how a single fundamental reality could do anything, for there is no apparent happening in what it is thought to do. It is difficult, for example, to understand what action there is in God's creating the world or in having Aristotle's unmoved mover think. If there were two or more equally fundamental realities, then we might suppose that they also should just exist. There is one and there is another; neither should change or do anything, and that might be true of them if the two were at some "distance" from each other. In that case, though, there would have to be a third, more comprehensive, reality that embraced them both, and unless one or the other of them did something, we would not be able to think how many or what realities there are. Realities are distinguished from one another, it seems, by what they do; so it is, at least, with time and individuals.

Time and individuals are equally fundamental and they are together, but not in a third reality. They must each be what they are while they are together, and that requires some action on their part. Their action is that each comes to be inside the other, so that they distinguish themselves as inside and outside each other—and they each come to be inside the other through those portions of their being in which individuals continue to be singular and in which time passes. As present, time and individuals therefore both act and exist. In the future and the past they just are. They are present as they are doing something. The actions of individuals and the passage of time occur within those realities themselves. They must occur because of them, and because time and individuals are inseparable, their actions could never have been started nor can they ever end.

Within the present, then, constituting the present, individuals act and time passes. If individuals did not take hold of passing and freshly present time they would not remain present. They would pass away and become past. There would be no new present, time would not have to pass again, and time and individualness would be divided. It is because individuals must take hold of the time that comes into them that they continue to be present. Their hold, however, is a provocation for time to continue to pass. It thrusts itself on individuals and passes through and over them; it extends and relates them and it causes them to become, first partly and then finally, past.

The Interaction of Time and Individuals

Time's passage threatens to make individuals entirely past. Their basic action is to remove this jeopardy, though they act in other ways as well. Time, in turn, issues into presence and passes because of a jeopardy that individuals make for it. These two jeopardies occur together. Neither time nor singular individuals ever become still and safe from each other's intrusion. As individuals individualize a portion of their future being, they provoke to passage the time that is tissued with their future being. This passage is a threat to the persistence of individuals, and because it is, as individuals act and extend themselves, they unsettle time again. There is an endless willfulness in individuals; in time, or in its passage, there is a dumb necessity. Both time and individuals act to remove the jeopardies they make for each other only to introduce them once again.

What are these actions by time and individuals? How and when do they take place? Why is it that new present moments must endlessly come about?

When individuals act to individualize their future being they also incorporate the time that is suffused in it. Time, then, also acts. It comes to presence, and as it does, it brings with it some of the future being of individuals. These two actions can be said to occur in the present, but it is more accurate to say that, together, the actions *are* the present. They occur together because they overlap; neither could occur alone. Time passes because of what individuals do to it, and as it passes, it carries the future being of individuals along with it. An individual acts because of what time does to it, and as it continues itself, it takes into itself the time that is together with its future being. The time and being of the present are continuous with the time and being of the future, and they provoke them, causing them to become present as they are themselves becoming past. Time itself is a constituent in these two actions and in the passing that provokes them; it is thus more revealing to say that the actions *are* the present than to say that they are *in* time, though in a sense that is also true, because time is not only in the actions but surrounds them as well. Together, then, the two actions are the present and the present has some spread in it; something happens during it. This is true, however, only of the two actions together. It is not true of them so far as they can be considered separately: it takes no time for individuals to last and no time for time to pass.

This last observation will seem paradoxical because we think all activities must take time. How can two activities, neither of which takes time, combine to become a present that has some extent? The answer is that the contradiction—activities do and do not take time—is not real; the actions by time and individuals that make for the present are not separate activities. They are strands in one whole activity, and it is only because of their being together that there is duration as a present time. Although it takes no time for time to pass and none for individuals to last, the passing and the lasting that make for an extended present do not derive, as we will see, from either one of them alone.

Some trace of paradox remains in the idea that time and individuals become newly present if we think of them as moving into a place and of their moving as having to take some time. The idea that the present is a place, however, is wrong and very damaging. It is also difficult to set aside, probably because our images of things coming and going are so prominent. It seems easy to imagine that things that were future become present by moving into a place and then become past by moving beyond it; one place, always the same fixed place—as if things could come into it and so become present and then leave it without being changed. A somewhat better notion would be that the present is a place that moves, that things are in their own fixed place and that the present moves into them and then away from them while, again, they are otherwise unchanged, like a beam of light moving from thing to thing in a dark room. It would be sounder by far to think that the present is not a place at all but that it is, instead, a certain changing of time and individuals. It is a transformation from their being together in one way to their being together in other ways, where both time and individuals cause the transformation and both are affected by it. On this sounder view of the present nothing passes into or out of it. Individuals are present when they are making themselves singular; time is present when it is passing inside them. The present is the two of these strands together. It is a distinctive change of things and a change in them, so that our notion is not that these changes occur in the present but that these changes, involving time, are themselves the present time.

What we should see, then, is that the present is not a place but the "time" of activities; it is when individuals are caused to act to last, though not unchanged, and when time passes through singular individuals to get outside of them. The present is the heaving together of the being of time and individuals. Time's passing never occurs apart from individuals' acting, and individuals never change apart from time's passing. Together, they are an action that has an extent derived not from either of its strands but rather from their affecting each other.

What is it about time and individuals that enables them to be or come together as a present? They are never apart; they are together in one way as a future and in other ways as a present and a past, and they are the same or continuous throughout. The issue of their becoming present, then, is how and why there is a certain change in their way of being together, and the answer is that in a present, time and individuals are unstably together. Present individuals are always being made past by the time that is passing inside them. In turn, that passing time draws into individuals the future time with which it is continuous. This time carries with it the future being of individuals—future time and being are inseparably together—and the individuals that are still singular take hold of it and form it and also take hold of the time that carried it into them, subjecting it to themselves. Doing this, in turn, causes still more time to pass and more of the being of individuals to become present, and these activities must continue. Time and individuals in the present, and in becoming present, are phased with each other. There is time's becoming past and individuals' becoming more concrete and definite; there is time entering into individuals' activity and individuals' continuing themselves—time and individuals, time and individuals, paired, each pair containing a jeopardy to the continuity of time and individualness. Time's passing tends to shear individuals apart, and individuals' acting tends to shear time apart, but then time and individuals act to reduce the jeopardy, and their doing so continues their activity. Time and individuals are never apart. The present, however, is when their being together becomes unsettled and when, for a moment, it becomes settled once again.

The present, then, is not a place through which time and individuals pass, entering and then leaving it. It is, as it were, the *when* of the activities constituted by individuals and time affecting each other. In the present, time and individuals are as much a becoming past as they are a becoming present, each freeing itself from the hold the other has on it. Then, as time enters into individuals and as individuals take hold of it, each subjects itself to the same divisiveness it had acted to escape. The holding and passing in the transformation of being and time are opposite vectors in the activity that is the present. For both time and individuals, being present is an achievement: the individuals that continue themselves in the present have persisted and individuated themselves afresh; time has recovered, or is recovering itself, from the hold that singular individuals have or have had on it. The jeopardy for each is owed to the other, and it is always renewed. It is because individuals are endlessly willful and time is dumb that there must be new moments endlessly.

Time's Passing

Time's passing should be like the other passings with which we are acquainted; otherwise, we would not know what its passing means or have a basis for understanding it. We know that from time to time we pass things and they pass us, and the notion of things *going on* is familiar. Still, it is difficult to understand time's passing because time is so unlike the other things that pass. Comparisons are certainly not obvious. In fact, many philosophers have said they are so remote that, strictly speaking, we should not suppose that time passes even if it is real. Can we nevertheless find enough sense in the comparisons to say something about time's passing, even if it is not strictly accurate? Whenever we have some insight into fundamental themes, we must take our language beyond its familiar applications. Can we do this to find a sense for the passing of time, so that time's passing is like, though still different from, the passings that take place in time?

When we say that something is passing we refer to ourselves or to a point: what passes has not yet arrived here or there, now it has, and now it has passed beyond it. What passes must pass a point (whether or not the point itself passes something else), and it remains the same before and after it continues in its direction and passes the point. If something reaches a point and then turns around, or if something comes into existence at a point and ceases to exist while it is there, it has not passed anything. The most prominent sense of "passing," then, supposes that a thing moves in more or less one direction, that there is a point or place, and that the thing that passes that point exists before and after it passes it.

It seems obvious that these requirements cannot be met if we think of time as a moving line or a point, and it is because they cannot be met by a line or point that time is often said not to pass. If time, for example, were like a line of infinite length and if that whole infinite linear space and all that is in it were to move, it would not pass anything—unless we were outside it and it passed us, but even then we could not know that it was passing unless we had reached into it and marked a place that we then saw receding from us. In that case, though, if we could mark a place in time, we would have to be in that time ourselves, and there would be another time of our own from which we would see the mark receding from us. The notion of a linear time's passing and our knowing that it passes is incoherent: it supposes a time outside of time, it supposes our being in it but also our intervening in the passing world, and it attributes to us a capacity for knowing that is either a little less or a little more than God's. Whatever is true of God, it is not true of us that we are both in and out of time and that we can do what we would have to do to know that time is passing as a whole.

Nor can the requirements be met, as some phenomenologists try to meet them, by thinking of time as a point, a present in which we are conscious of first a certain content and then another content—a different content for every *now*. This would give us not time's passing but the appearance of its passing, and the appearance is irresolvably ambiguous: does the *now* move into different contents? Does it light them up for its companion consciousness? Or do different contents simply come into the present and to our consciousness? Does our thinking cause us to have different thoughts? Or is it our having different thoughts that makes it appear we are doing something? There is no way of telling. In either case, there is no account of the content into which we move or that moves into us. What was it before our moving consciousness becomes a consciousness of it? When is it, in or out of time? And if it was because of the content's moving that we became conscious of it, what is it in the content that causes it to move? Why is it that, of all the things that might be thought, so little comes into the light of mind? These are difficult issues about the nature and activity of thought, but, whichever way they are turned, they do not resolve the question of whether time moves or is moved past anything. Something moves—but what? The obvious difficulty that remains in the common answers, line or point, is that we cannot see time move or pass anything: nothing that we can know seems to be moving outside of it, and even if we think of our consciousness as being now, we cannot confidently conclude that it is our *now* that moves. We may be prisoners in the cave. Things come into and out of mind. It is not sure, though, that they are real enough to be said to pass.

These difficulties about the passing of lines and points of time are so great, the themes about a changing consciousness so subtle, that it is not surprising so many philosophers have thought there to be no sense in the idea of a passing time. And there is no sense to time's passing if time is a relation or a line or a point. There is a sense of its passing, however, or we can construct or discover or define one, if we think of time as being real and inseparable from individuals.

We cannot say that there is a moving time unless we can both show that what moves is time and find something with which to contrast its moving. If we are not to find this contrasting thing outside of time, then—if there at all—the contrast must be between time and something in time itself. What might that be? It must be something in the present, for it is only in the present that there is activity. If time moves at all, therefore, it can move only in the present, and if it can pass anything in the present, the only entities it can pass will be individuals: the present consists of time and individuals. The obvious difficulty in the idea that time passes individuals in the present is that it carries them with it to the past. It therefore does not pass what moves along with it.

There is, though, a sense in which time does pass individuals in the present, or in which it passes a part of them. In the present, time does not pass beyond individuals or even separate itself from them, but there is a part of each individual in the present beyond which time has passed. It has passed that newly present part of an individual that its own passing has caused to come about. The newly present portion of an individual is together with the time that brought it into that individual, but the further time that is already passing in the individual is the agency for the new time and being that continue it. *That* passing time, the time that causes the new being to become present, has *passed* that new being, although it did not *pass by* that portion of the individual that it caused to come about.

This is an unusual and constructed sense of "passing." It is the sense that, in the present in which time passes, time passes what is becoming present because of its own passing. The rationale for this sense is that, in the present that is both a coming to be and a passing away, the passing part of time, and also of individuals, has passed that portion of an individual that is only then coming to be definite. This is something we can see when we think that, in the present, individuals are becoming past while they are also becoming present.

There remains only the disturbing note that this sense of having passed but not having passed *by* something is not what we usually mean by "passing," and that is so. Should we therefore say that time does not pass or that its passing is only metaphorical? The answer is "no," because what we usually mean by "passing" applies only to what already exists, to what is thought to exist continuously, and to a passing that itself takes time: it takes time for someone to walk past someone else. "Passing" does not, in the same sense, apply to the passing of time or to the present, which is the only "time" in which the passing of time could occur. Still, a remnant of our more familiar sense remains.

What has passed a portion of an individual in the present is the same before and after it has passed it. The same time has passed—the time that is passing is the time that was itself caused to come into the individual in which it passes and that in turn causes more time and being to come into that individual. Taking note of the differences between time's action and the actions we usually understand as "passing," this is ground enough for saying what we can think and might even see, that time passes in a present. A cause is, in some way, prior to its effect, and if the causality of continuing individuals takes place within the present, then the time that is within the present and is the cause of the further being of an individual's also being present has passed that further being; it has passed it but it is not yet past. If the time that is passing in the present were past before individuals were continued, individuals would not last, they would not be continuous—if they continued to occur at all—and time's passing would not itself be continuous.

We have already considered why the passage of time occurs and how and why it must occur. The notions that time passes and that individuals persist and change to reduce the jeopardies they cause each other is not a dramatic device. It is an emphatic statement of the point that, in being together, different basic realities are the causes and the conditions for the changes they each must undergo.

These conceptions of time and individuals and of their jeopardies differ from the basic conceptions in many other philosophical views: that is their unfamiliarity. The main difference is that most of the more familiar views suppose that there is permanent matter or a permanent something in enduring entities, that the entities move or are moved, and that their motions and changes are measured against one another.

By contrast, the basic notion of this essay is that the *stuff* in a new action by an individual comes to be in it as the time of the new activity passes. This notion—now perhaps less unfamiliar—and its supporting arguments and concepts have, I think, argument and consistency of construction in their support. They seem to provide suitably, without paradox, for the newness of what is new in each moment. They also provide a rationale for the novelties of time as it is present and passing and of individuals as they individualize themselves in a new present. These newnesses must occur, because time and individuals reach into each other. Something of each of the specific newnesses has no specific prior cause. It is new in a new present, configured then and there, but not unintelligible because of that. If we deny the novelty of time and individuals, we deny that the present is real; if we deny that its occurrence has a rationale, we deny that the past and future are real as well. It seems, however, that there are no grounds on which these denials can be justified.

CHAPTER FOUR

THE DIMENSIONS OF THE PRESENT

T HOUGH IT seems paradoxical to say so, the present is the part of time in which time passes and in which individuals act to remain in a present time. The paradox seems to be an endless regress—time passes in the present, which passes in the present, which passes in the present, and so on, and there seems to be a contradiction in having individuals run to stay in a place from which they can never get away. The seeming paradox and contradiction come about when we think of time as if it were a thing in time, doing the kinds of things that such things do. The remedy seems obvious: avoid comparing time with the kinds of things that are and act in time. If time is real, however, and there is something to be known about it, it must be compared with something, and what is there to compare it to except for things that are in time?

This seems to me to show why our thought about time is almost always open to criticism. We know that the concepts we use to describe what occurs in time do not apply, at least in the same way, to time itself. Still, those concepts, and the comparisons with things that are in time, are the most important and perhaps the only terms we have for describing time. We have no alternative to using them. The question is how to use them without being misled by them, without taking the comparisons too far. Perhaps the best that we can do then is to balance comparisons, to make one comparison and then an offsetting one, and hope to see something about time in the contrast of the two.

One very broad idea that can be used in such revealing comparisons is the idea of *dimension*. We say that both things and time itself have their dimensions. For example, things persist and have a size and move at a certain rate; these are some of the dimensions of the things that are in time. What if we were to think of present time, or the present itself, as having dimensions, too? Philosophers have talked about the present's having or not having a length. What about its having a breadth, a depth, and a rate at which it passes? We should consider all the dimensions of things as also being dimensions of time; then, when the comparisons between time and the things that are in time are jarring, we may well be able to see something underneath the opposition. Paradoxes are profound instruments for provoking and expressing thought. Let me review the dimensions, one by one.

The Extension of the Present

This is the view I will argue for: the present is extended but not in the way that a line has a length. It is extended by both the individuals that are present and the time that passes through them. There can be no measure of the present's length, however, and we should not think of it as being so many completed clocklike motions long or even as the unit that measures the lengths of other times.

The argument begins by thinking again of the old idea that the present is a point, either ideal or real, and seeing again that in either case that there is no extensiveness or successiveness in a present time. Most philosophers think that we can establish a point *for* measurement but that the point is neither a point *of* time nor a point *in* time. For them, time is just not real; the present is ideal, and there is then only the difficulty that we cannot say when it is that things occur. On the other hand, some philosophers think that time is real; they stay with points, with real infinitesimals, with *nows,* and there is then only the difficulty that nothing can occur in a present time. The philosophers who take the latter view hope for clever ways of unraveling Zeno's paradoxes; these seem to them only sophistical. Ideal points, then, or real ones with nothing happening in or at them—is this the alternative?

There is a further view that almost combines these options. It is the idea that there are special kinds of occurrences in the present and that the present is not quite a point but like one, at least in not having successive parts. This is the idea of a present that is extended *far enough* for something to occur in it, though the occurrence is present *all at once.* Can such a conception be constructed and shown to be true? Whitehead thinks so, and I think so too, though in a way very different from Whitehead's.

Consider Whitehead's view, to which I have already referred in the first chapter. The issue now is how the present can be long enough for something to occur in it but short enough for what occurs in it to occur all at once. In *Process and Reality,* the idea of such a present is part of the conception of an actual occasion. An actual occasion, according to Whitehead, is the process of something becoming actual, and all processes, Whitehead thinks, ultimately consist of actual occasions.

Whitehead's view is especially interesting, and especially clear, when it is contrasted with Aristotle's more familiar view of change. Aristotle thinks that when substances change, *they* actualize their potentialities; the actualization makes for a change in the substance itself. A substance, for Aristotle, is something that is actual, here and now—that person, that tree, that rock, that chair—and when a substance actualizes its potentialities it gives up one property and comes to have a contrary one instead: a person who is not sunburned becomes sunburned, a tree grows taller.

According to Aristotle, when a change occurs there is an interval between the contrary states of the substance. Both states cannot exist at the same time, so one can measure the time it takes for a change to occur by marking off the distinct, contrary states—a change in things is like going from one place to another—and by comparing the time of the change to other changes that are also going on. It is difficult, however, to do this exactly for certain kinds of changes, because it is difficult to be exact about the contrary states. For example, although it is true that we go from not being sunburned to being sunburned, we go by being a little sunburned, then a little more, and then a little more—and we have to wonder how these potential states are distinguished one from another and how long it takes for each of them to be actualized. Are there distinct and contrary states? Does the actualization of some take longer than the actualization of others? Or should we suppose that each actualization must take the same very small amount of time? Whitehead supposes that there are distinct states and that their actualizations take the same amount of time. He also supposes, in a fine account of occurrences, that when we talk about the actualization of possibilities we do not need the notion of substances at all.

Like Aristotle, then, Whitehead thinks that there are actualizations, but he doesn't think that the actualizations are changes *of* substances or changes *in* them. The final real things, he thinks, are processes, not substances, and all processes are ultimately occasions of actualization. There is no need, Whitehead says, to think that actualizations are caused by something more real than themselves or even that actualizations occur inside of substances, though these are Aristotle's views. Actualizations simply occur; what occur are actualizations, and because they do not occur in a substance we cannot talk about measuring how long it takes for them to occur. There are no intervals *in* an actualization (for Aristotle, the interval is *between* one actual state and the actualization of another). That means that in an actualization, there is no interval between states, so that everything that occurs in an actualization occurs at once.

The major themes in Whitehead's view seem to me sound. There is nevertheless something wrong in the notion of the time of an actualization or in the notion of actualization itself. The sure sign of this is that there is too much about actualization that Whitehead's conceptions cannot explain; for example, his ideas do not explain why actual occasions continue to occur or why they are as big or as long as they are. There should be a rationale for these two points. That the world goes on in unit processes of the same length cannot be accidentally true. Still, none of Whitehead's conceptions can explain these important results.

The main conceptions Whitehead uses to define actual occasions are "data," "pulsation," and "forms." He says that occasions emerge from data. They arise naturally when "creation produces" a "natural pulsation," "each pulsation forming a natural unit of historic fact." The data are "the full context of the antecedent universe as it exists in relevance to that pulsation," and to give an occasion a direction and a sense for its own completeness, there are also forms "harboured in the nature of things, either as realized forms or as potentialities for realization." This is Whitehead's detailed way of saying that an actualization consists in something propulsive that takes account of what precedes it and that also has its own direction.

How does an occasion come about? Why do they continue to come about? Whitehead says that an occasion emerges from data; the data, however, do nothing themselves—the forms that are in the past do not act—and what Whitehead calls "potentialities" do not actualize themselves. The vital fact for occurrence, and for continuing occurrences, seems therefore to be in what Whitehead calls pulsations, in a pulsation's seeking after forms that will make it definite while it actualizes them in turn. It is as if there is a swish of *ongoing* that wants to become definite, a flash of ambition that wants a direction, or, in Plato's terms, a fluxing that needs to be informed. For Whitehead, a pulsation seems almost to act as its own demiurge to actualize the forms that are made available to it. When the process is complete the forms will be saturated with the pulsation, and the occasion will be actual and past. It is or was a process only as a single pulse, and another pulse will then presumably arise. Why?

Whitehead has no answer to this question or none that can be understood. Pulsations are produced by "creation," but we do not know how and why. Creation, for Whitehead, is neither God nor even an act of God's. God is a process in the universe, not its creator, and God provides for only some of the forms that are actualized in occasions. Creation is something else, and though, on Whitehead's analysis, we cannot understand it, we can see why he thinks it is real.

Whitehead's intuition about creation is that, at each moment, there are new additions to everything that in any sense already exists: at each moment, there are not merely new arrangements of data and possibilities but also a newness that makes for the occurrence of new occasions. I think Whitehead's view is that this kind of newness is owed to creation, not to anything that already is, not even to God. Consequently, there is no understanding creation. There is nothing behind it; nothing even conditions it. It is the extreme reality that enables the items that can be connected to come to be connected in actual occasions. It is itself continual, but there is no reason for its being so. It just is, and we must think carefully what our patience should be with the idea of such an ultimacy. Perhaps we have to suppose one; one hopes, however, that we do not.

There remains the much smaller matter that was also to be understood, the notion that an occasion has an extent or that what is present has a length. For Whitehead, the extent of an occasion is not owed to its data or its forms. They are not the kinds of things that have a size. The extent of an occasion must therefore be owed to the pulsation that is the basis for its actuality. What Whitehead is saying, then, is that an occasion is extended because its pulsation is extended. The process of actualization is the pulsation's becoming definite because of the forms of definiteness that enter into it. The process, the complexity in the process, occurs all at once because it takes place in one pulsation. The pulsation itself, however, has no complexity; its extension cannot be said to be all at once because there is no "all" to it. There are no parts of it. The difficulty in this idea is that, again, we are without an explanation: an occasion is extended because its pulsation is extended, but there is no understanding the sense in which a pulsation is extended, and we are therefore without an explanation of an occasion's occurring all at once and without an understanding of a present's having length. Whitehead's fundamental conceptions seem not to resolve the important issues of the necessity for new occasions and for those occasions having length. They point toward resolutions, but they stop short, usually with a possibility that depends on a possibility and without that interdependence of conceptions that makes for a necessity. It is not certain that Whitehead's conceptions can be easily revised.

Can a notion of an extended but nonsuccessive present be constructed in some other way? Or is the notion contradictory and beyond all sense? Can some of Whitehead's insights about novelty and complexity be preserved? Can we say that there are occurrences in the present and that they are all at once? I think that the answers are "yes": the notion that answers them is that something that is becoming present is becoming actual, not by actualizing forms or possibilities, as Whitehead thinks, but by forming itself on something already actual in that present time. What becomes actual in an individual in the present can become actual because a part of the individual is already actual.

To understand this we need to review the previously made observation that even when individuals are present they are also partly past and partly future. In each new moment, as individuals act, they make singular and actualize a part of their own indefinite future being by forming that part of themselves on that further part of themselves that has already become definite or is becoming so. Additionally, time comes into singular individuals and passes through them in the present. There is, then, this complexity: individuals act to continue themselves and time comes into them and passes through them to a past beyond their singularity. In this action of time and individuals the time that is in individuals and the individuals that are in the time extend each other. An action in the present is extended not because it is in a time that is itself extended but because time and individuals extend each other in the actions of which they are the parts. The extension of the present, then, comes about as the present—and it comes about because, in the present, an individual's action moves in one direction and the time that comes into it moves in another.

This last observation is a version of the familiar idea that actions go from the past or the present toward the future but that time moves from being future to being present and then to being past. The actions that consist of individuals' lasting and time's coming into them also move in these directions, and it is this moving in both directions that makes for the extension of the present. The extension comes about because the strands of an individual's acting and of time's passing do not pass each other by, as if they were on different tracks; instead, they enter into one another, filling each other out. As inside each other but also as continuing in their own directions, each extends the other. Time comes to have its duration through a present because of the individuals that are in it, and individuals endure or persist because of the time that courses through them.

If time and individuals could not be in one another time could not pass and individuals could not act. Each would stop the other by not yielding for the other a place inside itself. The world would be stilled. It is obvious that the world is not still and that, because there must always be singular individuals, it can never stop. The present is when the world goes on. It is an ongoing in which individuals extend time and time becomes the basis of their persistence. This extension is one of the differences between the present and the other parts of time; it is also one of the differences between individuals as they are present and as they are past and future.

The present, then, has its length as a kind of complexity, but not the kind that Whitehead imagines. Its length, its complexity, is owed to individuals' being in time and to time's being in singular individuals. By themselves, if we could think of individuals as being by themselves, individuals would have no length. This is also true of time. Together as a present, however, as the components of an action, the two affect each other. In that action there is a coming to be singular and a becoming past, and these must occur together. An individual comes to be singular at the same time that the time in that individual becomes past. The coming to be and the becoming past do not occur sequentially; they are not outside each other. They are inside each other, and the action they constitute, therefore, cannot be condensed or occur in an instant because its components stretch each other out. Each has a real direction—a going forward and a becoming past—and having these directions, the components cannot be confined within an unextended point.

In each moment, then, individuals come to be newly singular. In that same moment they also become past. What is passing does not occur first, to make room in an individual for what is coming into it, nor does the becoming occur first and thereby push out what is becoming past. The two occur together, and both occur because of time's entry into an individual and its recovery from the hold that the individual has on it. As time passes it makes something of an individual past; it is also made to pass by the reaching, provocative going forward of the individual. The ceaseless change in individuals is therefore not wholly a succession of comings to be. Most of the puzzles and paradoxes about change are due to our supposing that change is entirely a coming to be. Perhaps we think of it in that way because we think that change is much the same as motion, but the changes in individuals do not, as motions do, go only in one way. In a present there is both a future's becoming present and a present's becoming past, and individuals and time are spread between the two.

We should, then, see the following about the present: (1) the time that is present cannot be separated from the action that it causes and constitutes in an individual; (2) such an action is complex; it is both a coming to be singular and a becoming past, and because of their different directions, these components of an individual's lasting extend each other some; (3) occurrences are complex because time enters into individuals and passes to get beyond their singularity, making them partly past even while individuals are making singular that being of their own that a provoked time brings into them; (4) there is some indefiniteness in the present about what is going on and some indefiniteness as well about the extent of the present; but even so, (5) the extension is real; it consists of the temporal complexity, the coming to be and passing away, in an action itself.

The question these notions seem to evade is how long, exactly, the present is—what portion of a second? This seems a simple and direct question, but it really is miscast. The misunderstanding in it is, again, the idea that if the present has a length, it must start, go on, and then come to a close, that it must have a first, a next, and then a last—that the present is like a line. An extended present, however, is not a line. It is not even like a line. The challenge is to say what an extended present is or is like. Recently the most frequent answer has been that it is like a pulse or beat, that it is spread out but still all at once. This comparison, however, though it seems suggestive, is not ultimately of any use. Time does not pass in the simple way that it suggests.

In the image of pulses or beats there are also intervals: pulse, interval, pulse, interval. We can recognize and count pulses and beats because of the intervals between them. There are no intervals between present moments, however, and pulses and beats that have no interval between them are continuous and not throbs at all: there is nothing separately emphatic in a continuous note. There is, then, no contrast between these images of line and pulse. The issue about time's passing remains, however, whether or not the images help.

The issues we are concerned with are the nature of the continuity of time or actions and whether there is consecutiveness in a present time. There are different views: the view that these continuities arise from the density of sets of instants in a linear time and the persistence of objects (but this is also the view that harbors paradoxes about the reality of motion and change) and the romantic view that there is a basic flow of things, that the division of time into instants is a reflective analysis of past passage, not an analysis of the passing in a present that is itself without components and cannot be analyzed. There is also Whitehead's view that occasions are momentary but that they occur sequentially, without interval, though there is a difficulty then about when—present or past—an occasion can be said to have its length.

My view in this essay is that time and action are continuous but that, even so, they are spread out in the present, that what occurs in the present is also, without an interval, succeeded by what occurs in a new present but that from present to present individuals are not unchanging entities. In this view, themes from otherwise different conceptions of continuity are combined in the notion that individuals are their actions. Their being present is both their coming to be and their becoming past, and their being continuous with their successors is owed to their complexity. What comes to be in one present becomes past in the next, so that there is an overlap or a partial lasting moment to moment, even though individuals do not persist unchanged even over that period of time. We come back then to the conception of a whole action in a present, one that has a length because of its being both a coming to be and a becoming past. These are the changes that time and individuals cause in each other when they stretch each other out.

Presents are the final units of passing time. They cannot be measured because measure does not apply to them. If we attempt to measure a present, making the mistake of waiting for the present to begin so that we can time it to its close, whatever clock we use will move from present to present, and all that the clock could show is that it was present when what it was timing was a present time. Presents consist of actions, and they are extended because of time and individuals. They are, however, neither a set of instants nor any number of completed motions long. In the present's lasting for a moment, the coming to be and passing away of individuals are the real units in the actions of individuals and time.

The Breadth of the Present

In the present, time is both inside and outside individuals. As it is spread outward from the inside of individuals, it is the same as space. So space should be said to be present too; indeed, it is only as being present that space exists. There is no space in the past and none in the future. Space is not an eternal background over which time passes and on which the motions and distances between past, present, and future things are located. Space comes to be continuously. Despite its great stability, despite its seeming differences from a time that passes, in the present, it is the same as time: it is spread out from the inside of the individuals that provoke it to pass.

Our ideas of space and time are very closely connected with the ideas we have about objects in space and time, and how we conceive of objects affects our ideas of space and time. In what direction, though, do the connections go? Are things related spatially and temporally because spatial and temporal properties are essential in them? Or do they have spatial and temporal properties because they are always *in* space and time? The ideas of space and time and objects are very different in these two views.

For example, if we suppose that objects are intrinsically spatial and sized and always now, then there will be spatial and temporal relations between the objects but there will need not be a real and separate space and time. On the other hand, if objects become spatial and present, space and time will have to be real enough to lend or give or constitute the spatiality and temporality of the entities that might then be said to be in them. The first idea has been dominant in Western cosmological thought—the ultimate entities are bodies and they are in themselves spatial, extended, sized, and they are always wholly at a present time. There are, however, very strong reasons for thinking that this idea is not accurate. The view I will argue for is that the space and time *of* entities, or of *individuals,* are not theirs intrinsically but are due to and acquired from space and time.

The course of the argument will be (1) to show that it is uncertain, even on scientific grounds, that things are intrinsically spatial and that there is no real space outside them. Then the question is (2) how the space that is supposedly essential in bodies is connected to the real but empty space beyond them. The answer is that there is no connection, so, (3) if we are to think of there being spatial entities in space, we must think not of bodies but of individuals (or of entities like individuals), and we must think that those individuals acquire their spatiality from space itself. They will, therefore, have an intense spatiality, a spatiality that is a concentration in them of the space that is also beyond them. These two spaces, though *located* differently, are nevertheless really the same space, both inside and outside individuals. And finally, (4) this unusual conclusion and the ideas that lead to it will be reviewed and summarized.

1. Many philosophers and scientists think that bodies are essentially extended. They have a size and they are at some place at a given time. They also think that we need not posit a space in addition to the space of bodies, not even to provide the fields in which measurements of distances are made. Bodies and their motions can be used in making such measurements. One body, for example, is half the size of another and it is so many body distances away. Size and measure, then, seem not to argue for there being a space and time beyond the space and time of bodies themselves.

This will be true, though, only if a large number of suppositions are made, some of which are unwarranted according to modern physics. For example, if bodies are to measure other bodies and the distances between them, they must be moved around in the course of making the measurements. There is then the question whether their sizes or the distances remain the same while the bodies are being moved. Their size may be affected by the speeds at which they move—supposing whatever we must suppose to measure the speeds—and they may also be affected by the space through which they move and even by the length of time they move. Very strong suppositions about bodies, motions, times, and perhaps space itself are needed to assure us that the measures of size and distance by bodies are uniform, and there are grounds for serious doubt about some of them.

There are other reasons for thinking that the space of bodies is not the only space there is. These are about geometry and motions. Ideas about geometry have changed radically over the last two hundred years. Geometry used to be thought of as the science of the properties of space, but when non-euclidean geometries were formulated, many people came to think that neither logic nor space itself favored one geometry over another, that geometries do not *describe* anything and that, therefore, space itself is not real. Recent developments in physics, however, have led us to reflect further, and our notion now seems to be that space is real even though it does not have all the properties set out in any one geometry or doesn't have them everywhere.

This last idea has grown out of thinking about why some geometries are better than others for describing motions in certain regions of the cosmos. Its insight is that we can not only describe motions but think about their causes as well. In the old interpretations of geometry, the causes of motions were never considered. They were thought to have nothing to do with space. The causes are dynamic; they produce the motions, and when the motions are described, the causes or conditions can be left aside. Our notion now seems to be that, in some motions, there are contours that are not caused by anything prior to the motions themselves. They must, however, be caused by something, and the imaginative conjecture is that they are caused by the space in which the motions occur. Space causes or contributes to the shapes of motions as they occur, and because it really does this, because it really affects motions, space is said to be real. The truest geometries are therefore those that describe the notable configurations of space itself; they are the ones that most accurately describe those large motions that are affected by the space in which they occur.

The idea that space has configurations and that it affects the shape of bodily motions rules out the idea that the space of bodies is the only space, but it also leaves us uncertain as to how the space of bodies is to be understood. Are we to think that there are two spaces, the space of bodies and a space beyond them? Or must we deny that bodies have a space of their own?

2. If bodies are intrinsically spatial and space is also real, if these two spaces are the same in nature, there must be something else that is essential to bodies besides their spatiality. Otherwise, we would not know that there are entities in space; there would be no real difference between space and bodies, there would just be a lot of space. The definition of bodies as extended enables us to identify them only if, as in Descartes, there is no separate space. Will it really suffice, though, to

think of bodies as having two essences, one of which is space? What is the other essence, and what connection must it have to a body's spatiality? The soundest answer to these questions goes, I think, in the direction of Leibniz's view that there is one essence to bodies and that it is not spatiality. The spatiality of a body derives from its activity. Its essence is therefore some power or activity of extending and limiting itself, of pressing itself out so far and then holding itself in. A body is thus not something that is spatial and is then in space; it is rather something nonspatial that is *in* space and that, in one way or another—and perhaps not uniformly—limits itself to a certain extent of space. This notion of a thing's spatiality requires a notion of that thing's activity and its acquisition and occupation of a space. If it, or something like it, is sound, we are done with the notion of bodies that are spatial, passive, and incapable of initiating action. We must think of the things in space as being activities or being in action; we must think of them as individuals. How is it then that individuals become spatial, have a space of their own, and are nevertheless continuous with the space beyond them?

3. The spaces of individuals are intensities of the space that extends beyond them: there is at the present a single space, and the spaces of singular individuals are concentrations of it. This is an unfamiliar notion, but I think we will understand it if we remember that individuals are actions and that their activity defines a place in the present. An individual's space is not a static property; an individual is not itself static. Its spatiality, therefore, comes about continually as an individual persists. More accurately, an individual's persistence is the individual's spatial track. We can then see that an individual's essential activity also explains the intensification of space in an individual.

The spatiality of a singular individual must be acquired continually. Where, when, how, and why does the acquisition come about? These may seem eerily like the old questions about souls, which are not themselves bodies but come to have them. Indeed, on some important points, our views about individuals and their spatiality resemble the old answers to those old questions.

Like souls, individuals are not spatial before they become present. They are not spatial when they are future, though they are not then singular. They become singular and spatial when they become present. Their being is made present by time, and they become spatial as they continue the being of the individuals that are already present. Individuals become or continue to be spatial as they act and as time passes. Nothing outside of them or time creates and inserts them into space. Through their own action, they cause the space in which they continue to be.

The strongest objection to the idea that actions are spatial is that, unlike actions, spatial *things* are thought to be substantial. Spatial things are solid; their final parts seem to be impermeable. Actions do not seem to have the same solidity.

The compelling principle about the substantiality of bodies is that two bodies cannot be in the same place at the same time. This principle defines the meaning or the conditions for there being a body or for there being two of them. It has, however, a compelling analogue for individuals and actions, namely, that two individuals cannot initiate the same action. Individuals continue themselves, they form themselves continuously, and as they do, they oppose and resist one another. Their resistance to one another is, therefore, not an occasional feature of actions, as it is for bodies; atoms, for example, may or may not bump into one another. Individuals, on the other hand, cannot continue to exist without holding off one another. They are always resistant, always, one might say, showing their version of solidity.

The solidity of bodies is not the same as the resistant outsidedness that individuals have in lasting, but as regards explaining change and motion, the notion of action proves no less helpful than the notion of a solid body. The notions of space and time that are involved in action are less familiar than those involved with bodies, but not only are they of equal use, they have the further advantage of being less obscure. There is, for example, no way to explain how a body is in space if space is real and no way to explain the conditions of motions if it is not. There is no such disadvantage in thinking that individuals continue to become spatial when they come to be singular.

Our conclusion, then, should be that individuals are not intrinsically spatial but that, as they act and time comes into them, they acquire their spatiality. They are not inserted into a separate time or space; their coming to be spatial is not miraculous. Individuals are inseparable from time, and in the present, when time is both inside and outside them, they are also inseparable from space. When they become singular and present, they become spatial: singularity, presence, and spatiality occur together, at the same time, as it were.

These last phrases, however, remind us of the question it is always appropriate to ask when distinctions are introduced, namely, whether the distinctions have not already been supposed, so that they are not really introduced but are only reinstated and reinstated confidently because of having been presupposed. The expression that prompts the question is "time is inside and outside individuals." Does this mean that individuals already have a space of their own? What else could time's passing into them mean? Is it true, then, that individuals are intrinsically spatial?

No, they are not, but they are always spatial and always acquiring new spatiality. As they are present, they are already spatial, and they have acquired the space they have; it in turn helps them channel the time that continues to come into them. Time's coming into and passing around individuals presupposes time and space but not that they are intrinsic to singular individuals. They are the time and space of the present; they must themselves become present, and the new presentness and new size of individuals have to be acquired in their continuing action. Time's passing in the present leads to time's continuing to pass. Space in the present prepares the way for the next moment's space. Individuals acquire their spatiality continuously.

There is therefore no circularity in the idea that the spatiality of individuals is owed to time and that it comes about as time enters into and passes around them. The present temporality and spatiality of individuals are presupposed in describing how individuals make themselves definite in new present moments and how they continue to be spatial as they act to last, but an individual's present spatiality is not intrinsic to it. It, too, is acquired; it presupposes a former spatiality, which presupposes a former spatiality, and so on, indefinitely. There was no time at which everything was future and individuals had to become spatial for the first time.

There is no reason in the requirements for explanation why we cannot hold that the spatiality of individuals is owed to time, but the notion that individuals acquire their spatiality, however, should be developed further. We especially need to explain the idea that the space of individuals is continuous with the space beyond them and that there is a whole or single space in the present time. What is the difference between the space of individuals and the space beyond them? This was the question that could not be answered for the space of bodies and the space that surrounds them. For individuals, the answer is that the space of an individual is an intense space, but the space beyond it is not. The difference is in intensity. This difficult notion is the second concept we need to understand the space of individuals.

The intensity of an occupied space is not exactly the same as the density of a body. Density is a measure of the amount of matter in a body of a given size. The more the matter, the greater the density; the more (same-sized) atoms in a place, the more densely crowded the space. It is not certain, however, that whatever the number of atoms in a place, the place itself is affected by their presence. It might or might not be, but if it is, the only effect is that its curvature is changed, not its quantity. The notion of a quantity of space in a place, or something like quantity, is the notion needed for intensity.

The space of an individual is intense because there is more space in an occupied space than in an empty one. This will seem paradoxical or senseless if we think of space only as a measure of size and distance. It will also seem senseless if we think that space is homogeneous and unaffectable. Can a sense nevertheless be given to this idea? Some such notion is needed if the space of individuals is to be continuous with the space beyond them and if the space of an individual is *its* space because of the individual's being in space and time.

The image that suggests a sense for "intensity" is that space is folded back on itself in an individual. There would be more space in a space if it could be folded and the folds were to lie on top of one another, as a piece of paper might be folded, thicker in the over-lapping areas and thinner elsewhere. The image is not a description: space cannot be picked up and folded, but something like a folding of space occurs in an individual's lasting because of the directions inside its activity.

There are, as we have seen, two directions in an individual's lasting. As it lasts, an individual reconstitutes itself in the present to continue to be singular. In that same present, though, it is also ceasing to be present and becoming past. These opposing directions in an action make for the extension of the present. They also make for the intensity of the space of a present activity, because the coming into being and the becoming past of an individual each have a kind of space and the actions are inside each other, thickening the space of an individual's activity.

The coming into being and the becoming past of an individual do not occur at the ends of its activity. An individual's continuing is not its forward edge, and its becoming past is not the part of it that is nearly gone. Both occur throughout the activity; one cannot occur without the other. It is because of the time and being that come into individuals that individuals are made to pass away or become past. It is because of what is already definite in them that what comes into individuals, even as it comes into them, comes to be shaped and formed. Coming to be present and ceasing to be present are therefore spread through the whole of the present, and they are inside each other.

The coming into being and becoming past of an individual affect the space inside of it. It is not, however, that coming to be and becoming past each have a separate space and that their separate spaces are combined. Neither has its own full-fledged separate space, but the two have a space together, and the space they have is more than the space either would have if it could occur alone.

The space inside individuals is different from the space surrounding them. There is no activity in the space outside individuals except for the unresisted passing of time, and there is no forward component in this passing. How, then, shall we describe the difference between a space inside an individual and the space outside of it? The difference is, at the least, that what is inside individuals is more complex than the time and space outside them. The lasting of individuals is more complex than the passing of time, and the space inside individuals is more complex than the space beyond them. Still, the space inside individuals is the same as the space outside them. How shall we interpret the difference so that it is a difference of the spaces themselves? The answer, though tinged with metaphor, is that the space inside an individual is thicker or more intense than the space outside of it.

In all accounts of space and time, complexity is what makes for their dimension. An infinity of instants, for example, is said to make for an extension of time, and points make for a line, lines for planes, and planes for solids. Each of these collections is an extension that is due to the *outsidedness* of things that are somehow together. The suggestion here is that, in individuals, there is an extension consisting of *insidedness,* an extendedness of time as a present and an internal extendedness that is also an intensification of space. The intensification is not found outside individuals. It is the difference between what happens inside and outside of individuals that makes for the difference between the space of individuals and the space of space itself.

We have the two notions we need: (a) the space of individuals is not intrinsic to them; individuals are spatial when they act and come to have space inside of them. (b) The space that is in individuals is more intense than the space that is outside of them. These two claims imply that, as apart from individuals, space is not an extended continuum. Instead, it continuously becomes because of them. As time comes into individuals and passes around them and as it passes through them to overcome the divisions that individuals tend to make of it, time becomes a space; it is then the time common to all individuals. Space comes about because of individuals, because of their interplay with time. Time would not pass and there would be no space if there were no individuals. It is only as individuals take time into themselves that time becomes an extended field configured by individuals, spreading through the individuals as they persist in being spatial and spreading beyond them as well. Individuals configure the space they are in by their persistence. In turn, space makes for their extension. As they act and time passes, space passes as well, though individuals occupy the same amount of space, or nearly the same amount, over short periods of time. We normally locate individuals by considering where they persist; their persistence is their spatial track. They occupy a wider space in other of their activities, however. In their basic persisting, they have their smallest size.

4. These claims reach further than many physicists find they need go, but they are neither incompatible with physics nor at odds with what other subjects show. There are works, for example, of painting, sculpture, architecture, dance, drama, and music that seem to shape in unusual ways the space and perhaps the time they occupy. Different colors bend, divide, thicken, or thin a space; one will compress the space of a room and another lengthen it, and sounds of different sorts will perhaps shorten, lengthen, or intensify a time. It is not that the works represent a different space and time or that their representation of these realities is skewed; instead, their configurations of space and time are simply not the same as those we are accustomed to apart from art, and we can describe the differences only by dramatically modifying the language we use in our usual activity.

The space and time in works of art are real and not subjective, as real as the space and time of any other individuals. They appear subjective when the works are set in a larger context where we can no longer deal with them as works of art and when the measures appropriate to acting in the space and time of everything are also used to measure them. Held off as works of art, as alone as we can let them be, they are measured by the eye and ear. Well-made works help us into themselves; they can also help to close or consummate our experience of them. While we are in them, though, they are controlling; we act and contribute to their space and time. They are each, as we act in them, as the works take us into them, a world unto themselves, and it is as if their space and time were theirs alone.

We are not generally able to sustain our sight of works of art for long, but even when set in larger compass where they are no longer seen as works of art their lesson remains: individuals configure the space and perhaps the time they occupy. The space and time of works of art are no less real than those of a more extended world, they are simply what space and time become in them. Space and time are real under the conditions of constructing and appreciating works of art, and they are also real apart from them.

Individuals provoke the occurrence of a common space and time. These extend individuals and individuals affect them. Because of their doing so, space may not be uniform in its spread; whether that is so depends on what individuals there are and where they are. These are contingent facts, not settled by the requirement that individuals exist in a common present that is a space as well. It is a further question whether, as there might be, there is also a dilation of time.

The Depth of Individuals

Individuals are suffused with time, it penetrates them through and through, but it does not overwhelm them and keep them from acting. Individuals are more than tints on a mighty, passing time. They act even while time is passing through them. There is a depth in them and they act out of it. Even in their depths, however, individuals are not beyond the reach of time.

There is literally a depth in individuals, which like length and width is a dimension of them or of the place they occupy. When we think of individuals as able to act, we think of their having depth in another sense as well, and not just metaphorically. There is something in them that enables them to act. If individuals were like atoms, if all their changes were motions caused by forces acting on them from outside, there would be no change inside them; they would be the same through and through and always what they already are. When, on the other hand, we think that individuals originate their actions and can move and change themselves, we think of something like an internal force, something like a potentiality or a power or a capacity to realize possibilities. We are right to think that there is an inside to individuals, only the notion of a power is so obscure that it does not help us understand the inside of an individual.

What is a power, and how does an individual have and use its powers? The difficulty here is simply that things and their powers seem too different to be together in a single entity. The things we imagine to have powers are what they are, they are actual and here and now, but the power of a thing is not actual; it is something that can be used or exhibited; it is something in reserve. How, then, does a thing *have* a power? Its power is in some sense inside it, but that means that while the thing is otherwise all definite, with every part of it in place, something that is only potentially actual is inside it but not quite anywhere. There is also the question of whether a thing has the further power of being able to use its own powers. How and when does it use them? How does it manage to change itself? What is it that acts to affect the change—the thing as it is? And what does it act on and with? Or does the power itself act, exhibiting itself and affecting the thing that has it?

There have been ingenious answers to these questions, but the fact that none of them is convincing shows that our conceptions of "thing" and "power" have not been sound. Still, conceptions like them are not dispensable. What seems most to cause the difficulties in understanding them is, once again, the idea that the things thought to have powers are thought to be wholly in the present time. If we also think that they can change themselves we must suppose that they have a capacity to change, so that a thing will have parts of different kinds, one that has to do with what it is, the other with what it can be in a later time, and we do not see how a power can be in something actual without being actual itself.

We will have a sounder notion of "thing" and "power" if we move away from the idea that things are wholly present and suppose again that individuals are singular in the present but extend to the future and the past. This leads to a sounder notion of power by having it be something that comes into singular individuals; power is something that individuals come to have. It is in them only as it is being exhibited, and individuals always become empowered because they are always acting and having something that is not present coming into them.

Individuals are always acting, they are never paused. Inside them, at their depths, they form themselves continuously, which becomes evident as change. This forming is something like a power's being expended in an action. An individual has the power it expends, but it has it only as it is expending it. There is no reserve of power already inside of it. What comes to be the power that an individual expends is its own, but while it is unexpended it is not inside of it—it might be thought to be future to it. As individuals act, their own future being is always being brought into them by passing time. This is what empowers them.

Some of the future being of individuals comes to be present in them or to empower them because the individuals that are singular and present pull on time and future being, and that pull starts them into the depths of individuals. The pull is the result of an individual's holding itself together while time passes in the present. Because singular individuals are continuous with their future being and their time is continuous with future time, as the time that is already in individuals passes and the individuals hold themselves together, they pull on those portions of themselves that are not yet present.

An individual's holding itself together is the innermost strand of its action. There is a coming to be and a passing away in an individual, but these two strands of its action must be kept together; otherwise, an individual would be pulled apart. What is becoming past could be separated from what is coming to be or get too far ahead of it; there would be a vacant place in the individual where there is no action, and that is impossible. The basic action of individuals is the holding together of what comes to be and what is becoming past; this is the lasting of an individual.

As an individual persists nothing in it is unchanging, nothing remains the same underneath the action and the change. Individuals are suffused with the passing time that changes them and causes them to change themselves. In the course of persisting, the future being that is carried into individuals becomes active; it becomes the new being of the singular individual, and as it becomes more and more definite and then past further being is drawn into the individual. Individuals reconstitute themselves in each moment. The power they have for doing this—the being and time that become active—comes into them.

The notion of something inside and at the depth of a thing contrasts with something's being outside it. The inside of an individual has to do with the start or fresh continuing of its activity, with its making singular what had been continuous with it but outside of it. When an individual acts, it starts its action from inside itself, at its depth, where time and the future being of individuals come into it. It is there that the power of individuals is first exercised.

The depth in individuals is the first part of their action, and it is continuous with their continuing. It is the joining of the present and the future; it is the transformation of the future being of time and individuals into their continuing activity. There is no separation between individuals and their future being and therefore no bottom to individuals. Even when they are singular, individuals are not enclosed; they are not wholly in one place or time but spread beyond their being present. The time and being of the future are continuous with individuals before they become present and are transformed, and they continue them after they are transformed. This transformation must occur because time and being as they are future are not separated into strands, one for each individual, nor is future time divided into ordered moments of presence, one after another. The whole of future time and being bears on the individuals that are singular when they are present. The singulars cause the divisions in the time and being that continue them; this cause occurs in their depths.

Because individuals are continuous with the whole of future time and being there can be a feeling of an impending immensity and fullness beyond them, or we can imagine that this is how some of our feelings are to be interpreted. Future time and being do not have the dimensions that are found in the present, however; there is no length or breadth, and future being is not even definite. Still, if we must have an image for our thought, it should be that in their depths, where individuals are continuous with the time and being of the future, they are, as it were, joined to the spread of the whole of the future. Each individual is continuous with the whole of future time and being, which, if it had a size, would seem enormous compared to each of them.

Our image, then, might be of the whole future opening out at the depth of singular individuals, though the image is inaccurate because future time and being do not take up space. Still, there is a difference between the time that is inside individuals and the whole of the future time that has not yet been strained by singularities. We might also imagine that, though different, these two times are joined. This image, however, is also inaccurate and for the same reason. There is no separation, no ontological difference between them; they are, for example, not like the actual and the possible. They are different from each other because they are together with individuals in different ways, and it is at the depths of individuals that the difference is overcome.

The Rate of the Present's Passing

In every moment there are many individuals. They are contemporaries, and the simplest individuals will also be contemporaries in the next present. Individuals are continuously contemporaneous, even though each initiates its own action. It is as if each moves through time at the same rate or as if time moves through all of them equably. "Rate" is not a geometrical notion, like length, breadth, and depth, but a dynamical conception; still, it can help us understand that there is a whole and single present and that all singular individuals are in it.

It is not a coincidence that individuals are and continue to be contemporaries. It does not just happen that each of them is at the same time. Singular individuals are nevertheless distinct. How does it come about, then, that they are and continue to be together in time? What explains the fact of their being continuously contemporary?

Whether these questions have sense, and what that sense might be, turns on our conceptions of time and the things in it. Some recent constructions suppose that individuals' continued contemporaneity depends on how quickly things move or on what clocks might show and the systems in which motions are measured, as if there were choices, as if no clocks or systems of measure were more basic than others and none were able to measure everything.

Is it an observational question whether things are contemporaries of one another? Were we to think so—were we to think that things might or might not be at the same time—we would be supposing that some of them might be contemporary and others past or future relative to one another and that the distinction depends on where and how the comparisons are made. We would also be supposing that because there is no map of all the relative positions there is no common present for everything and that even for the things that are thought to be contemporary there is no common future or past.

Some of these striking notions are mentioned in modern physics in relation to how one establishes the time at which events occur. Physicists consider the location and motion of an observer relative to the motions whose relative places in time are to be established; they also consider the transmission of the signals needed for such a measurement. They construct systems for measuring the time of occurrences and compare the measurements established in the different systems. Some of them find it difficult to comprehend how actual and possible systems can be understood together and whether, in a universe of such systems, anything would really occur. The major philosophical difficulty in the usual interpretations is due to overlooking the fact that, whatever the measures of relative rates of motion or change, things or occurrences are intrinsically temporal. Systems for locating and comparing their relative "whens" will be no more than mathematical conveniences if we neglect their having a time inside of them.

The time that is inside individuals is not the absolute time so many modern theories in physics have found to be useless; that time is outside things. The time that is inside individuals is part of their activity of continuing themselves. It should, therefore, be presupposed even in the theory that motions and their times are entirely relative. A thing neither moves nor stays at rest unless it continues to exist; individuals continue to exist by reconstituting themselves, and they could not reconstitute themselves unless time were inside them. We should, then, be able to talk without confusion about both the time of the motions of individuals and the time in the actions in which they continue themselves.

Relative motions are relations between what seem to be the motions of things; they are comparative relations that involve the time it takes for things to change their properties, places, or the rates at which these changes themselves occur. Motion is defined by these relations and not thought to be a property of things considered separately. The relative motions of greatest interest are changes of place, and these presuppose that, relatively, things move themselves or are moved by something else. Calculations of these motions neglect all the changes in the relatively moving things except those that occur because of the motions themselves or because of the rates at which the motions occur. What one cares about is only where and when, how fast or slow, and whether there are changes of rates. Motions and their times have nothing to do with anything else.

The action in which individuals reconstitute themselves, however, is the *interior motion* in which they make themselves continuously present. It is not relative to anything else. Something in the individuals moves; their being and time are passing, and they are constituted of these passings. There is a change of their being and a temporal change as well. New presents with individuals in them come about whether individuals otherwise move or not.

It is a small matter whether the motions inside and outside individuals are both called "motions"; it is more important to understand the connection between the two, namely, that relative motions presuppose that moving or moveable things continue to exist and that individuals change inside themselves. Measures of relative motion are indifferent to such changes. Physicists can measure any kind of exterior motion, but, except in particle theory, they neglect interior changes and suppose that time is the measure only of the exterior motions and the comparative durations of things. This supposition may or may not cause problems for physics—this is for physics to decide—but there will be terrible anomalies for our understanding of the persistence and changes of things if we think individuals that are contemporary in one frame for measurement do not otherwise change but nevertheless become future or past to one another when some of them move and have their motions measured in different frames. Being present or future or past is not a matter only of *when* things are but most basically a matter of *what* they are, whether they are singular or, if not singular, past and definite or future and indefinite. Individuals continue themselves in any frame of reference.

Physicists make suppositions that allow for both simplicity and great comprehensiveness in their accounts of relative motions. These are suppositions about entities, the lines along which they move, and possible comparisons of the clocks that move along with them. When physicists are not confident that the clocks can be compared or that it makes sense to think of comparing them, they suppose there to be many times, not one. Alternatively, if there is a theory about the comparability of clocks, the entities whose motions they measure can be thought to be past and future to one another, though there is no intrinsic difference between the two. Some physicists then interpret the system of spacelike and timelike lines as a timeless world in which nothing moves and nothing really happens and in which the ideas of relative pasts and futures, despite their paradoxical popular use, are no more than names for the relations between the points that the physicists have located on certain lines. Relative pasts and futures are, for physicists, only nominal, or it is at least uncertain, if not false, that what they name is real.

Many incomparable times or a timeless whole of different times? Both these views are extreme. Physicists are led to extremes like these when, in the course of explaining things, they go on to explain what their explanations presuppose. What explains the real, we think, is real itself and perhaps more fundamental than anything we have explained. What defuses this argument are the uncertainties we feel over whether our explanations are the only ones possible and whether, even then, they are as simple as they can be. Both physics and philosophy have their extreme views, and each reads the others either critically or as consistent with itself.

My most concrete claim in this essay is that individuals are always continuing themselves; my most extreme view is that there is a single future and a single past. In its account of motions, physics does not consider the nature of the changes in things, and its extreme view is that things, otherwise alike in nature, can be in different times relative to one another if they are thought to be in different frames of reference. It is difficult to state either the philosophical or the physical extremes without apparent paradox. If either of the two were to be adjusted to remove or reduce the inconsistency between them, however—if there is an inconsistency—the adjustment should be made in the physicist's interpretation of time.

The reason is that the ongoingness of individuals is such a concrete fact that an interpretation of it is much less likely to be wayward than a result based on theories that are extensions of theories far removed from anything concrete. This kind of adjustment has, in fact, already been made in the notion that "relative futures" and "relative pasts" are only dramatic names for imagined points whose positions have been calculated in certain ways. Other adjustments might be devised as well, concerning the temporality of frames of reference, for example, or the nature of occurrences and ways of locating them in a space-time continuum. If adjustments could not be made in these ways—and not made just for the sake of surer compatibilities—they would have to be tried the other way around. Further adjustments in the very elaborate and often philosophically playful interpretations of physics seem so likely, however, that for now, at least, there seems no overwhelming bar to thinking that single individuals are contemporary and will continue to be contemporaries, no matter where or how quickly they move. Individuals can be contemporary even while they move or change at different rates.

It is obvious that the changes of individuals, apart from those that constitute their continuing, can occur at different rates. Their motions can also occur at different rates, depending on what is happening to them. That there are relative differences is revealing and can be explained, but whatever these sorts of differences, individuals that are contemporaries will continue to be contemporaries. The unity and singleness of time and the way it enters into their reconstitution ensure that this is so. The only way in which contemporary individuals could locate themselves in separate times (and the only way in which entities that are not contemporaries could make themselves contemporaries) would be for each of them to deal separately with time and have time respond to them one by one. The future might then come more quickly into some of them, or the past might slow some of them, so that they would stay present for a longer time. These, however, are foolish conjectures. There is one time—one future, one present, and one past. Individuals are together with time as a whole and it responds to all of them together. It passes into and through each of them, but not in one case slowly and in another at a faster rate. If it did that—even if it could—it would not be a whole and single time. Nothing, then, not even the rate at which individuals move or change, can alter their alignment in time.

The passage of time in and through individuals is the most fundamental motion in them. Because all other kinds of motion and change depend on it, in the being and becoming of singular individuals, time does not have a rate in the same sense as the rate at which the singulars themselves move and change. Rate is a relative notion; one individual moves or changes more quickly, more slowly, or at the same rate as another individual. Time, however, is not a thing in time and its passage is not relative to the motions that are in time. It passes as it does whether the individuals it helps constitute move quickly or slowly. The sense we found for the notion of passage turns on time's passing into and through individuals. This sense is slender but sound, and it should not be lost in our unavoidable comparisons between time itself and the things that are in time.

There are images that turn on the comparison and suggest that if processes can be fast or slow, the rate at which time itself passes might also change. This might be so, but if we were caught up in such a change, we would not notice that it had occurred; we and our clocks would speed up or slow down, too. The point of such images, however, is not to present paradox but to argue that time does not really pass or that it is not real. The images, however, are not serious. "Passage" does not have exactly the same meaning for time and for the things that are in time. One has to do with a change in individuals, the other with change of place and rate: the fact of their difference, however, does not affect an understanding of time's being a part of the change of things nor the sense of time's being real.

Dimensions and the Present

The reflections of this chapter have been formed from two opposing traditions of philosophical thought, and they do not stand entirely in either one of them. One of the traditions maintains that what is fundamentally real is unchanging; the other, that change or becoming is the fundamental reality and that nothing, not even the totality of things, remains unchanged. The importance, the weight, of these traditions is incalculable. We are in them and we think in them. Still, they contradict each other, and though both cannot be right, we are reluctant to give up the insights of either.

The themes in this chapter are attempts to reconcile the traditions. Their widest claim is that there is not one fundamental reality from which others are derived but that there are different realities, equally fundamental, and that the ongoing of the world is constituted in these realities being together, even while they are distinct. Two of these realities are that which makes for there being individuals and that which has been called "time." Their being together in different ways accounts for the future and the past and for the ongoing that is the present of both time and individuals.

The reconciliation in this broad view is that neither the being nor the becoming that traditionally have been thought to be fundamental is really so—not that some other reality is more fundamental. Instead, there are two fundamental realities and they are together. Each considered separately is what the one tradition would call "being"; together, there is transience, process, and change—what the other tradition calls "becoming." There are beings and becoming; realities that are together are also distinct. There should therefore be a twining of the traditions: because individuals and time are each real and are inseparably together, being and becoming are equally fundamental and, by being so, they ensure that the change of the world, the newness of the world at each moment, occurs within all there is. There is no explanation for this newness occurring in any other way. It certainly does not arise from nothing.

It would relieve reflection, and confirm it, if there were a way of proving this without concluding it from a group of austere arguments. If only we could see that it is true or even that it is false and that something else must therefore be true. Our sight, unfortunately, is not so clear. There is little discipline in Western thought about the mood of mind in which the final realities might be disclosed to us. Although Eastern and Oriental thought includes disciplines of meditation and provocation that are supposed to lead to an acknowledgment of what is ultimately real, there has been no consensus in Western thought about how such an acknowledgment might come about. There are Pythagoras's advice and Plato's curriculum; there are practices of prayer, spiritual exercises, and meditations about the road to God; there are principles of knowledge, rules about methods, ways to improve the understanding, and maxims on how to make our ideas clear. There are also doctrines that what is real discloses itself, whether or not we are prepared, in intuitions or insights that we cannot induce, that come on us unexpectedly, and that may be either clear or vague. There has been little agreement, however, on how the mind might be brought directly to what is real.

The most prominent of modern themes about method is that we are to ask questions, to search for what is disclosed to us, and to see how it is disclosed. We suppose that the real will finally answer us, so we become inquirers, which is, we think, though aggressive, within our right. We have the right to ask questions; we have the right to know. Our individualistic spirit can be harsh when we have not reflected on the communion that should exist between us, as questioners, and whatever answers us. In years past, it was often thought that there are some matters about which it is inappropriate to raise questions; the hand should be on the mouth, others are to be addressed in pious petition, not in contentious spirit, and we should wait hopefully for an answer that might, even then, not be disclosed. Even so, all such matters can be made into the answers to questions. When can and should we ask our questions? What questions should we ask and how should we ask them? Everything can be brought into an inquiry, even those realities that will, perhaps, be understood only when we see why their necessity puts them almost beyond questioning.

Questions presuppose alternatives. We may find an answer or not; if we do, the answer will be about one thing or another, and it will be either true or not. Each part of an alternative is a possibility. It is possible that we will find an answer and possible that we will not, but a possible answer is only possibly true and possibly not. Were there to be an actual answer—and not just a possible answer we are confident is true—the possibilities about truth and falsity would be, in a certain sense, removed. The things we ask about also have their modalities: there are some perhaps whose mode is possibility, others are actual, and there may be some necessary beings. When we ask about things, though, we bracket their modality.

Is x a prime number, yes or no? The question makes it seem as if it were possible for it to be prime and also not prime, though this clearly is not so. The easy resolution of this matter is to distinguish the modality of our knowing from the modality of the proposition about which we ask: I do not know that I can prove x to be prime and I do not know that I cannot. In a state of ignorance, leaving aside the intrinsic modality of what we ask about, everything is or seems possible, a belief Anselm attributed to the fool.

There are much more difficult cases—the Kantian antinomies, for example (indeed, the prime number example may be more difficult than I suggested). Kant says that we are inclined by habit to question without end, though the limiting condition for the sense of questions is the conditions for the possibility of experience. Use our concepts under these conditions and we make sense; use them uncritically, without staying to those conditions, and even the law of noncontradiction fails. Questions and answers, the argument goes, can make sense only within the limits of experience or language or if they are effective in a certain form of life. Only then will the questions have possible answers. They are about what is actual and, therefore, they are first about what is possible. The modality that is actual is the possibility that remains when one of the alternatives in answering a question is removed, as if the remaining answer were affected by the removal and no longer merely a possibility. A necessity, however, never had and never has an alternative; of necessity, the possible has one and, at one time, the actual had or should have had one, too.

This array of modalities holds not only for our knowledge but for the things that we can and do know about and even for those realities that we somehow must have always known about. The great project for knowledge is to align its modalities with the modalities of the realities we know about. We do not know enough, or do not know in the right way, if all we see of an ultimate reality is that it might be real or that we have a reason for thinking that it is. What must be should be known not in conjecture but with surity: necessity matching its necessity, for example, as in the illumination of the ontological argument or in our knowledge of mathematical truths. Likewise, we don't know that something is a fact if all we know is that it is possibly factual.

The awkwardness in all this is that we cannot come to know what is necessary or fundamental by answering questions about it because questions presuppose an alternative in what we ask about, but in reality there is no alternative to what must be the case. If we raise questions about it, then, we are not acknowledging it as necessary. We are thinking of it as if it were a fact, and this shows the knowledge we will acquire of it to be incomplete. We come toward knowledge of the necessary from *below,* and we will not come to adequate knowledge of it unless we can make a leap, unless we can see that what we think of as having an alternative cannot really have had one. It is not certain that we can make this leap, but if we can and do, we see something different and we see differently from how we had before. Plato imagines that such leaps are made in dialectic, where we are driven beyond a contradiction to see the forms themselves, but such leaps may or may not be possible; what is necessary need not of necessity be known. What is poignant in all this is that we try to move toward certainties about necessities—Plato also says that we have a dimmed sight that they are there—by the best method we have and it cannot take us there; it can only take us to something that is neither necessary nor necessarily true.

There is no remedy for the limitation of this method, but there is another, supplementary method, and the two can be joined. Together, they are the method of speculative philosophy. One is the method of asking and answering question. In the cases in which we are interested, it ends in acknowledging as less than necessary something that is true of what must be; it never gets beyond seeing the necessary as a choice between alternatives. The other method begins with such sight as we may have of what is fundamentally real and attempts to extend it in imagination. We try to imagine the state of things in which a fundamental reality would not have to be; we try to imagine a lessening of its necessity and an alternative for it. This cannot succeed, but it need not fail entirely. An imaginative test reveals something of the reality's necessity and provides an arena for connecting our sight of what is most real with what we have learned through inquiry.

From the side of sight, we try to imagine what there cannot be, an alternative for a necessary reality; from the side of inquiry our last thought is of one side of what was, throughout our inquiry, an alternative; these two, thought and imagination, can be combined and blended thoughtfully and imaginatively, as I think they are in speculative philosophy. The paradox, then, is that through a kind of matching, what we cannot really ask about is brought near the reach of inquiry, while from the side of inquiry, we come to sense that there is more to the real than the answers to our questions have revealed.

It is this way with time. It is a fundamental reality. It is always there. We cannot therefore simply ask what it is and whether it could have begun or ever end. There is no absence of it; there is nothing against which it can stand in contrast. Our understanding of it, then, must be cast by its difference from and likeness to the other sorts of things we think we understand. We have some sight of it, we ask and answer questions about it, and we try to blend the sight and the sense we have. It is easy to favor one side or the other and almost impossible to balance them. When Augustine says that he knows what time is when no one asks him but that he does not know otherwise, he expresses his sense, and ours, of time's reality, but Augustine was not right about what it was that he knows when no one asks him. His own explicit questions about time compare it to the times we know, but his theory about the past and future turns implausibly on the length of time it takes us to say what we remember and anticipate. Augustine had a theory, for all that he knew but could not say, and we must have our theory, too, no matter what sights of time seem so compelling to us. These must be set out and elaborated, and whatever we say must be explained. Whatever our sight, it is always vague, but there is also a texture of argument in which we experience and think, and we must feel for the fittingness of the two, sight and thought. The main issues of this essay are developed from a sense that each moment is new and that there must continuously be new moments—but then, the meaning of "moment," the nature of its "newness," and the necessity for there continuing to be new moments have themselves to be explained. Our first sight cannot certify our constructions and we must always ask whether we are preserving it. We should also ask whether we are enhancing it in the construction of our concepts.

These last sections on the dimensions of the present are about the quantity of present time. We often talk about measures of time, and there are theories about the knife-edged present and the eternal present in which a notion of length is applied to time itself. Time, however, or the present, has more than one dimension. All the dimensions apply to it. To say how that is so, even to say what the length of the present is, requires turns of meaning that are, looked at from one side, unusual. Still, the sight that the meanings give us is not all metaphorical. The things that are in time have dimensions. Time, as constituting them, has dimensions, too. The dimensions of each are alike, as alike as the outside and inside of things can be.

PART II

THE PAST

CHAPTER FIVE

THE REALITY OF THE PAST

T HE PAST is a part of time. It consists of individuals and time, as the present and the future also do, but the way that individuals and time are together as the past differs from the ways they form the other parts of time. In the present, for example, individuals and time contend with each other. Individuals try to hold time inside themselves while time passes to avoid being divided by them. In the past, by contrast, time dominates individuals. As time becomes past it transforms the individuals in which it was present, depriving them of their singularity and making them part of the fabric of a vast, stilled time that is as real and full as the present and is effective, too.

This notion of the past depends on the idea that both time and the being of individuals are fundamentally real: they cannot cease to be. Those who think that one or the other is not real will also think that there is no past, except as we remember or infer what has occurred. They will also deny that the future is real. They think that the present is the only time, or the only point from which we measure time, and they may also think that entities are real only when they are present.

The strongest arguments against the reality of the past are that we have no experience of it and that nothing we do experience requires us to think that it is real. What we experience is present or it is present to us. If there were something in it that we could not explain, we might have to infer that something not present is also real, real enough and in such a way to explain what we did not understand. Inferences like these always contain some uncertainty; nevertheless, we must make them occasionally—though almost no one thinks we should infer that something past is real to explain some fact about the present. The reason for this is the very common idea that what occurs or happens does so from the present *on,* and almost no one thinks that what is past can affect what succeeds it in time. If there were an explicit argument against the reality of the past, it would be that what is real must have some effect; what is past can have no effect; the past, therefore, is not real.

These strong arguments against thinking the past to be real depend on the notion that when things change or act, their actions *proceed* from the present; there is a going from one present to another present. They also depend on the idea that as the actions go on, nothing in them is left behind. Whatever changes or acts does so from moment to moment, present to present. Any part of it that does not enter the new or continuing action ceases to exist; it does not persist uselessly in a past time.

There is something obviously right in these ideas, but there is also something wrong: there are too many troubling questions that the ideas do not answer or do not answer well. Why do things act at all, and why do changes or actions continue to occur? Why do actions seem continuous with the actions that preceded them? And what is it for a thing to change or act? These questions cannot be answered or answered well because, on the view that actions or changes consist wholly of a thing's going on from the present, there is too great a distinction, too great a separation, between a thing and the changes that come about in it: the thing remains present, but the changes have ceased to be. If we distinguish things from their actions in a certain way, we will wonder about the connections between them. We know that we need some distinction between a thing and the changes that come about in it, but what distinction shall we make? Can we make a discerning distinction while preserving the ideas that usually seem so obvious—namely, that the things that act are (wholly?) in the present and that changing is (entirely?) a going on from the present?

These questions provide a direction for discussion. I will test the notions that present things change or act and that these occurrences are a going on from present to present. I will attempt to use these ideas to answer some of the obvious questions about changes and actions. If the answers are satisfactory, they will show us how to distinguish things from their actions, and we will also understand their connection. We will see how things are involved in the changes that occur in them and whether they cause them or are involved in them in some other way.

If the answers are not satisfactory, if they are false or obscure or ambiguous, we will know that there is something wrong with the ideas—either with the idea that acting entities are wholly present or with the idea that their actions go only from the present on. If this is the case, we will have to revise them or construct other ideas of "entity" and "change," and of "the present," too, and we will have to consider whether the new ideas give us sounder views.

Some Questions about Action and Change

Why do things change or act? Why do actions or changes continue to occur? The only answer ever given is that, in one way or another, something *causes* things to change or act. Different philosophies interpret the questions differently and have given different specific answers to them, but the answers are in general the same: what changes or acts is mainly caused to change or act by some other reality, and because changes and actions continue to occur, there must finally be one or several realities that cause all of the occurrences but that are themselves not caused to act. Plato, for example, thinks that the flux continually unsettles things and that the demiurge must always make them definite again. Aristotle says that substances change because they are lured into change by the unmoved mover; there is always an aspiration in them for further form. Descartes thinks that God creates things in each moment, and for Leibniz, though monads are entirely actual, they can seem to change from state to state. Hume's secret springs flow all the time, and, according to Kant, the sensuous manifold is always changing, though we cannot know why. There are forces that cause particles to move, and vitalities course through living things. No philosophy that supposes actions to be always and only a going forward locates the whole cause, condition, or occasion for action in the acting things themselves. Each supposes that things act or continue to act because of the actions of other sorts of realities, and these realities also cause the coordination of the actions or changes of the things.

Given that other sorts of realities affect a thing's changing or acting, what do the things themselves contribute to their own actions? Other realities do so much, what do the things themselves do? What do we do, for example, if all or some part of what we do is caused by something apart from us? Not much, if anything. The causes seem to do everything. Plato, for example, thinks that things do nothing: their ongoing is owed to the flux, and the demiurge does everything else. Aristotle thinks that substances provide the aim for the ongoing of their actions but they do not cause the ongoing itself; none of the four causes concerns it. For Descartes and Leibniz, substances do not even construct the aim of their actions. Hume and Kant say that we cannot know what things really are, what they do, and how they do it. The issue is no plainer in more recent philosophy, and it never will become plainer if we continue to suppose that things are wholly in the present and that their changes or actions are wholly a going on from the present, for if things are wholly present, there isn't very much to them, and there will, therefore, be very little that they can do. Still, they must contribute something to their actions or the occurrence of the changes in them, or else their actions would not be their own; they would not be able to change themselves. What is it that they do?

The usual answer is that things are the *centers* of their actions or of the changes that occur in them. They make their actions out of the forms and stuffs and passings that are either already in them or brought into them. In general, what they do is hold themselves or bring themselves together. When a thing changes or acts, then, there is a great deal going on around it that the thing itself does not do—it is done by a flux or matter or demiurge or forces or by whatever makes possibilities relevant—and these are thought to become part of a thing's action or to be the causes or conditions of it. The action by the thing itself, though, or the change within it, is only a small part of what is *going on.* There would not be these goings on if there were not also things that could change or act, but the little that the things themselves might do cannot account for there having to be changes or actions, for their passing away, for the coordination of the actions of different things, or even for the fact that a thing's successive actions are so fitting and seemingly continuous.

These philosophical constructions about change and action are massive. They start from something obvious—that things change and act—and explain what things are, what they do, when and how and why they do it, and why and how they are coordinated in doing it by supposing *in a certain way* that there are mighty realities conditioning what things do. In these suppositions, the philosophies make more precise their first ideas about the things that persist and change and act; some notes in the first and obvious ideas must be modified and refined. There is nothing wrong in doing this. The first ideas may not have been altogether sound; then too, we may not have been searching enough about just *what* must be explained and *how* to explain it. It is the *what* and *how* that lead us to conceive of the mighty realities that explain everything.

We cannot come to sure understandings of change or action without constructions of these massive sorts, filled with suppositions about more fundamental realities. If we could, there would be no point in making them. We must therefore follow the constructions carefully and see how the realities that have been supposed are connected with our first notions about the natures of changing things. If they are not connected well enough to explain the changes, that will be because (1) we have conceived of the wrong realities, (2) the first notions about the natures of changing things are wrong, or (3) we have made mistakes about what things are to be explained and how to explain them. In the philosophies I have outlined—the ones that have dominated our thought about time and the things that are in time—all three of these mistakes have been made. What exactly are the mistakes? Where do they arise? Would another line of construction be sounder?

The most familiar constructions begin, as I mentioned, with the obviously true claim that change and action occur from present to present, but because they suppose that present to present is the only direction within a change, the constructions require further suppositions about what might become present, about whether it is real before it becomes present, and about the realities that cause the present to come about. All these suppositions characterize change as an occurrence that is wholly a going *forward,* though its causes or conditions are supposed to be powerful realities that are not themselves in time. No suppositions, however, are ever made or even considered along a *backward* line or one that goes into the depth of things; no suppositions are made about the past or future being real. The past is never thought to be real because it would have to *turn around* to contribute to what comes to be in a present time, it would have to go *the other way,* and it is so obvious that this cannot be done that almost no one even considers that the past might have any effectiveness and, consequently, any reality.

If an action goes on from the present, what affects it must either come out of what is present, be a rearrangement or reformation of what is present, be manifested in what is present, or be put just in front of the present, close enough that the thing itself can act on it. Nothing past can affect an action in these ways. Consequently, rather than suppose that what passes continues uselessly to exist in the past, almost all philosophers have supposed that it ceases to exist. There are things and their properties and actions, and as the properties are changed and the actions pass, they cease to exist, while the things themselves, distinguished so sharply from their properties and actions, remain. For almost all philosophers, the present is the only time at which the things that act and change can exist, and their explanations of change and action depend on their supposing so. It would seem obvious to them—perhaps too obvious even to consider—that nothing past can in any way contribute to what goes from the present on, as they say all action does.

The basic notions in all these philosophies are that things are wholly present and that their actions are wholly a going on from the present. One or both of these notions should be changed, however, because the explanations based on them are too obscure for us to understand what things are and what they do. The answers to our questions about change and action show this. Why does a thing act? Because of another kind of reality that, of itself, always acts. How does this other reality cause things to change and act? How does it account for their being in continual and coordinated change? The answers are unrelievedly obscure because it has never been shown that there is an effective connection between the things that are actual or present and the final and powerful realities. It is just supposed that, in a certain way of explaining things, there must be a connection. We can see the connections between things that are in space and time, but what is the connection between the things in space and time and those realities that are apart from them? What is the connection between things and the flux that is supposed to unsettle them, or the final cause that is supposed to lure them to change their incidental forms, or the God that Descartes thinks conserves them by re-creating them? Connections were not even made between a thing and its own changes or actions. Those two are also too sharply separated: properties are changed, actions occur and go, but things remain. It is therefore almost entirely uncertain what a thing does, why it does it, what it does it to, or what it does it for.

Connections between things and the realities apart from them are not made because they cannot be made. Things that are wholly here and now cannot be essentially connected with anything else. They are worlds unto themselves, and nothing in their natures shows that they are what they are because of other things and that they cannot be what they are unless they are essentially connected with realities of other kinds. In fact, except in Descartes, no attempt has ever been made to show that, in their own natures, things are connected to other realities. When philosophers have tried to show that there must be such connections, they have not appealed to the natures of things but to the fact that the things change and act. Even arguments about change and action fail, however—they never quite show that things in time are connected with the more powerful realities—because things are so sharply distinguished from their changes and actions that even if the final realities were effective in causing changes of them, the changes never reach into the things themselves. Things, changes, final realities— they are so unconnected that there can be no understanding how the changes can be changes *of* things or *in* them.

In the constructions we have been considering, things have moments of transiency that are caused not by those things themselves but by a reality of a very different kind that is not in time; this transiency attaches to the things, so that through their changes, they are connected somehow to the reality that causes or conditions their change. However, the transiency does not attach to them or even affect them; if they respond to it at all, they respond inside themselves, so there is no real connection between the things and the great realities. Forms never quite get into things; what changes in substances are incidental properties; atoms are not affected by the forces they are said to transmit; it is not certain that minds are touched by the ideas they have; and we remain uncertain whether anything is really given for actualization. Along this line of thought, the simplest, plainest, and strongest doctrine is Descartes's: things do not change; they are continually and directly created by God and perhaps do not ever stand apart from him.

If we think of things as sharply separated from their changes and actions, as so many philosophers do, we cannot understand how their changes and actions are really theirs. If we also suppose that the changes and actions are continually caused or conditioned by other realities, it will be impossible to see how things wholly here and now are connected to those realities. The idea that things are wholly here and now and the idea that their change or action is wholly a going on from the present are inseparable; they go together because things are supposed to be connected with realities that affect them continually, causing their changes or actions to be of certain kinds. We cannot, however, connect this idea of things with the idea of there being mighty realities of a very different sort, so that neither the idea that things are wholly here and now nor the idea that their actions are wholly a going on from the present can be altogether true—even though there is something obviously right in both of them. Other notions should be taken as the basis for our thought about things, time, and change; these notions should lead us to different kinds of questions, and the questions, based on the sense of the notions we start with, will give us very different views.

Revised Notions of Action and Change

Our revised notions should preserve the ideas that things are here and now and that their actions are a going on from the present. They should also characterize change or action or transiency as in the very nature of the things in time and suggest what kinds of *inner connections* there are between the things that are present and other sorts of realities, avoiding in this regard the kind of obscurity we have just seen. These two requirements lead to the notions we need: there must be an intrinsic complexity in the things that are here and now, and what makes for the complexity must explain why and to what end things change, act, and last continuously.

Things are here and now, but that cannot be their whole reality; if it were, they could not change themselves. They must change themselves, however, at least to persist, and they also must change to take account of the different things that become components in their actions.

What kind of changes can things make in themselves? What must they be to change themselves? They must change not into something else but in their substance, change the *what* of what they are even while they continue to be the same. They must change but remain the same. There must, therefore, be more to them, of them, or in them than there is as they are present, which leads to the idea that, in some way, things are already partly future, a notion much like thinking of them as having a potentiality. The idea that things are wholly here and now seems obviously right because they cannot now also be at another place or be in any other time; this is true, however, only if we think of things as being in some other time *in the same way* in which they are in the present. Things cannot be in two presents or in two places in the present at the same time, but they can be both present and future if they are in time *in different ways*.

To explain how things can change themselves, we must think that things, or individuals, are not wholly here and now. They are future as well, though there is a difference between them as they are present and as they are future; the difference is in their relation to time. Individuals must also be partly past, because when part of the future being of an individual becomes present, it becomes the acting, changing part of that individual; it is the individual as lasting, as continuing its action, and an individual can act continually in the same ways only if it is continuous with what it was, if it is affected by the passing and past part of itself, if it is apprenticed to itself. The passing part of an individual—what becomes its past—cannot cease to be when it is passing or when it becomes past. It must continue to be; otherwise, what a singular individual comes to be, or what comes to be in it, will not continue it, will not act in ways that it has acted, and will not come to have its definiteness. Individuals must be future and past as well as present. They are always changing and changing themselves, which could not occur if they were wholly here and now.

Our starting notion, then, is that time is as much in individuals as they are in it. To understand how individuals can change themselves and act, we must suppose that there is a past, present, and future part of individuals. One change they make in themselves is to transform the portion of their own future being that is brought into them. This change is a going on, something is coming about, but the whole change that occurs in an individual is not a going on. If we set aside the notion that things are wholly here and now, we must qualify the only notion of change that can go along with it. We must say not only that there is a going on in an individual as it changes but that there is another change as well: as something comes about in an individual, something also becomes past. As an individual changes, there is both a going on and a becoming past, and these occur, as it were, at the same time.

We must therefore set aside the idea that what comes about ceases to exist after a time. This idea of ceasing to exist goes with the notion that a change is wholly a going on from the present, that something is brought about in a thing and when the thing changes again something else is brought about, the new something replacing the earlier something; the earlier does not become past but passes away, and the thing in which it was brought about remains, unchanged by what has passed away. This idea is not altogether wrong, however, for just as it is true that there is a going on from the present in the changes of things, it is also true that something in an action passes away or ceases to exist. What is not true is that *all* that has come about ceases to exist.

The crucial distinction is between what in an individual becomes past and what in, or attached to, an individual passes away and ceases to exist. The individual itself comes about, its substance changes, but the changing part does not cease to exist—it becomes past. It is transformed during the change, but as it is becoming past and when it has become past, it is still real and continuous with that being of its own that is coming to be present and singular. What passes away altogether is what came to be for the first time in the course of the change or action, what comes to be in the interaction of individuals. It exists only in that interaction and it ceases to be when individuals become past and no longer interact; impacts and resistances, for example, exist only in a present time. They are wholly creatures of the here and now. There is, then, a difference between what comes to be present and what comes to be *in* the present: the former has some reality in both the future and past; the latter exists only in the present—it is what is derived from individuals as they act and come together in an action, and it ceases to exist when their action is at an end.

Individuals are always changing and they always interact. As every interaction is completed, something that was in it ceases to exist— namely, what came to exist *in* and during the action itself. The changes in the acting individuals themselves, however, do not cease to exist. These changes are the transformations that occur in them as they are becoming past. The past consists of individuals together, individuals as changed. It consists of completed changes, but these will seem unreal if we think that changes are only something that things do, that things are so different from their changes that the changes come and go while the things remain present and unchanged. Completed changes, or the completed parts of changes, will be real to us if we abandon the notion that things are distinct from the changes that occur in them and if we think, as we have reason to, that the changes inside individuals are the individuals themselves. A change is not transient stuff attaching itself for a moment to an unchanging thing; it is a node of change in beings that are themselves spread out in time, the transformation in individuals as they heave themselves forward and as what was present in them becomes past. Individuals change and act in the present, which they could not do if they were not also, in some ways, past and future. The changes in individuals are the individuals themselves, and their own past and future being bear on how these changes come about.

A change is therefore both a coming to be and a becoming past. These are its strands or directions. They occur together, inside each other; neither occurs first. What comes to be does not force what is present to become past, and what is passing does not leave the present to make room for what is coming to be. Coming to be, passing away, and becoming past occur in the present because of the way that individuals and time are together. Time causes individuals to change and act, to reconstitute themselves in each moment, and to become past. Time passes, too, but not of itself: individuals cause it to pass.

The major implausibility in supposing the past to be real is the idea that past things are impotent to affect what comes after them. A past that does nothing, that cannot bear in any way on what is going on, is not real. The questions, though, are what change and action are and what must be supposed to be real to explain their occurrence. In the notion that the past is not real, the idea is that change or action occurs in the present, that it is a going forward where the past is wholly gone from the present. If something past were real and could have bearing on action, it would have to *turn around* and reenter the present—it would not be past at all. Since this notion of the past's reality is so plainly implausible, the conclusion that most philosophers reach is that nothing past is real; the definiteness of a change or action comes into an individual from somewhere else.

These notions of change and action are unsound, however. Change is a becoming past as well as a coming to be, and the definiteness of what comes to be in an individual is not due to the unusual agency of realities apart from individuals. It is due to the obvious agency in having what comes to be form itself on what is becoming past, while what is becoming past owes its further transformation into its final definiteness to the past itself.

What is past does not have to turn around to act on what is coming to be, as it would if a change in individuals were entirely a coming to be. Because it is also a becoming past, and because the becoming past and the coming to be overlap, what comes to be can form itself on what is becoming past *while* it is becoming past. Causes do not cause from the present on; they cause from the past to the present but not by turning around, not by getting themselves into the present and joining in some going on from there. What is past and what is passing act on what is coming to be from where they are. What is passing does so in the present, where something is also coming to be, and individuals are continuous throughout these times. It is not, as Plato and Whitehead think, that a definite something comes into what is present; instead, what becomes definite in the present becomes definite by forming itself on what is definite and past.

We have yet to describe the past and explain how things form themselves on it, but the claim to its reality is settled, at least in outline. The main argument against the past's reality is that we do not have to suppose that it is real; we need not suppose anything that it is real enough to explain. What unsettles this argument is that to explain why things last and how they do what they do, we must suppose that they change, and there will be no explaining how they change if they are wholly in a present time. No matter what the contribution of other realities to their actions, things themselves must change to persist and to accommodate themselves to the things with which they must interact. The changes in them are not mere rearrangements of stuff that is in them now, nor can the changes consist of things that come to be in the present and then cease to exist. We must think of things differently; we must think of them as individuals that are not wholly present but also partly past and partly future and that, when they change and act, act through their whole being, their past and future as well as their present parts. Change in individuals, then, is not just a coming to be. It is also a becoming past, and the past and what is becoming past are therefore effective in change, serving to make definite the part of them that is coming to be newly present. The past is effective in change because change is a becoming past as well as a coming to be and because these strands of action occur inside each other. The grand argument against the reality of the past is therefore reversed—our new conclusion is that there must be a past because individuals continue to be, and they become definite by forming themselves on what they already are and were.

Philosophical Argument and Conviction

We can argue that something is or must be fundamentally real, but even if the arguments are strong and persuasive, we always want more conviction than they—or any arguments—can provide. The arguments tell us no more about the reality than what we have argued for—that it is the only reality that can explain what we thought should be explained in the way we thought it should be explained. We wonder then if we might not experience that reality or otherwise come to know more about it.

We hope to supplement our philosophical argument with new experience or a new and compelling clarity in understanding our previous experience. Most philosophers would probably think this a vain hope because they think that experience and argument are either not independent of each other or not independent enough. Their view is that we cannot know what experience shows about a fundamental reality unless we are already persuaded that there is such a reality. An experience, therefore, cannot confirm an argument about something's reality; rather, it can be thought to be an experience of that reality only because we have already argued for the reality, because we otherwise believe in it. Our arguments that this or that is real thus must stand on their own. All our conviction about there being a particular reality finally derives from them.

This view is almost entirely sound. Our experience is never, of itself, revealing; so far as we understand it, it is interpreted by ideas we already have. It may also be that any revision of our ideas comes not from experience itself but from our adjusting ideas to one another, removing contradictions, for example, or recombining and generalizing our ideas. This theme is beautifully expressed in one of Plato's images: to know the real, to see what things really are, to come to certainties, we must turn away from what most of us think of as experience.

Still, this critical view is not entirely sound. There are features of experience in which our ideas about what is real can be more or less confirmed. These features have to do not so much with *what* we experience but with the *value* of the experiences to which the ideas lead us. This is an unusual idea—that we may come to conviction about philosophical ideas because of the value of the experiences they lead us to—and it must be justified.

This chapter has been filled with arguments about the past's reality and about how the past helps to explain change and action. Even if we could find nothing wrong in them, however, these arguments would not be convincing if there were not also intimations in our experience that the past is real or something that we would be willing to interpret as such an intimation. Shored by such intimations, the arguments will seem sound and revealing; they will even help us toward a further understanding of some of our experience. For example, we sometimes feel restrained or even burdened because of what has occurred and think that there are fewer possibilities for us than before; old things seem to still be going on, and we wonder at the difference between *being* responsible and *having been* responsible for something we have done. These feelings and ideas are very vague, but it can seem to us that we will understand them more clearly and to a greater depth if we think that, in some way, they have to do with a real past: it is the past, we may come to think, that is a restraining burden on us. We feel either the past or the burden of it, and because of it there are now fewer different kinds of things that we can do. We *are* what we *were,* but never quite the same and never altogether different, and we look again and again at "are" and "were" to find the sense in their ambiguity.

If there are, then, tones or hints of certain kinds in our experience or the language we use to describe it, the arguments that the past is real will be borne out by experience. The arguments may also change our experience somewhat, or our understanding of it, or they may change the sense in some of our language. We will be clearer about some things and there will, perhaps, be differences in the importance that things have for us. The idea that the past is real will lead us to a fuller interpretation of some experience, and that will be a change in experience itself—for the better we suppose.

This might seem to be all the assurance that we can have that the past is real: the arguments against the past's reality seem unsound and even incoherent; there are, however, other explanations of change, action, and the efficacy of the past, and some dense portions of our experience seem to be made more clear by thinking that the past is real. There seems to be nothing more that can be added.

There remains the question, though, of whether these ideas of the past's reality will be sustained. We argue and argue in philosophy about what of necessity exists without ever being certain that our arguments have the same full measure of necessity. It is uncertain whether the idea that the past is real will continue to throw light on our experience. It might or it might not—we cannot say now what interpretations of our feelings will seem to make them most revealing. It is because of the possibility of new interpretations that philosophy goes on and on, waiting for the formulations of revised conceptions and counter-arguments, to which there will or will not be responses. There might, for example, be some new version of the idea that the present is the only time; it might be used to argue that what we thought was a feeling about the past is really a feeling about present moments wherein something that has since ceased to be has caused an effect. There then might be counter-counterarguments on behalf of a real past, and so on, until we lose interest or come to think that philosophy is vain and that, from its start, our issues have not been set out properly.

The central issue in having a philosophy sustained is, however, not a matter of arguments alone, even when the arguments are in some way confirmed by our experience. It is about ideas and action and the character of the experiences we will have when we act on the ideas—though even then it is not only whether experience sustains ideas by confirming them. It is mainly whether, when we act on the ideas, *we* are sustained in the experiences to which the ideas will lead us; whether the ideas lead us to the fullest life to which we can aspire and that the real can ask of us. Ultimately, philosophy is sustained only if it sustains us, and not only those of us who construct its arguments. A philosophy is sustained if the meaning it gives to common experience and common sense helps us understand what a full life is. It will not be sustained if, over time, it leaves us feeling that full lives are very different from what our philosophy implies.

There are two very strong objections to this idea—that philosophical notions do not make a real difference in what we might do and that, even if they do, a philosophy is not true, or finally true, because of the goodness of the life to which it leads. Together, these objections seem to be a stern counterargument: the truth of a philosophy neither can nor should depend on what is good; there is also the lesser argument that a philosophy should not be thought true simply because it would be good for us to think that it is true. The issues in these objections are deep, and they could be discussed separately. It will not depreciate their importance, though, to examine them together and to argue that our ideas about what is real do have a bearing on our actions and that the experience that occurs in and after these actions has a bearing on whether the ideas are true; it will be as if the degree of the goodness or fullness of the experiences is a measure of the extent to which the experiences confirm the ideas and the ideas sustain us.

To see that this is so, we must first examine the position of philosophers who do not believe that ideas about what is fundamentally real have any bearing on what we experience. These philosophers think that such ideas have no meaning, or are only structural or grammatical, or are simply too abstract: they are beyond the sensing and doing of experience and action. They think that believing there are carousels in the park can affect what we might do but that we are not affected by believing, for example, that there is an unmoved mover; an unmoved mover is not an object toward which we can act. They base this criticism on an analysis of meaning and on notions of what can be known and often summarize it in questions about what difference it would make in our experience whether or not we believe universals to be real or solipsism to be true. They claim there would be no real differences. We would not stop doing the kinds of things we had done before and start doing other things instead. Everything would be the same, only we might describe things differently. They think, however, that a difference in language alone is not a *real* difference; it does not require a difference in what is real. There is no difference in things that requires them to be described in English rather than French, and there is none that requires us to call them instances of universals or not. These philosophers conclude that no belief about the reality of the past or of time can affect what we do; we would act in the same ways, no matter what our beliefs about them. The same consequences will occur whether or not we believe the past is real. What happens, then, does not confirm or sustain either view. The method of differences shows that there is no difference between the two.

The objection and the basis for it are perhaps deeper than I have suggested; nevertheless, they are based on a distinction between the kinds of concepts that have meaning and those that don't, and the distinction is much too severe. The objection also looks for only one kind of difference between actions—the difference between doing one thing or doing something else—and this difference is supposed to be obvious. The ideal, yet infinitely unlikely, case for these critics would be one where there are two people in identical circumstances who have identical desires, dispositions, and abilities and all of whose beliefs are identical but one, with that one being about whether something is finally real. Do these persons act differently from each other? Only the one belief could cause a difference in what they do, but it is imagined that their actions are not different, that no effect is caused by the difference in beliefs, and it is then concluded that beliefs about what is finally real are ineffective and perhaps insignificant.

Whatever else one thinks about the concept of meaning in these critics' view, their ideas of action are not deep enough. They see that there is an inner side to action, that our ideas affect what we might do, but their view of this inner side goes only to the first layer of our thought. It supposes that ideas are *directions* about what to do. Then, as in the example, where everything is the same except for two ideas, because the two persons' actions are the same, the different ideas are said not really to be ideas, or not really directions on which the persons act. Some of our ideas may be useless and parasitic on the ones that can direct us in what to do, but there is also a greater depth from which our thought about action develops and in which ideas about what is real have a different role: namely, to define the nature of our action and to approve or disapprove of what we propose to do. The ideas are connected with what we always aim to do, and we may be more or less clear about them. Ideas about what we always aim to do are the basis for our approvals. It is in using them that we make our actions deliberate.

An idea of what we always aim to do is an idea of a general or comprehensive end. Such a notion is not a generalization of what we aim to do in any particular circumstance; we could not settle on a particular end if we did not have first a comprehensive one. Now it must be possible for our actions, whatever the circumstances, to have the character required for us to approve of them, and what is possible is, at least, not precluded by necessity. Our notion of a general or comprehensive end contains or supposes ideas about what is real and real of necessity; it also supposes the idea that what is most approved by us, what is most fulfilling for us, is not precluded by what is fundamentally real; it is, we think, really possible.

Some ideas about comprehensive ends seem stronger on this point, for instance, that what is real prescribes an end for us instead of merely making one possible. Plato and Aristotle, for example, think that this is true of the Good and the unmoved mover; we aim toward the Good though we see it only dimly, and we are to imitate the unmoved mover as far as our natures will allow. Plato and Aristotle correctly see that our end will not be comprehensive if it is not addressed to the most fundamental of realities, but their views are about the ends of everything. The comprehensive end of human action must still be thought out, and we must think it out without being as certain as Plato and Aristotle that we know what is finally real and without supposing, as they do, that the end the final realities seem to provide for us also provides an acceptable conception of our fulfillment.

We need to have our notions of what is most real bear on the ends of our actions and then to see whether we feel ourselves as fulfilled as we feel we could be. If the actions we endorse do not provide for a full life—and fulfillment is not the same as pleasure or even happiness—then we must conclude that there is something wrong with our ideas about what is real and perhaps think them through again. On the other hand, if we are confident about our ideas, we must decide whether those notions of ours that measure fulfillment are deficient or extravagant. We judge these measure for measure, then—thought articulated in action, feeling articulated in thought—on the supposition that lives are full if our actions grow out of sound ideas about what is real. We measure our conceptions of the real by our actions, and we measure the fullness of our actions by our conceptions of the real.

It is mistaken and trivial to suppose that ideas about what is fundamentally real do not bear on what we do, and we are trivial, less or more, depending on how we think that the ideas, or the realities themselves, bear on what we do. These ideas do not relate to action by being about the objects on or toward which we act. They bear on our actions by defining them, by being the basis for our approving them, and the realities themselves are finally the indirect objects in the comprehensive aim of our actions. They make a difference to our action, but the difference cannot be seen. A more revealing rendition of our previous example of two persons with but one differing idea would therefore be to have their actions look the same but really be different because their intentions are different, because they conform to different comprehensive aims. Even so, it can be very difficult to say exactly what anyone of us ever does.

It should make a difference in our actions whether we think that time and the past are real, but it is difficult, perhaps impossible, to say what the difference is. We cannot set two actions before ourselves and point to an item that is in one and not in the other. The idea that the past is real does not affect an action by directing us to anything that is around us, and a person who believes that the past is real cannot explain to someone who does not what difference the idea makes. As the idea affects that person's aim, however, it makes *all* the difference in the meaning and importance of the things on which we act.

Suppose, for example, that I did something yesterday or a year ago or many years ago. Should I say about my having done it that I *was* responsible or that I *am* responsible? The obvious difference is between past and present tense, but though a great difference, it is not the only one. Along with the difference in tense comes a difference in the meaning of every other term. There is, for example, a difference in the meanings of "responsible." Cause and accountability mean virtually the same thing in the belief that I *am* responsible; they are different from each other and related only by principle in the past tense: what I *was* in one sense responsible for (cause), I *am* also, but in another sense, responsible for at a later time (accountability). What does this difference in meaning come to? Not much, perhaps, or perhaps a great deal; for some of us, there are also differences in the feelings that underlie our thoughts about the responsibility.

Some of us may feel, for example, that once done is over with and we can be impatient to have things done; there is no past, and we also feel that there are always new beginnings and we can always start again. Those of us who think that the past is real will feel instead that once done is never over with, that things go on, that there are no new beginnings, that things work themselves out, and that what we are doing continues what we have done. These different thoughts are imprecise; the largest part of them is feeling. Perhaps those who feel the weight of the past will not act in perceptibly different ways from the former group; still, things are measured differently for them: they are more or less important, they have an age or not, they are close to them or behind them, and each of these terms, and other terms as well, has a different meaning for the two groups, so that there will be differences between them in what they think and feel that they are doing, no matter how much alike their actions seem.

Someone impatient with these notes about thought and feeling might respond by saying that things are what they are regardless of our feelings and that these feelings, the different subjectivities, should be put aside when we try to decide whether the past is real. This would be a harsh response, however, because its own suppositions lie on one side of the argument. The response is made on the basis of doctrines of meaning, of strict connotation, which is supposed to be independent of time, as if no one in fact ever meant anything; the response also begs the question of whether the real is what we can come to know it to be. Even so, the response acknowledges that there are differences in feelings and thoughts that we can interpret as being ideas about the past's reality. What it denies is that these should make a difference in what we finally think. Nevertheless, they do make for differences, both in what we understand our actions to be and in whether we think that they are good or important. There are also differences in what we come to think, as we come on our own and through all the devices in which we become practiced to interpret our feelings and to consider whether they are appropriate to what outer or inner phenomena led us to them.

It is not important for this discussion to say whether the feelings that are interpreted in the idea that the past is real are deeper, finer, or fuller than those accompanying the idea that the present alone is real. The question of which view is sound would not be genuine if we had already settled which view is most consonant with the widest and deepest range of our experience. The point of this argument is that, beyond and after our philosophical arguments about whether time is real, one view, as we act on it and as it affects the meanings of common sense and experience, will come to seem more and more obvious, whereas the other will come to seem more opaque and abstract. This will happen as we come to consider whether our aims are not merely possible but are also the fullest aims that we can have. The thoughts and feelings out of which we act, our sense of the importances of things, have a depth on which we have some hold. They are continuous with the feelings our ideas interpret. It can happen that our ideas do not fit the feelings that they interpret, and we may feel that we have to change them. It is a common notion that we have to change our ideas if, when we act on them, what we expected did not come about. It is a large but not ill-defined extension of this idea to think that, over time and in a broad course of experience and thought, the idea of time's reality will come to seem sound or not depending on which idea of time most fully fits the comprehensive aim of a fulfilling life.

Is the past real or not? The simple summary philosophical argument we can be sure of is that the past is real because individuals must change, which they could not do if they were not, in each moment, becoming past. Perhaps counterarguments will be formed or qualifications made on several points; philosophy will go on. The question may be changed or even dropped, perhaps as being only a fashion of the time, but whether it is dropped or continued or comes in some other way to seem more settled will be because, beyond all argument, there comes to be a sense that the ideas interpreting our deepest feelings about time help to define the aim in which we have the fullest, widest, and deepest life. I believe that the past is real, and I have some reason to hope that this judgment will be sustained. I must admit, however, that I am not certain it will. This is not the same, though, as admitting that there *is* some real doubt about whether the past is real.

CHAPTER SIX

BECOMING AND BEING PAST

Becoming Past

WHEN INDIVIDUALS change, some part of them becomes past. What is it to become past? Many philosophers would say that things become past simply by being succeeded: one action or event follows another; when the second occurs, the first has become past. Something becomes past or passes away when something else follows it in time.

This view is not false but too limited. It says only *when* something becomes past or passes away—when it is succeeded—but not *how* anything becomes past or *what* it is when it has become past, if it is at all. Does it still exist? Is it like what succeeds it, different only in being earlier in time and no longer eventful? On the other hand, if there is nothing in the past, if the past itself is not real, how has what just occurred lost the existence it had? Was it only a configuration of constituents that are now related differently? Was it broken up in the formation of its successor? If the relations in what occurs are more internal to the constituents, have they been preserved in a successive occurrence, so that nothing really becomes past at all?

These further questions are not often asked; the philosophers who mention succession are not usually interested in passing and the past. They are interested in the process of coming to be. They think about something's coming to be, then about something else's, and then something else's. Some of them think that what occurs is wholly a coming to be. They would be distracted by a question about what had become past. To answer it, they would, as it were, have to look over their shoulders and note that what had come to be has already been succeeded. There is perhaps nothing else that they can say about something that comes to be once it has become past. Something's having been succeeded, however, is not a cause of anything's becoming past but rather is concerned only with something that is past or no longer exists. What are the causes or other agencies that make things past or pass away? They may be as mighty as those involved with there being new occurrences.

Individuals and their actions are forced to become past. Becoming past is not something they had aimed to do, nor had they aimed to change in the ways in which they are transformed in becoming past. Individuals are made past by the time inside them as it passes and as they change and act. They do not first come to be, then change, and then become past; they become past as they change and act. They originate their changes and actions. There is, however, a passing in them that they do not originate—the passing of time—and this passing is what makes them past. In all that they do, individuals aim toward the future but they also become past.

The past is not a place to which things go. It does not begin at a point on a line, the point immediately before the present time. There is no location for the past, neither spatial nor temporal. The past is a part of time and, like the present and the future, it is not set inside a further time. Individuals and the changes and actions they originate become past when the time that had been in them becomes past, when time overcomes the hold that individuals have on it in the present, when it comes to be outside them, and when it makes those changes of them that make them past.

As I previously noted, most philosophical accounts of the changes of things are about what comes to be. Their great theme is that something becomes actual, that something that had been possible or potential comes to be here and now. A possible world or a possibility is created or embodied, or a thing realizes one of its potentialities or achieves one of its aims. Coming to be involves either an entirely new entity or a change in something that already exists. Details differ in different philosophies: Platonists talk of possibilities or aims; Aristotelians, of potentialities and final causes. Whatever the details, however, these accounts are only of what comes to be or the process of coming to be, and those who think that these are the only kinds of changes correctly suppose that, after they have occurred, there are no additional and different kinds of changes by which what has become actual becomes past. Things don't first become actual and then become past, changing first in one way and then in another, as if the changes occurred in successive moments that are oddly within a single present time. For the reasons that have already been given, we should not suppose that the changes or actions of things are wholly a coming to be, but neither should we invent an additional successive action by which what comes to be is changed in becoming past. The resolution of this tension is that the change and action of individuals are complex: change is a coming to be that is also a passing or becoming past, and the coming to be and becoming past are, indeed, not successive but occur together in a present time.

Our notion is that change and action in an individual are both a coming to be and a becoming past. We will, however, understand neither of these if we think that they occur successively, on the same level, as it were. The idea that most helps us to understand them, discussed earlier, is that individuals have depth and that they act outward from their depths even while they are forming themselves anew in those depths. Individuals are not unchanging substances or actualities whose changes or actions are incidental to what they really are. They are always changing, and they are not distinct from their changes, but they also last, and they do this by reconstituting themselves continuously. The coming to be in an individual's changing is an individual's forming itself, which takes place in the depth of the individual. The becoming past in an individual's action is its acting outward from its depth. Coming to be cannot occur in the future, and becoming past cannot occur in the past. Both occur within the present, not sequentially but together, as a coming into and a going out of the depth of individuals.

The moving vitality in coming to be and becoming past is the passing of time. Time comes into individuals. It is provoked to pass into them, and it carries into them that being of their own that had been future and is formed to become their new insides. The future being of individuals is their own being, but at each moment a part of it is made to be singular and inside them. There is no impermeable core in individuals. As future time and being are portioned to individuals, individuals form themselves anew. The future being of individuals does not of itself come into them but is brought into them by time as it passes. Where many philosophies suppose that things change by incorporating the being of the definite possibilities that are made available to them, the notion here is that the future being of individuals is entirely indefinite, that it is brought into individuals by time, and that it becomes definite in the present as individuals continue to be. Time is not merely a measure of coming to be. It is the "coming to" part of the process that is the being of individuals.

Time is also the passing in the changes in which individuals become past. Individuals act outward from their depths. The power that carries them into change and action, whether they will or not, is time's passing. Individuals have insides, they have depths, but they do not have reservoirs of power inside themselves. There exist no quiet powers inside us waiting to be quickened. Power is the same as passing in change and action; change, action, and passing occur constantly, and new passing, new power, are continuous. Again, time is not simply a measure of the length of the passing of an individual's change. It is in the change itself and is the individual's power, not merely a measure of its manifestation. There are not two processes, the passing of time and the manifestation of power, but only one. Individuals and time are in each other in the present. Time is the passing in an individual's change and action and also what transforms them and makes them past.

The passing time in individuals changes them by making them act outwardly and, as they act, by turning them *inside out.* Time does this as it itself passes outward from inside individuals to free itself from the hold individuals have on it. It thereby binds itself more closely with the time that had been inside other individuals and with the time that was outside them as the space of the present. This heave of time is a coming together of all the present times in all individuals, their coming to be together in a way that they had not been together when they were present. As time passes out of singular individuals, present times coalesce into a sheaf of new past time and time dominates the individuals it carries and transforms into being past.

The passing and the passing outward of the time inside individuals are what make individuals change and act. Individuals express themselves outwardly; they change themselves and shape their actions, and as they do, they also form themselves at their depths. Individuals are never without depth. In their actions, what had been in their depths comes to be outside what is now their new insides. Individuals are always being turned inside out. This constitutes their becoming actual, and while they are becoming actual, they come to have new insides— their future being is taking something like the form of a possibility or potentiality.

How does a present become past? The time that is present passes to become past by passing from inside individuals and by coming to an unstrained unity with the time that had been in other individuals. In the present, even while time is inside individuals, it is together with the time in other individuals, though this unity is strained; it is nearly sheared into the separate times of singular individuals. This is how individuals jeopardize time's being a whole and single reality. Time passes to become a stable and less-distended unity, a time without a space, settled in itself and ordered into the time that is already past. Individuals unsettle and trouble time when it is present; they tend to divide it, and it passes ceaselessly and dumbly to remove the jeopardy. It always succeeds, but it again exposes itself to the same jeopardy: as each moment becomes past, another moment becomes present. A moment that becomes past is settled, however, and the individuals that are carried in the moment are settled, too.

What changes are there in individuals as they become past? How are individuals transformed? The most striking change is that they are no longer singular, they no longer resist one another. In the present, individuals oppose one another even when they act together; they are outside one another even when they are close and they keep one another from penetrating their insides. As they are made to be past, however, as they are turned inside out, individuals meld into one another; they lose their singularity without losing the definiteness they have come to have. As we become past, we become completed portions of change and action; we become much different from what we were when change and action were going on. Individuals, strained toward separateness in the present, as time is also strained, become as unified in the past as the time that has itself become past.

With opposition, resistance, and singularity shorn from individuals because of time's becoming past, all the relative or relational characters they had when they were present cease to exist. These are the characters that individuals have because they oppose or resist other individuals—the sound, touch, and smell of things, their sensibilia, their appearances, and their spatial relations, which arise from individuals' contact with one another. As individuals become past and no longer singular, however, the qualities that depend on their affecting one another when they are singular are not sustained. These qualities are creatures of the present. They pass away and do not become past.

The individuals themselves do become past, though, as they are or were in their changes and actions. The massive motor powering change and action is time's passing, and there are changes and actions—rather than flux or sheer transience—because time passes inside individuals. Individuals shape, form, aim, and spread through their changes and actions. Their relational characters are attached to the changes and actions, and these pass away and cease to be. They are what they are because of the individuals. There would be no relational characters if individuals did not come to have their own definite characters. It is in their definite characters that individuals become past, however, and in the moment of passing, relative characters collapse and individuals are unified with other individuals with which they are or were contemporary. Together, they become the single fact of the world's momentary definiteness. The distinction between individuals, the contentions that were among them in the present, are at an end.

Individuals become past by being made to be past. There is a passing in them that they neither start nor control; it is the passing of the time inside them. Time forces individuals into change and action, where they shape and aim what is passing in them, having it be something that they do or that is happening to them. In the course of their changes and actions, individuals are also transformed because of time. Time itself is changing, overcoming the contention it has with individuals. It becomes less strained toward division and more unified. The time within singular individuals flows together; the space that was time as time was continuous among separate and opposing individuals is intensified as a purer time, and time ceases to pass and becomes past. It overcomes and dominates the individuals it contended with in the present. Individuals, made to change and act by passing time, have their natures transformed in corresponding ways: their singularity and their opposition and resistance to one another are overcome; the conditions for their having relational characters are undermined; and their formativeness ends. They have been turned inside out. Their definiteness, the definiteness of their action, becomes past. They are inseparably together with other individuals, unified within a whole and single moment's time. Individuals provoke time into passing; by passing, time overcomes them, connecting them both in a different way from how they had been together in the present and from how they had been connected with everything that is already past.

Though time and individuals become newly past in each moment, they do not add new moments of time or new individuals to the past. The time that becomes newly past is, or was all along, continuous with the time that is or was already past. It is the same time, and the individuals that become past are or were continuous with the being of the individuals that are or were already past; they are the same in being. What is added to the past, or what is new in becoming past, is the definiteness that individuals achieved in the present. Perhaps the strain that time comes to have as it contends with individuals becomes past, too. New characters, new definiteness, are added to the past, not new beings or new moments, and these characters come to be past as time and individuals pass from the straining, contending passage of being present to being wholly inside the time that dominates them. It is as if becoming past is a heave of the world, like a passing wave. We need not wonder whether and how that which becomes past attaches to what had, until now, been the whole of the past. The time and individuals that are newly past were never separated from the time and individuals that are past. They have changed only in their way of being together with one another and with the time and individuals of the past. New beings have not been added to the past, nor has the past been made larger and longer. Because there is new definiteness for the past in each moment, however, we must think about how this definiteness is ordered—we must consider the nature of the past.

Being Past

The past is real, and it affects everything that occurs in the present. It affects what things become. Individuals change and act as they do mainly because of what is past. What is the nature of the past? The most accessible description of it I can give is to contrast the past with possibilities. What is in the past is like a possibility that that has been affected by being actualized.

The idea that when things change and act they actualize possibilities is a well-known philosophical view. My notion is that the past explains many or all of the issues that have so often been explained by supposing possibilities to be real, and I think it does so better, more clearly and directly, and with less mystery. In view of what possibilities are supposed to explain and the difficulties in understanding these explanations, I think it will be easily seen that there can be another, better explanation of the issues—that the past is real and that what is in it contributes to forming what comes to be. Possibilities and the past do not address precisely the same issues; each defines them in its own way. Still, the issues are enough alike that the different explanations of them can be compared. I will start with what has been said about possibilities. There have been many subtle doctrines about them, for example, in Plato, Aristotle, Leibniz, and Whitehead. In all these accounts, though, the nature of possibilities is generally the same.

Possibilities

What are possibilities? What do they explain? When philosophers think about possibilities, they think about the changes that occur *in* things. Anyone who thinks the only changes that can occur *to* things are changes of their positions will not think about either possibilities or the past except to wonder where things might have been or where they might be made to go. When philosophers think about something becoming different from what it was, however, many of them think that the change involves possibilities. The thing is what it is, but it can also change. It can become this or that; it can come to have different properties or relations. What it *can* become—not just what it *will* become—are possibilities. Possibilities are the properties and relations that a thing does not now possess but that are, in some special way, relevant to it. They are real, even when they are not possessed by the thing for which they are possibilities or, perhaps, by anything. They are real because things can change and possibilities are the entities that can constitute their change. So if it is possible for things to change, what can come about in them must be real before it in fact comes about. What comes about in things could not have come from nothing; that would be impossible. If a thing can become an X, Y, or Z, it is not impossible for it to become anyone of them. The X, Y, and Z, therefore—the *whats* that can possibly come about in the thing—are real.

A few finer points should be added to this general account:

1. It is important to distinguish a thing from its properties, some of which are the possibilities that can be actualized in it. In almost all accounts of possibilities, possibilities are properties or certain kinds of relations. They are actualized in things, but they do not wholly constitute the things. We can thus say that at different times the same thing has actualized different possibilities: it was this, it is not that, and it can become something else. What it is possible for a thing to become is only a part of it. The rest of it is, as it were, already actual.

2. Though *what* things can become is somehow real before it is made to come about, possibilities are not in the future. Usually, the philosophers who think that possibilities are real do not think that the future is real. For them, what is possible, what can come about, is really apart from time—properties sometimes are said to be eternal, for example. Someone who thinks that they can be brought about will

imagine a present in which one or more of them will occur. It is only when possibilities are actualized that they are in time.

3. There are always many possibilities for a thing, not just one, and the possibilities are related to one another. Indeed, the possibilities for everything are related to one another. Each possibility is, for example, said to have an opposite; a thing can become beautiful or not, and both are possibilities for it. Because they are contradictories, however, only one of them can be actualized in one thing at one time. Actualizing one possibility might be the same as excluding its contradictory and, perhaps, vice versa, so that while possibilities must have contradictories, the two cannot be in the same thing at the same time in the same respect. Many possibilities can, of course, be actualized at once, only they cannot be contradictories: a tomato, for example, can be large and red and sweet and round.

Properties can also be linked so that when one of them is actualized others must be actualized as well. This is thought to be true of possibilities related in terms of specificity. Something can be red or not, but in either case it must be colored; something can be square or not, but it must have a size and shape. Such linkages make us think of ladders or hierarchies of possibilities, as if there were classes of possibilities that were themselves possibilities, and so on, up and up, until at last we reach the most general kinds of possibilities and there is, perhaps, a single, final possibility that is actualized when any possibility is actualized. Plato's name for this supreme form is the Good.

We are to think, then, of arrays of qualities, properties, or relations. For some of the things in time, some of them are possibilities; it is possible for them to be actualized in things. For all things at any times there are always some possibilities; for certain things at certain times there are certain possibilities; for others, there are other possibilities—and there may be qualities that will never be actualized. It may even be that there are qualities that will never be possibilities; there may never be things—not even possibly—for which they are possibilities.

4. Because qualities are distinct, because they are opposite to one another, and because they are linked to one another, they constitute a domain of an incalculable number of interconnected entities, some of which, at one time or another, are possibilities for the things in which they may be actualized. The domain is usually said to be complete— everything that could ever be a possibility is already real, and no new possibilities can come to be. There is nothing from which a new possibility could come. From time to time we think of possibilities we

had not thought of before, but though the thought of them is new, the possibilities themselves are not. It is supposed that they were already real and are implicated in other possibilities that we know about, which explains how we can come to think of them.

5. Thinking of possibilities is the only way to acknowledge them. We cannot imagine them, for they have no sensuous characters. We conflate imagining them with imagining what the things in which they are actualized will be when the possibilities are actualized. We can imagine a green tree or a generous person, but we cannot imagine generosity itself or even green itself. We can only imagine the objects in which they may occur; it is as if those objects are sensuous and give the possibilities such sensuosity as they come to have. If we want to find out about possibilities, if we want to know what they really are, we ultimately must think about them without images. Plato's images of the cave and the divided line represent such a move to purer apprehensions of such realities.

We are, then, to think that when things change, possibilities are actualized in them, that the possibilities are themselves entities apart from time. When they are considered as relevant to the things in which they can be actualized, they are thought of as possibilities and logically related to one another, though only some of these relations bear on the order in which the possibilities are actualized. These entities are unimaginable but real: they are the definitenesses that things can come to have, and they are real because they are what make it true that things can change and become definitely this or that.

Possibilities and Change

Can possibilities explain that things change, or are changes better explained by the effectiveness of a real past rather than by something apart from time? These two kinds of explanation are in some ways alike; in others, they are opposites. To compare and contrast them, I will consider three large themes about future, present, and past actualizations: what gets actualized, how it is actualized, and what happens to possibilities after they are actualized.

1. There are more possibilities than will come about—there must be more, for if the only real possibilities were those that will come about, they would not be possibilities but necessities; they would be what must come about if anything is to come about. What comes about, then, is always only a portion of all possible positive outcomes. We

must wonder, therefore, why just those possibilities come about and not others and why with all the possibilities, things so often change in the same ways, why there is so much regularity in the world, or even why there is regularity at all.

In the case of our own actions, the outline of the answer is very clear. We choose among possibilities, or we think we do, and we enact what we have chosen. The course of action we have chosen, the state of things that we want to have come about, will come about depending on our efforts and on whether, in the circumstances in which we act, other things support our actions or get in our way. What about the actions of animals and other living things, however? What about nature generally? Is there something analogous to choice even here, where there is no deliberation by the things in which the possibilities are actualized, or is there something else limiting or restricting the number of possibilities that natural processes might bring about? Both answers have been given—something like the first by Plato, Leibniz, and Whitehead; something like the second by Aristotle.

Plato, Leibniz, and Whitehead think that only certain qualities are made available for actualization. Something like a selection is made from them, not just for this or that thing, but for everything at a time, so that what comes to be actualized is the next stage of everything in the world, not the possibilities for each thing considered separately. There are, as it were, two stages for actualization: first, among all the qualities there are, only some are relevant to the things in which change is to occur. Because of their relevance, these qualities are the possibilities. Second, among the possibilities, only some will come about, and Plato, Leibniz, and Whitehead think that actualization requires there to be a choice from among those possibilities; Leibniz goes so far as to think that actualization consists of choice.

"Choice" is perhaps too metaphorical a term, but the sense of the term is sound: what one thing becomes depends on what other things become, and these in turn depend on what was possible for each and all of them. There is a fittingness in things and there are regularities, and if the only explanation for their occurrence involves possibilities, then from the plenum of entities that might be possibilities, only some of them will have that relevance to things that makes them possibilities, and from these possibilities, some and not others will come about. This suggests something like selection, perhaps made with a view to having the world continually be as intelligible or as good as it can be.

This view may appear extreme and unusual, but it seems necessary to complete the thought that begins with seeing that things can change, that, at each moment, there are different possibilities for what will come about, and that only some of these do come about.

One might take a partly different view, as Aristotle does: what can come about is limited by the things themselves. Substances have natures, and the only states that can come about in them are developments or manifestations of their natures or states incidental to the manifestations. Elephants can do only what they, in being elephants, can do, and because they are elephants, only certain things can happen to them. The natures of things make for both the world's general order and its finer order, things by nature aspire to manifest their natures so as to make themselves, as much as possible, independent of other substances or unaffected by them. The natures of things define what is possible for them, and their own aspirations direct them more specifically. According to Aristotle, their aspiration is directed toward a single being that lures all substances into their activity. Aristotle thinks of it as an unmoved mover, and all things, within the limits of their natures, imitate it. What substances can do, then, the changes that can occur in them, is limited by their natures, and the specific aims of their action express an aspiration for an ideal. For Aristotle, as for Plato, the world always has a value and its value ultimately depends on what limits and selects the aim for what can come about.

2. How do possibilities come about? Plato says that things participate in forms; Aristotle says that substances actualize their potentialities. This is what each of them means by "change," that a continually present, unstable, characterless something comes to have all the definiteness that it can have, loses it—or some of it—and comes to have a different definiteness instead. Plato thinks that what comes to be definite, or as definite as it can be, is the flux; Aristotle thinks that it is the matter of substances. Further, there are orders of the definiteness in any change: many forms are linked in any change, and all substances have many formed matters. The flux and unformed matter lie at the base of every change. It is in them that possibilities are actualized.

For Plato, participation is the flux, the whole flux—not one piece of it at a time—having qualities and relations of certain kinds, distributed throughout itself. The flux itself has no intelligible character. It is like an unsettled sea, and one cannot say whether it has the same degree of unsettlement throughout or even what "throughout itself" means. The question is how the characterless flux comes to have characters at all and why it comes to have the characters that it does. Nothing about the flux explains this. There is nothing definite in the flux itself, not even a germ of future order, and the characters it has at any particular time do not cause the characters it comes to have at later times. The characters that come to be in the flux do not hold it tightly enough to affect it or cause it to flow in only certain ways. Nothing that either is or was in the flux is the source or cause of the qualities and relations that come to be in it. A flux so little understood can come to have its characters only because of something that is altogether apart from it and perhaps of an altogether different nature. What causes the order in the flux is the forms, or some of them: the flux participates in the forms.

Participation does not mean that the forms are taken into the flux or are subjected to it. There is no relocation of the forms; they do not move. Moreover, things do not take aim at one form or another, though in his simplest expositions Plato writes as if this were so; rather, the whole flux participates in the forms by becoming like them, or like some of them, by becoming as much like them as it can and for as long as it can. The being of the flux becomes like the being of the forms, but then, because of its endless restlessness, it does this only momentarily, again and again.

In participation, the flux is affected by the forms. It thereby becomes ordered and intelligible—as the forms themselves are—but only for a moment and then it is ordered again. Why and how does this happen? It happens because of the flux and the forms: the world goes on, and the flux is the cause of its going on; its participation in the forms is what orders it as a world. The "how" is just the flux's imitating the forms. To Platonists, matters seem quite simple; the answers to questions of why and how seem obvious.

Must the flux imitate the forms? No, but if it is to imitate anything, the forms are the only things it can imitate. Can it imitate them more or less extensively and more or less well? Perhaps the world might be less or more ordered and its order might be less or more finely grained. Must something lay hands on the flux to ensure that it is ordered and ordered well? It would be picturesque and not very helpful to suppose so. Finally, and crucially, could not the flux come of itself to have an order without there being forms? The forms are not put into the flux. They are not imposed on it. The being of the flux changes of itself. Why even suppose that there are forms? The issue does not arise in quite this way for Plato, whose myth posits a demiurge that forms the flux according to the forms. There must be patterns for the forming so the demiurge will know what the flux can and perhaps should become; even so, the forming of the flux by the demiurge is not a molding of it—no hands are laid on it. It is more a persuading of the flux to become like certain forms. Again, therefore, the forming is by the flux itself, the forms remain apart and are imitated, and one can suppose or not that there is a demiurge, a gentle persuasion between the flux and forms.

Aristotle's doctrine of actualization is a variant of Plato's view. Instead of supposing, as Plato does, that there is a totally unorganized flux to be formed, Aristotle argues that there is no flux, or in his terms, no last matter, entirely without form. Aristotle then supposes that everything that comes to be is either a further forming of what already has some form or a loss or replacement of forms. If there were an analogue for this idea in Plato, it would be that something definite in the flux at one time causes some other definiteness in the flux at a later time.

In his discussion of changes in substances that have both form and matter, Aristotle notes that although substances have natures that do not change (though they may develop some), their matter can take on different incidental forms. Because of the order of formed matter in a substance, changes can be more or less extensive; one can paint the wood of a desk, or take a desk apart and use the wood for other purposes, or even burn it. For Aristotle, then, actualizations are the forming of a substance's matter or the forming of its proximate matter. It is perhaps not always clear what the forming of matter is—it does not always mean giving a shape to stuff—still, Aristotle may have no other meaning for the term, for he has no notion of a change *in* matter itself. For him, forming a matter is always doing something *to* it, while the matter somehow always eludes the form or does not permit the form to penetrate it. The form, therefore, always shapes its matter, and a new or different shaping seems to be what is going on when a change occurs. When a substance changes, it comes to have a different incidental property either because something else that already has that form imposes it on the substance or because the substance already has the form in a diminished version that it then develops.

For Aristotle, the possibilities or potentialities of substances have no reality in themselves. The forms of everything that can possibly occur are already actualized in substances, somewhere and in some way—

perhaps part for part in different substances—and whether the possibilities will come about depends on whether the substances that have the forms will act in certain ways. There is no separate domain of forms, no separate possibilities. A form is possible if there is a substance that can come to have it (considering the substance's other forms) and if there are substances that already have it, or parts of it, and can impose it on the waiting matter of the substance in which the change can come about. Here, too, matters seem quite simple.

3. What happens to possibilities after they have come about or been actualized? Either they remain present, or, if something else occurs to take their place, they simply cease to be. They never become past because possibilities have no power of their own and the being in which they were actualized always remains present. There is nothing in which they could become past, and they cannot sustain themselves as forms alone. Because participation and actualization take place in a flux or matter that is always present and always the same, what comes about in them can never become past. All there can be are configurations of the same flux, the same matter.

For Plato, forms do not do anything. They are not even, as it were, put into things, and things do not take them into themselves. To call them possibilities is only to say that portions of the flux will become now like some of them and now like others. The forms are unaffected by the flux's activity, and the moment of resemblance passes while the flux, so to speak, remains.

Whitehead's construction of these Platonic themes differs on several points, perhaps most importantly in that Whitehead does not think there is one flux that participates in the forms. He thinks there are, so to speak, many little fluxes, as many as there are actual occasions. Whitehead also thinks that in each moment there come to be new fluxes, as many as there had been before. What happens to the old fluxes after they have formed themselves? Whitehead says that they have indeed become past; he has a doctrine of real past entities, and the notion crucial to this doctrine—indeed, any notion of a real past—is that the stuff formed in the present does not remain in the present; either a new stuff comes to be, as Whitehead thinks, or a stuff that was future comes to be present, as I believe. The crucial idea for any notion of the past's reality is that the stuff of becoming itself becomes past. If you suppose that becoming is only the changing of forms in a flux that in some sense remains present, you must conclude that there is and can be no past. If you suppose instead that there is a forming in a flux that itself comes to be present, you must conclude that there is and must be a past. What has been formed in the present is sustained in the stuff that it has formed and that itself becomes past. Plato's supposition is the more conservative one. For him, there is only the present and what is not in time. The stuff of the present—the flux—remains the same. It does not come to be or come to be present, it has its forms only momentarily, and what is passing in it is, Plato thinks, an image of eternity.

For Aristotle, and for the same reasons, there can be no past. All changes are effects on the matter of substances, and substances and their matter are always present. Substances have now these incidental forms, now those. Change is a change *to* their matter; there is no change *in* the matter itself. Aristotle thinks that both a basic, unformed matter and a newly created matter are impossibilities. None of Aristotle's four causes can explain matter's coming to be, and like others of us, Aristotle supposes that what he cannot explain is not quite real. It is not surprising, then, that in his review of the causes his predecessors had mentioned, he found Heraclitus to be obscure. Aristotle conceives of a restless matter that has ever to be re-formed. He could not conceive, as Heraclitus does, of matter that arises endlessly and endlessly consumes itself, a view I think is very nearly true.

Possibilities and the Past

I will now sketch in detail some themes about possibilities, noting some variations between different views, to show by contrast the nature of the past. Those who think they understand what possibilities are should, when they understand the contrast, also understand the nature of the past.

The themes to be compared are *definiteness, indefiniteness,* and the *becoming definite* of what is in itself indefinite. Doctrines of possibility locate and connect these themes in certain ways. Possibilities are the items of definiteness. They are the *whats* that things can become, and, being the forms in things that could cause matter to take on different forms, they are either not in time at all or they are in the present. According to doctrines of possibility, the principle of indefiniteness is in the present; it is either an entirely indefinite flux or a matter that has basic forms. Finally, there are the processes of participation and actualization, both of which occur in the present; they are, respectively, the processes in which what is indefinite becomes definite or in which the matter of a substance comes to have different forms.

The contrasting notion involving the past locates and interprets these themes differently. In the contrasting view, the items that are *definite* are neither in the present nor apart from time, but past. There is one past, one domain of past occurrences. It is entirely definite, though it is not complete; rather, it is always growing. What is altogether *indefinite* is not a jiggling present flux but the future being of individuals. This is what is made definite, and it is made definite in a present, as individuals continue to make themselves singular, as their future being comes into them, and as they form themselves continuously on those parts of themselves that are already very definite and already becoming past.

It is as if, in contrast to the previous picture of possibilities, the past is a domain of actualized possibilities, all entirely definite, congealed, and past, as if change does not take place in a flux that remains present but in an altogether indefinite being that continuously becomes present, that forms itself as it passes, and that achieves its fullest definiteness in becoming past. The two notions have the same themes, then, or the same sorts of themes, but they interpret and locate them differently, and if one senses the differences from doctrines of possibilities and forms, one also sees the sense in the notion that the past is real.

In fact, I think we should go further and conclude that the past is real and that its nature is like what achieved and actualized possibilities would be if they were to become past and not cease to be. There is simply too much that cannot be understood in the notions of possibilities and forms and flux and matter. There is, for example, the unfounded claim that forms are discrete entities. There is their inexplicable being—what is their nature?—the supposed fullness of the domain of possibilities that precludes new possibilities, and the failure to explain both why only certain possibilities come about and the order of their coming about. There is also no explanation for there being only certain species and nothing that could cause new species to come about, nor is there an explanation for a flux that forms itself, though forms are altogether apart from it, and then unsettles the forms it has given to itself (whereas one might think instead that there is a kind of forming of a flux and then a new and continuing flux that must be formed in turn). There is, as well, the troubling notion that even when things change, they do not *do* anything but simply house the changes that have come about in them. Perhaps our clarity and certainty about these fundamental themes are limited, but there seems to me far too much that we cannot see in the idea that change is a coming to be and that what can come to be is a possibility. There are no comparable obscurities in the idea that individuals continue to make themselves singular in the present, that the time that passes through them also makes them past, and that individuals form themselves on those parts of themselves that are becoming and have become past.

The Nature of the Past

The past consists of what was becoming definite in a present; it became fully definite in being past. The past consists of what is fully actual. While individuals are present they are becoming definite and actual, and the completion of that process is their being past. Individuals are transformed when they become past, and the most prominent change in them is that their singularity is lost. In the present, individuals are singular and extended; they resist and oppose one another. They are spatial and outside one another. None of these features becomes past. What becomes past is the definiteness the individuals have achieved from inside themselves, and the definiteness of each individual is joined with the definiteness of all the other individuals that were their contemporaries. Together, they are the achieved definiteness of a moment of the entire world, joined to the past to which they have conformed. There is one whole past. There is no space in it and it has no length; duration and spatiality are only in a present time. We know that we should not think of the past or the future as if it were like the present, only at some distance away, but that is how we often imagine it. Considering what it really is, we should see that we cannot imagine it at all.

The past does not need anything to sustain it or make it effective. It consists of the being of individuals and of time, and they are as real in the past as they are in the present. The time that makes individuals past becomes past, too; it does not remain present, which is what the flux and matter are supposed to do. There is, as it were, a stuff in the past inseparable from the definiteness that was achieved in the present. The time and individuals that are the past are continuous with the time and individuals that are the present, and when individuals change and act in the present, their whole being enters into what they do; they do not change and act out of the present parts of themselves alone.

Most philosophers who think that change is entirely a coming to be suppose, as I noted earlier, that the past is not real. A few philosophers, however—Whitehead, Hartshorne, and Weiss, for example—suppose both that change is a coming to be and that the past is real. They are able to suppose that the past is real because they think that in each moment there is a new flux or a new exhibition of existence—and then they wonder what makes for the past's effectiveness. Their answer is that there is a mighty reality, a divinity, that takes up the past as part of itself and that its doing so affects the divinity's own activity of making available the possibilities for what can come about. Because they think of change as wholly a matter of coming to be, they think the past can be effective only through something else that affects what can possibly come about. This view, or something very like it, must be held by anyone who thinks that there is a past but that what occurs in the present is, through and through, a coming to be. What occurs in the present, though, is not just a coming to be, and there are no real possibilities. There is the time of the future and the indefinite future being of individuals, and they are continuous with the time and being of individuals in the present and the past. These sustain one another, and one need not suppose an additional and mighty reality to sustain any one of them.

Again, these brief notes about the nature of the past are a contrast with doctrines about possibilities, about the present's being the only time, and about occurrences in the present being wholly comings to be. If we see that changes are not wholly comings to be, we must think that individuals are indefinite in the future and active in the present and that they become past as well. The past is real and affects what is occurring now. We can see the effects, but we cannot imagine the past that causes them. We can imagine what past occurrences were or might have been when they were present, but once transformed and made to be past, they are not much like the present. In the present, individuals are *becoming* definite; in the past, they *are* definite. Their definiteness is what we think of even when they are present, and it is what we think of when they are past. We should not conceive of them through images, however. Such conceptions are thought, but as Plato says in his discussion of the cave and the divided line, images obscure our thought of some realities, and to grasp them, we must set our images aside and think of the realities themselves. This note about our thought of the past would be true also for possibilities if there were any; they cannot be imagined either. Our faintest images are that what is possible is something just coming into sight and that what is past is passing from our view. There are, however, no appearances for the past or for the possible; even when the real appears, we know the reality only through our thought of it. The appearances of things are only some of our reasons for thinking that what we think about those things is true. Where there are no appearances of what we think about, what we think can still be true, which shows that appearances do not mean much at all.

It is difficult to think about what is past and to understand how and why it affects what occurs in a present time. We know that the past has an almost overwhelming influence on what occurs now. It is a massive whole. We separate it into parts artfully and artificially, justifying the separations by supposing that they are the ones required to understand what has occurred, but no occurrence, however small, will be completely understood unless, in one way or another, we relate it to everything that occurred before it. Such complete understanding is beyond us. We therefore usually settle uneasily among contending notions of division: either we decide what we want to explain and then try to separate in the past those few factors that we think will explain it, or we think we know what real explanations must be, and we divide the past into portions to provide explanations of just those kinds. Both divisions give us the proper subjects of a demanding inquiry and art—the subject of history. The nature of the past suggests to us how history should be studied; how it is studied should also test whether we have understood the nature of the past.

CHAPTER SEVEN

HISTORY AND THE PAST

HISTORY IS about what people have done; about when, where, and why they have done it; and about what has occurred as a significant consequence. It can embrace the past of everything, and perhaps every history implicitly does. Everything that is present has a past and perhaps a history, but the history that most historians study is the history of the people whose thoughts and actions explain how or why or when certain other interesting and important actions or events have come about.

Who historians write about depends on what they want to understand. The "big" historians want to explain the large configuration of the public life of *an era,* to help us both understand the people of that time and better understand ourselves, even if the history is not our own. Smaller histories are said to have these same benefits, perhaps more intensively. Historians differ as to the scale and kinds of things they think it important to explain; they also differ about what they think will provide the explanations and even about what they think an explanation is. For all their differences, though, historians think themselves agreed that history is about the past—and, of course, it is. Few historians, however, think about how the past is real, and that unsettled issue affects their histories. The most obvious effect is that most histories are ambiguous.

The ambiguity is whether (1) history describes the past by saying what things were when they were present or (2) it describes what things are as they are past. Many historians seem to give both descriptions, first one and then the other, or to go back and forth between the two without recognizing their difference. In a historical narrative, for example, a historian may (1) "watch" events as they unfold, telling us what he or she sees, as if the historian has a more comprehensive and accurate view of what is going on than do any of the participants and, of course, more accurate anticipations; but (2) historians often will also say that this or that is important, that there are trends, that mighty forces are at play, that an age is coming to have a certain character, and that our own time is its heir. None of these claims, however, is about what was happening as it was when it was happening; rather, they are about the tenor and configuration of the past and its bearing on the present. Without realizing it, historians often shift from describing individuals and actions as they were when they were present to describing them as they are after they have become past—and this difference in what is being spoken of can occur without a change of words, obscuring what they mean through ambiguity.

For example, when we say that Augustus constructed an empire, built roads, and restored temples, we may be referring to what Augustus achieved through his administration, or we may be speaking not of him, or of him alone, but of a large part of Rome's past. In the latter case, "Augustus" is not a proper name but rather a focus or symbol that condenses the literal truth about the prominent organization of massive numbers of actions that have coalesced in becoming past.

This is not simply the difference between mentioning a vast number of actions and mentioning only a few in the knowledge that readers will suppose the rest. It is not simply the difference between merely saying that Augustus constructed a road and mentioning the engineers and soldiers who built the road and their construction sites, tools, and materials. The difference is that "Augustus constructed a road" can be about what he did as he was doing it or what was done as it was when it was finally done. This difference does not lie in the number of actions mentioned but in what we refer to and how we refer to and describe it.

If what is past differs from what it was when it was present, their descriptions should differ, too. Apart from tense, if the difference is not in the words themselves, it must be in the way they mean. "Augustus" means as a proper name when used in sentences about his actions as present; it means in a different way when used in sentences about his action as transformed and past. Some might deny that this admittedly subtle shift occurs, but it is real if the past is real, and the idea that different modes of grammar and meaning describe the different times of things can help us reconcile the disagreements among historians over (1) the extent to which history is factual, (2) the extent to which it is imaginative but not fictional, and (3) the extent to which and in what way it explains anything.

Contention over these ideas usually runs a course that begins with historians who think history should be done by describing the facts and letting them speak for themselves. Others, also concerned for the facts, think that our record of them is too incomplete for the facts to say much. One must, therefore—though carefully—imagine other, intervening facts and use them all to tell a connected story that shows things coming about the way they did. These notions of "fact" and "imagined fact" portray the past as it was when it was present; they use the language of present action, and the general idea of this kind of history has been criticized for supposing that facts can say anything for themselves and that the story connecting them, which is only imagined, can explain why or when anything has occurred.

According to other historians, there is a real connection between facts that need not be imagined. The connection has a cause that explains the course of history, namely, a mighty force that has an aim or end. Facts are expressions of it, and the facts are studied to reveal the nature and course of the reality that causes the facts to be what they are. Hegel, for example, supposes that Reason has been, and is still, active in the world; Marx thinks that there is a material base in history; some theologians think that God is also the Third Person of the Trinity. The central notion in such accounts is that what we think of as the actions of individuals is more fundamentally the action of something else that is taking place through them. Individual persons may qualify the action of the more fundamental reality, though what they can do either does not affect history or does not affect it much. We describe what occurs, then, by using the language of present action, and then we add what we must to account for the real connectedness in history, that these actions are stages in the action of a mighty reality. What really has occurred and will continue to occur is its exercise, its cunning, and its assumption of complicated and contentious forms. Its course must be made out, and doing this involves neither the discovery of an enormous number of specific facts nor a creative imagination. It is discovered in a distinctive historical investigation.

The complaint against this view is that it is philosophy, not history. An appeal to Reason, Matter, or God without reference to fact as well explains nothing in particular, and when it does explain something, the facts carry the burden of the explanation. It is not clear what, if anything, the grand realities themselves explain, so we turn again to the importance of the facts.

Are we now to have another round of argument, contending again that we must stay with fact but that imagination must give us a narrative, though a narrative that we only imagine does not explain what has in fact occurred? There is something sound in all three themes, and our hope should be to preserve their soundness while eliminating the contentions between them. We can do this by noting that what is in the past is very different from what was present and by considering which of these two options is the subject of each of the three themes: is it what something was as it was present or what something is as past? What history ultimately turns on is a conception of the past, and if the past is real, we can talk both about fact and about our having to imagine the real connections that things have when they are past. We can also claim that a mighty reality is effective in the world, only it does not differ from the individuals who act: it is the individuals themselves, as they are a single past. I will review the three themes in the light of this idea and try to show how they can be reconciled.

History and Fact

There is no question that historians should find out what really happened. Unfortunately, their notion of a fact is usually not finely drawn. A historical fact is, roughly, a significant public state of human things. It is also thought that there are always many facts. None is really general, perhaps, but some are complicated, and there must be simple ones. These are what make historical statements true. Some historians when they speak too simply go on to say that what one should do is discover facts and then connect them in a chronicle of true statements about what has occurred.

Nearly all this, though, is caricature. It does not distinguish between history and chronicle, it says nothing about historical connectedness, and it does not suggest what history explains or how it explains anything. Most of the caricature derives from the notion of fact. We can roughly repair this too simple picture by noting that historians never deal with all the facts; they never have them all—whatever that might mean—and they usually do not use all the facts they have. They deal only with facts within some frame, and within the frame, only with those that have become significant for us. One may then think that the narrative, the story showing the facts to be significant and hence historical, is a construction of the historian's imagination.

On this account of facts, the main work of imagination is not so much to invent the intervening facts that historians have not discovered but to connect the ones they have discovered, or at least some of them. Were we strict about facts, we would think that at any moment the world is filled with them; there are overlapping and successive facts, perhaps even facts about the connectedness of facts. Only a few facts, however, enter explicitly into a history, and one might think that the narrative connections between those few must therefore be imagined because they are not real. Facts are really connected only when they are densely arrayed; when only a few of them are connected in a history there is only a vestige of similarity to their real connectedness. One must wonder why we should want to imagine something so very thin.

Even so, it is also a caricature of history to see it as trying to say what a fact was when it was a fact, a crude science that searches for some facts and invents a plot to connect them and that, because it leaves so much out, says what is literally false about the connections of facts—though perhaps it is instructive in some other way. The rough repair about selecting and connecting facts does not take us far enough. It is too conservative and tries too much for the most established kind of respectable objectivity. Instead of thinking that history requires us to imagine connections between established facts, we would do better to think that fact and imagination work in it almost the other way around: the modest role of the established facts is to steady our imagination, and it is by imagination that we come as close as we can to discovering the "facts" of the real past.

Imagining the Past

When individuals and their actions are transformed in becoming past, they lose their interiority, their singularity, their sensuosity, and the indefiniteness and unfinishedness they had when they were present. We cannot really imagine what is past for it is not something that we can see. What things are as past is the subject of history, however, and we must imagine a surrogate for them. History is the work of imagination constrained somewhat by our knowledge of facts that were once discrete.

To construct a history is to resolve the previously mentioned ambiguity between what things were when they were present and what they are as past. I claimed that historians shift from describing one to describing the other and suggested that they could be clearer about which one they are discussing. The ambiguity, however, is not so simple, and something like it is irremovable, for history is not about what was as it was when it was present nor simply about what is past as it is past. It is rather about the past *as if* the past were occurring in a present time. History is the past imagined as occurring. The historical present is its grammatical form.

Of the many differences between what was as it was when it was present and what is really past but imagined as occurring now, one of the most important is that the definiteness of the achieved past is part of what we imagine is occurring, but that definiteness, which is only in the past, is not a part of anything in the present. As imagined to occur, the past contains notes that were never in a present time, which is why the notes about what things have become appear to be added on to descriptions of former presents and to cause their ambiguity.

Another difference—the most comprehensive—between what was as it was present and the past that we imagine to occur is that there is not much we must imagine in thinking of what was as it was when it was present, perhaps only some missing facts. In thinking of the past as if it were occurring, however, we must imagine almost everything—the space and time of the occurrences as well as their pacing and effectiveness. A historical narrative should not be construed as a plausible or even an interesting rendering of things as they in fact occurred. It is an imagined world in which imagined individuals are imagined to act in ways that real individuals never could have acted.

The imposture in supposing that history says what was as it was when it was present is that historians know, in telling or constructing the narrative, how it all comes out, but when things were as they were at a present, no one knew how they would come out. A historian's knowledge of outcomes affects either the telling of the story or the story itself. An impatient, unimaginative historian might foretell what will occur, which should make us wonder about the point of telling the story, but if a historian's knowledge of what became past enters into the construction of the narrative itself, then the story is not about what occurred as it was when it occurred but about what transformed individuals, no longer singular, have been imagined to do.

Because individuals are not singular in the past we must imagine them, and we focus on them by knowing something about what they were when they were present. In the past, they are sheafs of definiteness, inseparable from what we imagine others were. Augustus is a part of Rome—some part of Rome—but there are no divisions in the parts, which is why divisions have to be made imaginatively. It is as if the past were far away and nearly flat, so that we distinguish the few higher places we think we see and imagine in them "persons" who we also imagine think, speak, and act. Because the past has no space and no passing time for the actions we imagine, we imagine them, too—large when the actions are important and passing quickly when a lot is imagined to occur. The space and time of history and the causalities of historical actions are not intended to be reports of real occurrences. They are imagined dimensions and connections in the narrative, and different historians imagine them differently. Historians also imagine the dimensions of characters differently.

It is difficult even for present actions to say what one person is doing and who is involved in doing it, and it is far less sure for the past. Augustus can be imagined to have started the Imperial Age of Rome, and its fall may have started with him, too, but Augustus did neither of these alone. When he is a character in a narrative about the rise and fall of Rome he is not really singular; his effectiveness is never his alone. This is true of other characters as well. Relatively few characters need to be imagined in a history because the stories of many or most persons are imagined to be the same. Though the past is all definite, in a history, characters are general, like statues waiting to be named; any one of them, even Augustus, can stand for many persons who have not been imagined or named. Characters and stories are so often alike because in acting and becoming past, individuals are affected by the same whole past and they conform themselves to it. One of the great lessons of history is that things are what they are because of their pasts. We are taught this lesson through seeing that things were what they were because of their own pasts.

The past that historians write about also has a past, and that past formed itself on its own past. Narratives start with the past of the past with which they are concerned. The awkwardness for historians is that a past of a past itself has a past, leaving them unsure where their stories really begin. They begin somewhere, however, with the past that they think is needed for their narrative, and they go on to what they take to be the middle and to what seems, in their own time, the end. There is for us, in learning from a history, this same double sense of "past." We have a past, history tells its story, and the past that it imagines has its past, too. We are led consider whether we are, or can avoid, conforming ourselves to our past in the same ways in which history shows us that a past conformed itself to its own past. We may learn from reading Roman history that we have not done or had to do many of the things the Romans did. More recent history may show us that in certain large affairs we changed our ways of doing things a hundred years ago but that since then our stories have been very much the same.

History can show this double sense of past only because it is about the past as past. It is in becoming past that individuals complete their forming of themselves. When they are present they are not altogether definite, neither as much nor in the same way as they will be when they are past. When individuals are present we cannot see all the effects of their past on them; all the effects have not yet occurred. A historian who writes about the past as it was when it was present—though none can—will be writing about a present, not a past. Nothing in what might be written would show that it was about the past; one would have to somehow add that all this happened some time ago, but that addition would, clumsily, introduce our ambiguity.

The differences between the present and the past show themselves in an account of the past as past; they even show when we imagine that past as occurring. They show in the generality of characters, in the pace and contour of action, and in the moods and hues in which we sense the finality of what is being imagined to occur. We can think about the past, but as I mentioned, we cannot imagine it. It has no appearance; it is not much like what can be seen. By using what we think about the past, however, historians can imagine its occurring, and in the images and their motions there is something like the definiteness and the forms of definiteness that past individuals and past actions have. It is common to suppose that what we imagine is possible. History tries, in another kind of imagination, to imagine what is actual—the past. In even its greatest success, however, history may succeed only in imagining the possibility of the real past, and even then there is the question of whether, so far as the past is imagined, a history can be true, whether we can imagine the past as it really is.

This is not a question for factual histories; they are about what was as it was when it was present, and they obviously can be true, especially when they are short and dense. Some factual histories are so short and full of fact that some historians do not regard them as histories at all but think of them rather as economic reports or political or sociological surveys—reports, for example, of the fleet size, new construction, and loss of Roman merchant ships in the first year of Augustus's proconsulship or surveys of land holdings or divorce rates among Roman senators. The claims of these studies, whether or not they are histories, are that there were certain numbers of things at certain times, and the claims are true or probably true or not; we simply have to see the evidence.

There are also larger factual histories filled with records and registers, such as an account of the Roman campaigns against the Germans. Marches, battles, and changes of command are recorded, winter quarters are described, many facts are set out, and every sentence may be true. It is left to the reader to wonder about the direction and momentum of the campaigns, about wisdom in the administration of provinces, and about civic virtue, politics, and wars, as if the reader of such anecdotal histories were a historian of a different kind.

There is no question that in a history where there are claims about the facts there is truth or falsity, but there are also uses of fact in imaginative histories; all historians rely on facts, only some use them differently from others. Very different histories can use the same facts but see and weigh and tell them differently, which leads to the criticism that nothing in them is really true except the facts; the rest, the narrative, is imaginative art.

What this judgment fails to see is that there is a kind of fact that is larger than the ones cited in the narrative, and it is to this large fact that an imaginative history tries to be true. The large fact is a portion of the settled past; it is a fact of the final fittingness of things, of their being altogether in the past, but it is not a summation or a collection of facts about them. These, the facts, are what things were when they were present. The facts that history tries to represent are what things became in becoming past, and the only way we have imagined representing it is in a narrative about how a final fittingness came to be. There can be something true in such a narrative, but there is always and inescapably something false.

What is false is the implied claim that the final fittingness of things came about in a present time. An imaginative history describes the past as if it were occurring in present time, as if the past were becoming past—which it does not do. If it did, we could describe the past as becoming past rather than thinking of it *as if* that were happening. Something that occurs becomes past—the past does not become past—and things become finally fitting only when they have become past. A final fitting of things does not come about in a present but results from what already has come about. The ostensible narrative of a history is, therefore, always false because it imagines what is already past as if it were becoming past, but there is a fact that makes the *as if* possible, and that is why the narrative is history and not a fiction sustained only by an author's imagination.

The inescapable falsity in a history is the same kind of falsity that occurs in well-made fiction. A story, for example, is not just a sequence of incidents. It has a beginning and end, and the storyteller knows the story before telling it; indeed, the story controls the tone, rhythm, and emphasis in what is told. Yet the incidents are told one by one, and the story can seem improvised, as if it were not complete until the last incident is told. Storytellers know this is not true, and so do those who hear the stories, which is part of their delight.

The story that an imaginative history tells is also complete before it is told. Individuals and their actions have occurred, have been transformed, and have become past. These changes are presupposed in telling the story. The story is about a complete and definite past; the *as if* in it is about the past's occurring, and it is an *as if* because the past as past did not occur. What sustains the story, if it can be sustained, is that things have come to be together in the past. That is the fact to which an imaginative history tries to be true. It may or may not succeed; we will find out how far it does when further facts about what has occurred are found and we consider how, as transformed, they affect the historical narrative. They might show just what we expected, or they might show that the story had been too loosely or even wrongly conceived. We also make a judgment of a history's soundness by considering the history of later times: the story of a past should be the earlier part of an even longer story. A history of a later period, if sound itself, can be a criticism of an earlier history.

An imaginative history should be true of the past. The past should sustain the construction, and the history will be a fiction in the parts where it does not. The construction must be imagined, though, because there is not much in our experience of the past that we can describe. We sometimes seem to feel its weight or lightness, but we cannot see what things have become when they have become past. Instead, we must think of what they were, how they might have been transformed, and what their subsequent effects have been. We then tell what we have thought about through imaginative language that at the narrative's end may reveal the final fittingness of things as they are past.

Imagining the past as if it were becoming past is as close as we can come to knowing it. Imagining is not a substitute for knowing; it is a part of it. There is a good deal of imagination even in knowing a fact about what occurs in a present time; for example, it is probably only a conjecture on our part that a fact can be a fact in isolation or that a simple statement of fact can by itself be true. Still, many of us are more wary of imagination than of what seems to be a fact because imagining does not itself ensure that we have imagined what is true (though some very special kinds of self-awareness are thought to do this). It seems, then, that history is at best an imaginative elaboration of something that could not have been made up.

This is true, however, not of history alone but of all our knowledge of things outside us. What we claim to know is a construction on our part. Even if it is true, it could have been false. We think about how things might be together and the "might be" is imagined: it will be real or not. Whether the things we are thinking of are present or past will make a difference in what the things are and in the ways they might go together. History is a kind of knowledge different from the knowledge we have of present things, though, as noted earlier, many historians think they are the same. If, however, the past is real and history is knowledge about the past, it should not be criticized for being different from knowledge about what is present or was present, nor should it be criticized for being imagined, for there is no knowledge of things that is not imagined. It should not be criticized even for being, in general, less sure than the other ways we have of knowing things.

The critical assessment of history that has seemed to many philosophers to be the most sound is that history is not a high form of knowledge because it does not explain why things occurred as they did. All it does is recount their occurrence; it gives us information but not an understanding of why things occurred as they did. To come to such explanations, to the understandings and the further knowledge we should have, these philosophers think that we must go beyond history to something else that does not have to do with the past alone.

This higher form of knowledge has sometimes been thought to be a science, sometimes a philosophy or theology.

This assessment introduces the third of our themes about history, namely, its explanatory power. Even if history is not the highest form of knowledge (however forms of knowledge are distinguished and then ranked), it provides understandings and explanations of its own kind—the historical kind—and those critics who think that it should provide another kind do not really understand the goal of historical explanation, partly because they do not think that the past is real.

Historical Explanation

Many philosophers begin their criticism of history by saying that historians describe what has occurred; they then note that to describe an occurrence is not to explain it, and they depreciate historical knowledge for not explaining things. At the start of such critical reviews it is often unclear what the critics think history should explain and therefore unclear what they think the nature of an explanation ought to be. As discussion goes along both issues become clearer. It also becomes clear that, too often, philosophers and historians misunderstand each other: philosophical critics say that historians give no explanation for the occurrences described in their histories; historians seem to say that in describing occurrences they have explained them historically. Both are correct, but only because both think of different things as requiring explanation and each thinks of a different kind of explanation.

The philosophical critics think the question is simply why certain things have occurred. Their occurrence seems to be surprising and the explanation that removes the surprise is the understanding that in circumstances of a certain kind things of a certain kind always or usually occur. To explain why something occurred, we are to go away from the particular occurrence; we think of what kind of occurrence it is and of the kind of circumstances in which things of that kind occur. Then, the occurrence is explained as being an instance of the kind of occurrence we should have expected in circumstances of that kind. Thunderstorms and assassinations are both explained in this way. Explanation, critics say, appeals to law or regularity and to the circumstances in which they are exhibited. They shake their heads sadly at history, thinking that it will never explain why certain things occur if historians continue to insist that historical occurrences are unique and so specific that they cannot be understood by thinking of them as being of certain kinds or instances of laws.

The laws that these critics want historians to think of hold for things at any time, but *when* things are cannot be neglected in a history. Besides, historians are not concerned for single occurrences alone. They are concerned for many occurrences, not just the one or two that epitomize or dramatize the course and character of a period. Laws or principles that explain the occurrence of something whenever it occurs might do for some of the social sciences—for economics, psychology, or sociology—but they do not help with explanations in a history because history tries mainly to understand a different kind of thing.

The great philosophical historians have a much sounder view of understanding in history. They see, as most historians do, that there is a course in history and that things are ordered differently at different times; religion, commerce, politics, learning, and the arts affect one another in different ways within societies, and there are contentions between societies as well. The large questions for the philosophical historians are why history or a period of it has taken the overall course it has and what the causes for that course are, at least the fundamental ones. Their notion is that large forces must have been acting through history and that we explain the historical relationships of things by finding out which force is fundamental in what occurred. It may have always acted on the same principle, or in the same way, or toward the same end, and in knowing about it we will understand why, acting through the things that are at different times, the history of those times has the structure that it does.

So philosophical historians search the past for signs of what it is. They try to distinguish the fundamental from the derived, the kind of change that changes everything from those other changes that have only small effect. The cause of a course of history is not, they think, the past itself; they think that the past cannot act and that the cause of history is acting even now. It shows itself mainly in the kinds of conflicts within a society, in their intensity, persistence, and resolution. Different periods of history are, perhaps, defined by stages of the conflicts—a period starts with a conflict and ends with its resolution—and though there are differences between the periods, the stages within them may be formally alike. There may also be a direction in them over a course of time; the conflicts may become either larger, simpler, harsher, or perhaps the opposite. Philosophical historians search the patterns of past conflicts for the fundamental cause of a history, or if they think they know what the cause is or has to be, they distinguish and interpret the conflicts in certain ways. There have been notions that history is circular or cyclical, progressive or providential, rise and fall, challenge and response; it has been thought that there will be epochs and eras of history of very different kinds and also that history, or certain patterns in it, will come to an end at last.

The grand theme in philosophical histories, then, is that periods of history are distinctive as history and that there is a cause for their distinctiveness. They are not as they are accidentally; their character cannot be explained by supposing that at certain times people just happened to group themselves in certain ways and that their contention then just happened to take certain forms. Things are too much alike in any given period of history—people's thoughts, values, and actions—for the likeness to be altogether due to the separate activities of individuals. It is instead as if there were common conditions that affected all of them, some in one way and some in another. There is something in the air or in the material conditions of the time that explains the period's fundamental character. The explanation is that, being the kind of cause it is, having the aim and force it does, in the circumstances of the time its effect had to be this distinctive stage of history.

What is hardest to understand in these theories, insightful as they are, is how the great forces that determine history are effective through individuals. It is we who are in conflict and who are reconciled, but how much of what we do when we act as members of different groups is owed to us and how much to the realities that make us or lure us to act as we do? What natures must we have if we are responsible for so little of what we do? Are we just affected things, moved along by history's tide, or has that been our nature only up till now, when we have come to understand the forces acting on us and come to identify ourselves with them? Even if this last were true, there would still be forces acting through us, only we would not feel ourselves coerced by them.

The notion of a force acting through us is troublesome. If it acts through us, then we have no natures of our own or not enough force to affect our history, but unless we have such force, there will be no explanation for history's ups and downs. Why has the finest progress not yet been achieved? Why is providence not at hand? Why must there be a dialectic in history? The upshot of such reflection is that we cannot appeal to a fundamental force that shapes our history without also supposing that we ourselves have power to affect its course. If that is so, however, the course of a fundamental force will not explain how a period comes to have its cast. There is something deeply wrong in this sort of philosophical history. It is not wrong to think that there is a whole cast to a period of history or to think that it is owed to a single cause; what is wrong, it seems, is in our ideas of what the cause of history is, how it acts, and what the cause explains. We should think of a different cause, a different way of being effective, and something different for history to explain.

History does not primarily try to explain why something has occurred; it is not primarily occupied with causes for occurrences. Instead, it tries to explain why what occurred—for whatever causes—occurred just *when* it did. History is concerned with the *when* of things, and it can reflect on why then and not earlier or later or even why at all. In doing this, it must consider what has occurred, but it is the when of occurrences that marks them as historical. We take a when for granted when we think of the causes of an occurrence: whenever certain conditions are met there are certain kinds of occurrences, and we explain one of these occurrences by noting that the conditions have been met. In all this, however, there is no mention of why the conditions occurred just when they did—explaining that ultimately requires a noncausal kind of explanation. To explain *why* some event occurred we turn to the ideas of cause and law or to some other reality very different from the occurrence we want to explain. To explain why some event occurred *when* it did we also turn away from it, but not to a different sort of reality; we turn to other things of the same kind, to other occurrences that are in the event's past. They explain its occurring when it did.

In the final analysis, these two forms of explanation are not separable, though one is sometimes more prominent than the other, or one of them has to be given first. In simple cases, for example, when we know a cause, we explain why something occurred just when it did by saying when its cause occurred. The when of the effect is after the when of the cause, and we may even know how long it takes for the cause to take effect. Most often in history, though, cases are not so simple because we cannot readily make a distinction between a cause and the conditions that accompany it.

An occurrence is a cause of a certain kind only under certain conditions; striking a match does not always produce a flame. The conditions are other occurrences or states of things, and they affect causation in different ways, for example, by adding to the efficacy of the cause or by precluding conditions that would keep something from being effective as a cause. Because nothing can be the cause of the same effect in all conditions, for repeatable causes, the most that we can usually say is that whenever certain conditions are present, an occurrence of a certain kind will always be followed by an occurrence of a different kind: kinds of conditions and kinds of causes and effects occur at different times; we therefore explain both the occurrence and the when of an effect by referring to all these kinds.

This distinction between cause and condition is not used in a strict way in history because history is not content to explain an occurrence as an instance of a kind. More importantly, the distinction is inapplicable because historians do not know what the kind of an occurrence is until they have explained the event historically, after which there is no reason for them to explain it again in a strictly causal way. An action is not always obviously of any certain kind. That must be found out, and it is found out by seeing how the action came about. In history, the when of things often must be explained before we know enough to explain the why. Once the when is understood the why is superfluous; it would be gratuitious in a history of a war to add to the description of the event that what happened was a war and that, like other wars, it was owed to avarice.

The when of things is explained by searching their pasts for promptings and restraints, for openings and closures, and then testing these imaginatively and rendering them in a narrative about the fullness of the time of their occurrence. The actions that have occurred originated in individuals, and part of what they have become depends on the nature of those individuals. The actions may have been planned or adventitious; they may have been forceful, hesitant, deliberate, angry, skilled, or otherwise; but however far and fully individuals determine the character of their own actions, other individuals affect the actions, too. They may have invited an action, constrained it somewhat, or redirected it; they may have restrained others who tried to make it fail. For any given action, it is not a matter of necessity how many other things, how wide or long or deep a domain of things, bear on what came about. It is as though the vectors of that domain consist of many kinds of forces—some contending, some not, some resistant, some permeable, some cunning, some dumb, some enduring, and some shortlived—and had they and their junctures been different in any way, the action that is to be explained would have been different, too; it, the *it* as it occurred when it did, would not have occurred at all.

Historians try to order these plays of force and see their pace in time. They also have some notion of the time that is right for things, as we all do. They may see, for example, that something could have occurred at any time during a long period or that there may have been a crucial moment at which something had to be done if it was to be done at all, as if there were patiences and tensions in the course of time. Some sight of this often seems to prompt historical studies; historians may start a study because they are surprised that something came about at a certain time or because something else whose prospect seemed so strong did not occur. The upshot of the studies should be that, given all that supported the one occurrence and all that was against the other, there is no surprise in how things turned out. We understand why they turned out as they did: the time was full enough for the one and not for the other.

In explaining when things have come about, historians count on our being able to sense the fullness of a time. Historians seldom if ever appeal to the sorts of laws or principles that explain instances of things, but they always appeal to our sense of their different timings. This capacity to sense timings is deep in us. It is partly instinctive, but we go beyond instinct in becoming practiced about the lengths of time within which things can occur; some of the strongest disagreements between the old and the young are about when the time of things is right.

Our sense of timing serves historical explanation in something like the way laws or principles serve scientific explanation—it is general, and we appeal to it to explain why things had to come about just when they did. The two strongest differences between these kinds of explanations are that (1) our sense of the fullness of a time does not enter historical understanding as an explicit principle—it is doubtful that it could even be formulated—and (2) the occurrences historians describe are not described as instances of a principle. Because of these differences, instead of saying that history describes but does not explain, we should say that it tries to explain the when of occurrences in its own way, through a narrative whose turns and pace seem to fit and to specify our sense for the time of the actions that it has imaginatively described.

When historians construct their narratives they feel for the changing paces of actions. Their sense for the times of things guides historians even in first finding out what had happened: they think, for example, that something else must have been going on to make certain occurrences so important, and they will have notions of how quickly or slowly its consequences might have come about. In their narratives they diagram a feeling for the fullness of the time of past occurrences; they make it definite for us in renditions of action, and we understand why things occurred when they did when we come to feel that the narrative has captured the timing of the occurrences.

There is nothing like this in a chronicle. Historians use chronicle in the way we might use a set of diagrams to learn how to serve a tennis ball: all the stages that have been diagramed are in the serve, but when we serve we weld them into a natural motion; different speeds, tensions, and forces are smoothed through the whole serve. When historians use a chronology, their narrative weighs its items and choreographs them into the motion of historical actions. It is in the feeling of the "naturalness" of these motions that we understand why things occurred just when they did.

This understanding is in our understanding the narrative. If the narrative were merely descriptive we would know what happened but not understand any of the whys of the occurrences; we would have to go beyond the occurrences in explaining things. The historical narrative is an imaginative construction, however, and embedded in it is a rendition of a general sense or notion of the fullness of the times of things. If that rendition seems to us right we will not merely know that things occurred but also understand why they occurred when they did, just as we understand why the tennis ball was hit when it was when we see the timing of the serve. A general notion of the fullness of time has been incorporated, as if a principle that could explain the whys of things was used in the narrative in saying what we imagined had occurred. Because historical explanation is in the historical narrative, or in our understanding of it, we need not abandon it to understand why things occurred when they did. This also means that we need not abandon the past when we are searching for an explanation in history.

Those who think that the past cannot explain why something has occurred think, as we have seen, that there is no generality in it and that it cannot be a cause that could explain the whys of what occurred. They think that we describe what has occurred, that principles are needed to explain them, and that whatever causes the cast and tenor of a time must have been and still be a real and active agency. Though we can understand why these suppositions have been thought to be true, none of them is sound if the past is real. What we should say instead is that (1) history is an imaginative rendering of things as they are as past that does not describe what occurred as it was when it occurred; and (2) its primary purpose is not to explain why it is that things occurred. When we know that certain events have occurred, we also know that others like them would occur if comparable attending circumstances were to occur. We sort and order the circumstances, however, not to find the law that governs occurrences of those kinds but to find out the kind of the occurrences and above all to explain why they occurred when they did—before, after, during, and along with other things. The answer to this last question is always that "the time was right for their occurrence." The historical narrative saves this notion from being an empty generality by rendering it definite, by schematizing it; in the narrative account of the past's becoming past the generality of the fullness of time is made definite. It is the basis for our understanding why things occurred when they did.

Finally, we should say that (3) the cause of the cast and tenor of a time is a great and effective reality. It is the whole past of all that occurred at that time. This reality is not effective on things by producing them as manifestations or configurations of itself. This is the view of the philosophical histories that suppose causes to work from the present on. The past affects what is present while it is past; it affects the individuals that are present as they act and form their action on what is past. The past forms what originates in the present when individuals in the present form themselves on it. It is massively effective on them; all the definiteness that enters into the forming of individuals is owed to it, whereas all the novelties are owed to originations in a present time. The reality that distinguishes an era is not a reality beyond time, it is a part of time itself; it is the past, time and individuals together, and effective in a certain way. History does not have to be grounded on any other realities.

This threefold summary is, of course, not a neutral account of history, nor is it an account of what historians say about their enterprise and art. Historians do not usually make their basic suppositions explicit, even when they disagree with one another about what history is. We come, nevertheless, to some sight of these suppositions by thinking of the themes about which historians agree and disagree and by thinking of what is underneath them. This chapter brings many of these themes together, providing interpretations for them and reducing their contention, but the idea of the past's reality is neither suggested nor even much supported by the arrangement of the themes. It is rather that the idea of the past's reality led to arranging the themes in a certain way. This is the way anyone who thinks that the past is real will look at history. The unanswered question, of course, is whether this view of history is right about its richness and about its intelligibility and power. The theme in this that is perhaps least clear and most in need of support is that the past is effective in what comes after it. It should be explained and examined carefully.

CHAPTER EIGHT

HOW THE PAST AFFECTS THE PRESENT

WHEN DO causes cause? Do they cause when they are present, and do their effects occur only after the causes have become past? Or do causes cause when they are past, having their effects in what comes about after them? Does causation go from a present to the future or from the past to a present time? In either case, how and what do causes cause?

Many philosophers would be wary of these questions; most would think them miscast, for they think that causes and effects are separate events and that there is no further event wherein one causes the other, so there is no question of locating *causing* at the time of either the cause or the effect. Hume explicitly set out this view.

Hume says that when we search for the origin of our idea of cause, we remember that we have experienced pairs of past events that were very much alike; we also notice that, after some experience of such pairs, when an event like the first one in such a pair occurs we expect an event like the second one to occur as well. These events are a cause and an effect, and our expectation is the origin of our otherwise very unclear idea that the cause causes the effect. Our idea answers to a habit of expectation, not to some tie in the events themselves. The secret springs that make events occur are hidden from us; we have no idea of them. All we have is an idea of the regular occurrence of conjoined events and a habit of expecting that when one of them appears, the other will also appear. Our expectation fixes the direction of causation; an effect is what we expect. It establishes that the cause occurs first, but we cannot say that a cause causes anything. Questions about when causes cause would have to be about secret springs. Since we can know nothing about them, we can no more talk about the time of causation than we can talk about causation itself.

This view no longer seems so powerful, even to those contemporary philosophers who are sympathetic to its spirit, because we have seen that the notion of an "event" by definition precludes causation and has not itself been given a satisfactory analysis. Think of events as simple or discrete, so that an event does not consist of other events, and there obviously cannot be any causing inside it. Then, think of the events in a pair as independent of each other and the second need not occur after the first; the first does not produce the second, and there is no causation between them. There is therefore no causation anywhere, inside or between events. We would be willing to accept this result if it were derived from conceptions we are convinced are sound, but we do not know that the crucial notion of an event is sound. We do not even seem to understand it.

What we understand least about it is what makes for an event's being one event. In anything we think of as an event there are different characters, perhaps different constituents, and these occur over a period of time. An event is not momentary; it is something happening: there is an earlier and a later part in it. What kind of characters and constituents are there in events? How and by what are they held together? Does the earlier part of an event cause the later part to be what it is? What marks an event as ending or being closed? There have been different analyses of events, but all of them have had to suppose that it is the conformation of later characters or constituents to earlier ones that explains why or how the constituents form a single entity; the later parts fit with the earlier ones and somehow complete them. Ironically, the notion that leads us to think that one event does not cause another also leads us to think that there is causation, or something that is very much like it, within an event itself.

There must be causation somewhere, if not between events, then inside of them, and we must think about the time of this causation, too. We must ask whether the earlier of two events is the cause of the whole being and all the details of what comes after it, in which case the cause will cause in the present and its effect will occur later on. On the other hand, perhaps a cause is not the cause of the being of what comes after it but is the cause only of some of the characters that what comes after it comes to have, in which case the cause will be a cause only as the being that comes after it is present, and causing will go from a past to a present time.

To sort and order these issues, we should look not at pairs of events but at a single event—finally, at the smallest event possible. We should ask whether its parts or features originate in the event itself or whether something outside the event causes them to be in the event and to be just what they are. Then we will see where and when causes cause, from inside an event or from outside and, if from outside, whether from somewhere else in the present or from something in the future or the past.

The best-known contemporary analysis of this kind is Whitehead's conception of an actual occasion. Though it has already been discussed several times in this essay, it will be useful to turn to it again to see another point.

Whitehead thinks of occasions as atoms of occurrence. He says that what we usually think of as events, occurrences, or processes are very complex, but they have final parts, and those final parts are themselves something like events, occurrences, or processes. The final parts cannot be atoms of any other kind; they cannot, for example, be atoms that are merely capable of changing. According to Whitehead, the final parts of processes must be *actual* processes, actual occasions, and each of Whitehead's atoms is a new process, a new occasion; it is a process that forms itself then and there.

Whitehead's notion is that events, occurrences, or processes consist finally of atoms of activity. He calls these "actual occasions," and he says that the distinctive nature of their activity is that they form themselves. Activity, Whitehead thinks, cannot be derived from inactivity, so if there is a basic and underived activity, it must be one that is entirely self-contained, and the only nature that such an activity could have is self-formation.

An occasion forms itself from impulse, data, and aim. Whitehead says that there is a creative impulse for the formation of each occasion, that data are given for its formation, and that each occasion is also given a way of forming itself—this is its subjective aim. An occasion forms itself in a certain way from the data that are given for it. The data and the aim that are given for the formation of a new occasion are given either in the course of other processes or as a result of them. Because an occasion is or comes to be in a present and because Whitehead thinks that contemporary occasions do not affect one another, his striking view is that what is given to an occasion must have *come* to it from another part of time.

Whitehead thinks it plainly true that the data for an occasion are given or taken from something that is not present. Something is given or taken from the past, from the occasion that preceded it. Each occasion, Whitehead says, has its own predecessor. It does not form itself until its predecessor has become completely actual and past, at which time its successor becomes its successor by inheriting something of it. There can be sequences of occasions only if the successors of occasions line up on those that preceded them; they do this, Whitehead thinks, by inheriting something from them. What is past remains past, but a new occasion becomes what it will be by accommodating itself to its immediate past. Whitehead calls this accommodation an occasion's prehension of its past. There are perhaps options for an occasion in its construction of itself but it must prehend its past and accommodate some end as well, for it must aim at becoming the occasion it will be.

Whitehead thinks that an end is given to an occasion for prehension in the course of the continuing activity he thinks of as divine. His insight is that what an occasion can aim to be depends partly on what its predecessor has become and partly on what other occasions, depending on their predecessors, can become. There must be a way, then, of taking account of the pasts of all occasions in defining the aims of each and all the new ones. Whitehead therefore supposes that there must be a comprehensive and unending process that has an ideal as its own aim—an unending process can have only an ideal as its aim—and this unending process continually provides the aims for new occasions. The aims of all of the occasions taken together are at that moment a version of the ideal itself. Because the specific aims that are provided must take account of what has preceded the new occasions, Whitehead thinks that the continuing process—the divine activity—must somehow take up all past occasions in its own unending process of fulfilling its own aim. God's specific activity, Whitehead thinks, depends on the past that God has accommodated and on God's own ideal aim. This yields not the best of all possible worlds but the most ideal world that can come to be in any present time. Considering what the world has already been, this can be very bad.

On Whitehead's account, then, two constituents of an occasion—its data and its aim—are owed to something outside the occasion itself: one is owed directly to the occasion's immediate past; the other to the past's effectiveness in God's aim. Because of its predecessor, an occasion comes to have (1) an initial content, a fact or a form of fact, and also (2) an aim that it specifies in one way or another. No past occasion, however, acts to cause the occurrence of these constituents; past occasions are as actual as they can have become and there is no possibility of their doing anything. How, then, do data and aim become constituents in new occasions? They can do this because a present occasion consists of *activities,* and one of these is an occasion's prehending its predecessor. Past occasions do nothing to become prehended; they just are. Nor do they initiate anything in being prehended in the divine activity. Still, past occasions affect the occasions that come after them because of the ways in which present occasions form themselves. The past is doubly efficacious, but not by doing anything itself.

Whitehead's account of process is profound. There are, I think, no contradictions in it even though it is broad and complicated. There is some incompleteness and inexplicability, however, as I earlier tried to show in pointing out that for Whitehead occasions are wholly processes that come to be yet there is no necessity in his account for having processes continue to occur. Beyond these criticisms, though, there is the further question of whether Whitehead's view gives to things the sense of place, prominence, action, connection, and value that they seem to us otherwise to have. The answer to this question is uncertain because we think that there is a public world of action, but Whitehead's occasions are too inner and private to be its components; all actual occasions do is form themselves, and Whitehead says that once they are formed they are past, perished, and lifeless. They cannot act for there is no time for them to act. Besides they can not act until they are formed, but when they are formed, they are past; they can neither combine with one another in the present, as they would have to do if they were to act, nor even affect one another as they are being formed. It is not even sure that this conception of an actual occasion requires there to be a public world in which there are many occasions at the same time. The idea of process in actual occasions is very limited, too limited to give us a conception of a world in which things interact.

Whitehead's conception of occasions grew, I think, out of his idea that process is somehow the most fundamental reality. Everyone acknowledges that processes are real or that they seem to be, but most philosophers suppose that actions or changes, the kinds of processes that they usually describe, depend on something else, on something like a substance or a matter or a thing in itself, so that these and not the processes are fundamentally real. The strong, great counterargument to show that process is fundamental is that substances and matter, being what they are, would not and could not change or act unless there were a cause for their doing so; they cannot change or act out of themselves. There must therefore be something that causes them to act or change and to do so continually, and that cause must itself be a continuing process. There are Platonic, Aristotelian, and many other notions of what this process is. The imaginative venture that comes next in the counterargument is to think that what have been called substances or matter are not really separate sorts of things but configurations or divisions of process itself. Whitehead's refinement for this general idea is that there are units of the process of the world, and the only thing that he thinks can be a unit of process is a moment of actualization, an occasion that actualizes itself.

The strain in Whitehead's view—if his general idea is in fact that process is the most basic reality—is that in trying to turn notions that are prominent in accounts of substance into notions of process something important is lost, namely, the idea of a thing's *doing* something beyond just being or forming itself. There is nothing like this in Whitehead's notions and he has not persuaded us that such activity is not real at all. Should we reformulate Whitehead's conception of an occasion or reformulate notions of substance and try to make them more sensitive to themes about process? Contention like this—substance or process—could go on and on, but I propose a different course. Rather than argue that substance or process is fundamental, I argue that individualness and time are equally fundamental and that the process of the world is one of their ways of being together. This gives us neither the conception of a substance that one finds in the philosophies where substance is said to be the most basic reality nor the conception of process that one finds in process philosophy, but it does not diminish either of these conceptions to give prominence to the other, and that may be one of its advantages. Another of its advantages is that, with some readiness, it can draw insights from both traditions.

One of the insights it draws from Whitehead's thought is that what is past contributes to the process by which things form themselves. We can preserve this insight without also supposing, as Whitehead does, that actualities are so momentary that they can do no more than form themselves if we consider how individuals come to be singular in the present. Our theme has been that individuals are not wholly present, as substances and occasions are thought to be. Their being is also in the past and future, and as they come to be singular in each new moment, they act along with other individuals. Using these conceptions, then, we may be able to understand (1) how what is in the past and what is passing affect the ways in which individuals form themselves and (2) whether the past affects the order of all actions or the ordering of their ends and how it makes this contribution just by being past. Both suggestions can, I think, be developed without supposing, as Whitehead does, that there is an exceptional and endlessly acting entity that makes the past indirectly effective in a present time.

The Past and the Forming of Individuals

Though individuals do not have their whole being in a present moment, it is only then that they are singular. Their future being is undivided, and they lose their singularity when they become past, as if the singularities of individuals were winnowed for a moment from their common future being and then merged again when they all become past—not that there was once only a future time or that one day the only time will be the past. There are, were, and will always be presents, and individuals will be singular in them: we have already seen how singular individuals and time together define the present time.

Singularity is a moment of the being of individuals, it is the present moment, and when individuals are singular they continuously reconstitute themselves as time continuously passes into and through them, making them past. Individuals are not identical over a period of time in the same way that Aristotelian substances or Weissian actualities are the same, without a change *of* their being; they are the same by reconstituting themselves, by forming their future being to continue what they already are, and by having what they already are continuously become more and more definite and then finally definite as past. Singular individuals are moments of self-formation in the being of individuals. The passing portions of individuals and their being as past contribute to this forming. They contribute to the growing definiteness in singular individuals.

When individuals change and act there is more in what they do than we can see. We see only the outwardness of change and action, but these begin in the depths of individuals, where we cannot see, and they become more and more outward. Though there is a depth in individuals, however, there is no *bottom* to them. They are not self-enclosed, and their future being is continually passing into them while, in outward change and action, they are becoming past.

It is not an uncommon notion that our actions express what we are inside and that from considering an action, or what we can see of it, we can infer what an individual is or is like inside. This familiar notion wrongly suggests that there is a firm and permanent distinction between an individual's inside and outside, that what is inside never becomes outside but can only be represented by the actions that it somehow causes. There is, however, no permanent divide between what is inside and what is outside individuals. We do not always have the same inside while our outsides differ from time to time; instead, the distinction is temporal: what is inside comes continually to be outside, what can be formed becomes formed, and because there is no closure or no bottom for the inside of individuals, as time continues to come into them, singular individuals continue to be new on their insides, too. This being that is new in them, that is the new them, must be formed as it comes to singularity—and singular individuals themselves make their own being definite. The only parts of an individual that can contribute to this forming are the passing part of the individual and those that have already become past.

Aristotle's doctrine about the form and matter of substances can be thought of as a static analogue of this kind of forming, this inner and outer activity. Aristotle supposes that a substance is hierarchically organized. However simple the form of a substance, its matter is an already formed matter; in turn, this formed matter has a matter, and this matter is differently organized—perhaps less definitely or less fully— than the matter of the substance itself: a table is made of wood, but the wood is made of something, and that matter, itself formed, is in turn made of something else. The notion of an ordered organization of matter is logically completed in the concept of a formless first matter, though Aristotle does not think that matter without form can exist.

It is unclear in Aristotle how the form and matter of a substance constitute a unity; it is less clear how the "constituent" formed matters are unified; and it is especially unclear what the forms at any of the levels have to do with the action or actuality of substances. It is clear, however, that for Aristotle no new matter, unformed or only minimally formed, enters into substances at the lowest level of organization, makes its way to the highest level of a substance's organization, and then manifests itself in action. For Aristotle, levels of organization for natural substances are not temporally distinct.

What I am suggesting, though, is that there is a change in the being of an individual while it is present. There is a motion, a development, and an increasing singularity and growing definiteness. There is a coming to be and a becoming past in an individual, and the coming-to-be part of a singular individual is first inner and then more and more outer as it is becoming past. The being of a present individual is first something like feeling, then it develops into something like thought and finally into action, even while new feeling and thought occur. The being that becomes and continues the singular individual conforms itself to the way in which the individual was and is already acting, making itself more and more definite and becoming more and more outer, first present and then past. The Aristotelian analogue is static because an Aristotelian substance is wholly present. The being of an individual is not wholly present, however, which is why its forms are different and at different levels through the duration of a present time. In a present individual there is not only one strand of activity; the present is thick with coming and going.

The being that comes into a singular individual and continues it is continuous with it. Though it was entirely unformed when it was future, it is not altogether so as it begins to be made singular. Its most elementary order is owed to its being carried into individuals by the time that passes into them. There are *undulations* in the being and time that come into singular individuals because their way of being together is changing from being future to being present. Time is dominated by individuals when it is future; it contends with them in the present. It strains outward against the being of an individual even in its earliest passing, while that being in turn tries to restrain it. Such outward-inward strains are the habits of being and time in passage—they are somewhat like what Bergson points to when he says that duration is "attenuated" and consists of "pulsations"—and this basic or preliminary form of acting and passing enables the being that is new in individuals to enter them and to continue them. If an individual is complex, coordinated strands of being will enter it together.

The being that is new in a singular individual must not only be continuous with the being of that individual, it also must continue the individual's activity—not that it need repeat it, though it may. It must become that individual and continue to act in the way that individual acts, varying its actions within the limits of the individual's way of acting depending on the circumstances in which it forms itself and on the circumstances of its outer action. How does the being that comes into an individual come to continue it and its action? How does it come to have its way of acting?

The most familiar notion to suggest answers to these questions is that the being coming into an individual is *apprenticed* to the being already there, so that it comes to act in the way that the individual does; its apprenticeship leads it to continue the singularity of the individual. This apprenticeship is the older passing part of an individual leading the newer; it is the newer part following the part that is becoming past, never being out of touch, forming itself on the portion of the individual nearest to it. This forming is not an imposition, not an action of something from the outside penetrating the inside, but just the opposite. What is inside conforms itself to what is ahead and more outside. It is as if the apprentice, with his hands on the shoulder of his teacher, comes more and more to walk like him.

The most well-known doctrine of imposition is Aristotle's, for instance, the image of the potter and the clay or of a young person learning to be courageous by imitating courageous actions until the habit of acting as if courageous becomes ingrained in the youth. Platonic participation is also an "outside-inside" doctrine, though a very subtle one: nothing is imposed, forms are not templates for the flux—we do not know how the demiurge persuades it to shape itself—but it is clear that the flux does not aspire to the forms it comes to have.

Within an individual, however, the procession to the full definiteness of action goes the other way, from inside to outside, beginning with an almost unformed being. The first active forms of the being that comes into an individual, its undulations, are intensified because the being that is new to the singular individual is continuous with the being it already has. Time passes from the future to the past; in its own activity an individual strains toward persistence in a new present, and it re-forms itself to persist even while part of the present part of it is becoming past. It is able to do this when the being that comes into an individual comes more and more to act as it is already acting and has acted in the most recent past.

The being that comes into an individual cannot fail to conform to the being already in it. It has no other way to act or to contribute to the action of an individual. Its apprenticeship is its acting as the being that precedes it acted; then, as its circumstances become less like those in which it was first apprenticed and as less and less precedes it in the present, it becomes more and more dominant in the individual's acting. In this process, though it conforms to the being that is preceding it, it does not conform exactly. It comes to a somewhat different definiteness. This lack of exact conformation is why complex individuals both cease to be and, sometimes, are formed: when the individuals that constitute a complex do not conform closely enough to their earlier parts to continue their coordination new coordinations of individuals develop. Even in these cases, though, singular individuals continue, and the being that comes into them continues to form itself on them.

Perhaps the simplest summary contrast to this idea of forming is that it is like some of the themes in both Plato's and Aristotle's philosophies, but it is also different from both their views in emphasizing that (1) forms are the forms of the activity of individuals, (2) they are inseparable from the time that is in them, and (3) within individuals, forms grow to great definiteness as the individuals come to the presentness of action and are transformed in becoming past.

Plato thinks that forms are timeless and that something like them comes to be in the flux as a momentary definiteness in passing time. The characters in time are said to participate in the forms; participation must be supposed because the flux can neither generate nor retain any definiteness on its own. The organization of the flux therefore must depend on something apart from it and perhaps on something else that would explain the association of the two.

If we suppose instead that new and unformed being forms itself in an extended present that is already partly occupied, so that the activity that constitutes the present is partly formed and partly not, then the unformed portion of what is occurring will form itself on the part of itself that is already formed. This occurs continuously: less formed on more formed, more formed on still more formed, and the still more formed, finally, on the fully formed and past. The settled world of forms is not, as Plato thinks, apart from time. Something like it is settled simply and near at hand—the past.

The notion that individuals form themselves is thus something like the Platonic theme that the definiteness of the flux is its participation in the forms and that participation is owed to the persuasive or instructive influence of a demiurge. The flux is like time's wresting with individuals, and individuals are like demiurges, only they teach themselves to be definite, and the "forms" from which they learn are past definitenesses that are in time and not apart from it, though being past they do not move. Even so, they really affect the individuals that are present and in flux. The individuals form themselves on the "forms"—that is, on what they themselves have already become.

This notion of forming also contrasts with Aristotle's views. The major contrast is with Aristotle's idea that because of its form a substance is actual at every moment, which makes it difficult for Aristotle to explain how animate substances develop or even how a form continues to form its own matter. The least change that could be made in Aristotle's ideas to provide these explanations would be to think that, in a moment, a substance is not completely actual, that it is always actualizing itself, and that it is an efficient or a final cause of its coming to have variations of its own form. This would require massive changes in other of Aristotle's ideas—in his idea of matter, for example—but it would result in Aristotle's ideas more closely resembling the idea that individuals form themselves. They would agree that things possess a real "potentiality" for further form and that things can actualize themselves. Large differences would still remain, mainly about time, but even those differences might be reduced if we had a different understanding of what causes the restless aspiration of substances.

My notion of forming, then, is like but also different from the most historically important notions of form and matter. We cannot avoid making a distinction of the form-and-matter kind, but it is important in defining the distinction to think about the temporality of whatever we take to be or be like a *form* and also to consider whether *matter* is everlasting, whether it is always of its own nature in some kind of motion in "place" or in "passage," or whether it *moves* in either way because of something else. Matter and form are construed and connected here in the notion that an individual is always acting, that it is carried along by the time with which it contends, and that, in its action, it is always forming itself. Individuals do not slip from action to action, from moment to moment, unchanged by the changes they "cause." Their change is continuous, and because it is, their own future being continues to come into them; there is a new "matter" in each moment. It comes into individuals at their depths, and it forms itself as it comes to expression inside them. The activity of the new being of an individual continues the activity in which the individual was engaged. This can occur because the being of an individual as it is past, present, and future is continuous; it does occur because the being that is new to the singular individual forms itself on the being of that individual that is already past or that is acting outwardly or close to doing so. It is as if a singular individual holds onto it and follows its own earlier being as it moves along. In the continued forming of an individual, a way of forming spreads.

What comes into an individual, then, is affected by what precedes it. What is being formed is formed on what is passing. What is passing—all passings and all stages of passing—affects the being that comes after it, not by turning around and imposing an effect but just by passing, by having the being that is continuous with it form itself, as it must, in the way in which an individual more and more comes to act and in which it finally acts in that fullness that is its becoming past. It is as if there were generations within the being of an individual.

The causes of changes and actions—and one could say the causes of events as well, if events are not construed as discrete—go from the past to the present, from the earlier to the later. The earlier does not produce the being of what comes after it nor turn around and act on the being that comes after it. It would act twice in doing that—at least twice, once forward and once backward—and if it could do that there would be no need for it ever to become past. The being that continues an action follows on it because it is continuous with it and is carried by the passing to which time has been provoked. This new being—the stuff of a subsequent event—comes to be formed as it becomes present. Its own action is its forming itself, and it forms itself on the being and action that precede it. The past, then, is the cause of an individual's present and general form. It is like a final cause in reverse: the later *wants* to be like the earlier, only there is no "wanting" because there is nothing else that it can make itself be like.

The Effects of the Past

Our account of what causes the forming in the continuing activity of individuals is not yet complete because it has not specified the bearing of the past on what is present. It has so far dealt only with a connection between what is passing and what is becoming present. What about the past itself? Does it affect what comes to be present? As we have seen, there would be no reason to think that there is a past if it had or could have no effects.

The past is continuous with what is present, and it affects it just as what is passing does, not by acting on it but just by being past, by being the time and being in which activity ends.

In the familiar idea that actions come to a close when their aims have been achieved (or when it is clear that they cannot be achieved), changes and actions can start or end at the same or different times, some before and some after others; one child has graduated, another is still in school. It would be a coincidence or a contrivance if all actions were to end at once, but in each moment the activities of all individuals become past together and not by coincidence or contrivance. This need not mean that there are aims in each of the activities and that they are all achieved at once nor that all actions are completed together in some other sense. In each moment of each individual's activity, however, something does come about: the portions of the activities of all individuals that are contemporary become past together, at the same time; when the moment is over it is over for all of them. How is one to explain this?

In supposing that actual occasions are wholly a coming to be, Whitehead thinks of each of them as having an aim. He also thinks that all the occasions marvelously achieve their aims at once, even though they do not affect one another, so that all become past or exhausted together. Many others also take this sort of view: entirely independent comings to be, minute aims, and coincidental conclusions. Such a world would be very loose if it were not, as both Leibniz and Whitehead suppose, coordinated by God.

There is another explanation for the fact that at each moment portions of the activities of all individuals—equal portions at that— become past together. It is simply that there is a past, that passing time carries individuals to and into the past, and that individuals become past together as they form themselves on the past, as they make their last adjustment to one another and are overcome by the time that had been in all of them. The past is effective on individuals in the present by being a condition for the transformation that individuals undergo when they become past. Individuals become past together because they are contemporaries, because the same time is in all of them, because that time carries them apace to the past, and because they all have the same past to which they must adjust as they adjust to one another. Becoming past is as complex and interesting a process as coming to be. The role of the past in this process is (1) to be a condition for the transformation of what is present so that it can become past, and also, though derivatively, (2) to be a condition on what can come to be. This restraint on the formation of individuals is expressed by the principle that nothing can come to be present that cannot become past. When we consider the past's role in the transformation and formation of individuals, this principle will seem more meaningful.

(1) Not everything that is in an individual or an activity becomes past. Some of it, as has been noted before, ceases to be altogether: for example, relative characters and relations of individuals are not in the future and so do not become present; they come to be inside a present through the activities of the individuals that are present. Individuals themselves, however, become past as they act in the present, and as they do, at the depths from which they act, they renew and reconstitute themselves.

When individuals become past they are turned inside out. This change is important for understanding how the past affects the present. What individuals act out of has come out of them; a moment of their action is over and their singularity is gone. They retain the definiteness they have achieved, but as time passes to consolidate its own being—it had been distended, almost dispersed, among individuals in the present—it brings together all the individuals that had been contemporary and all the individuals that are already past. There is then the one being of all past individuals, and that one being is, as past, inside time.

Individuals do not change and act to become past. Their aim is forward, but they are in a kind of action even in their transformation into being past. They do not first complete their change and action and then become past, as if there were then only dried remnants of action that are swept along by time. Becoming past is part of an individual's action; it is a last part of an action that continues to go on. Passing time and individuals become past together, and in passing, as time consolidates its own being, individuals also consolidate themselves into their last definiteness. Their last definiteness is not another achieved character: first this character, then that, and finally a last character. It is the transformation of an individual or its action from doing something to having done it, from being active and being extended to being definite, no longer acting, and no longer in space and passing time. It is the change of individuals in which they come to be in time alone.

In philosophy, the nearest analogue of this last change, this last phase of an individual's action, would be the coming to be of a Platonic form or a Whiteheadian eternal object. These entities cannot come to be, however, because they are said to inform the only processes there are, because they are not themselves in those processes, and because those processes cannot produce anything that could be apart from them, least of all something more enduring than themselves.

For individuals, the themes are just the opposite. Individuals are their changes and actions; they form themselves, and their being extends to the past. As they come to their fullest definiteness, as they are becoming past, they do not remove themselves entirely from action but only from the present part of it, and then, in the definiteness they have achieved, time and individuals come to be together in a different way. Their transformation results in a new definiteness in the past, much like what the formation of a new Platonic form would be, or rather, what the formation of an incalculable number of newly related forms would be. Individuals do not become past one by one. They are joined together as they become past, so there is no question of many separate and single forms coming to be in the past. When individuals become past, time deprives them of their singularity, so that all the individuals that were contemporaries become past together, as a whole.

We have no picture of the unity individuals form in becoming and being past. For example, we are not to imagine that they lose their borders and spread into one another, as if there were a space in the past. What happens instead is that the ways individuals have of doing things lose their remaining generality and come to be together. In each individual there is a way of doing things, of being with other individuals; it is something like what they always mean to do. In the course of action these ways of doing things become more and more definite, and finally they become *the* way in which things are together; the generality of their ways of being together is gone. To use the analogy with Plato's thought once again, when individuals become past it is as if the flux has gone from all the forms that had been manifested at a moment, so that they are together as the form of all that had just been; it is as if that form had just come to be in the fullest definiteness it has in being exhibited. What makes for the singularity of individuals in the present is their activity, but as portions of their activity are made to close, the final definiteness that individuals achieve becomes the one whole definiteness of all there was. It is then part of the past.

In this transformation, this passing portion of the action of an individual, there is also an adjustment to the past itself. What becomes past continues the past; it is continuous with it not only in its being but in its definiteness as well. The past is not a veneer made from separate slivers of past present times. In becoming past, the question for individuals is how they will finally adjust their own natures. Because their natures made for their having had relative characters, the question is how they preserve their natures while their relative characters pass away. Their answer is that they form their *final* definiteness on what preceded them. This is also how they had become definite in the present, but now the only thing that precedes them is the past; they are the last part of the passing in the present. So they must form themselves on the past, and all individuals adjust themselves to the same past. Doing this is part of their adjusting to one another, and that adjustment is part of their adjustment to the past.

Individuals and their actions cannot become past without being transformed, and time's passing is what finally transforms them, but they themselves act in their transformation by adjusting to their contemporaries and to the past. The past is not the whole cause of the adjustment that individuals make to it, though individuals must at last conform to its definiteness. They must adjust to it; they must become past, but that does not mean they do not act as they are becoming past. Individuals contribute to their own transformation because of the difference between what is already past and what is becoming past. The past, however, does nothing. It only conditions what individuals do.

(2) The past affects what is in the present not by moving or changing or being an efficient cause of things but simply by being the past to which individuals adjust themselves as they themselves are becoming past. The sequence of action is that individuals always adjust themselves to the past: present individuals form themselves on those portions of themselves that are becoming past, and the being that is brought into them forms itself on that being of theirs that is issuing into action. The subsequent forms itself on the prior. Even while an individual adjusts itself to its contemporaries, it forms itself on the precedent being with which it is continuous. By apprenticeship or imitation, through the continuity of their being, individuals continue to act in the ways in which they already have, though never exactly. Forms are not inherited by singular occasions that reach beyond themselves to prehend the actuality of completed occasions, as Whitehead supposes. Instead, they are reproduced when the new being in singular individuals forms itself on its earlier parts and its past. The past affects what is present just by being what it is and by being continuous with the formative

action that occurs in the present. Subsequent being need not reach beyond itself to bring in or otherwise be affected by its past. It is continuous with it, and individuals are not wholly in a present time.

The largest alternative to this view is, as we have seen, that individuals come to their ways of acting and perhaps to their actions themselves not because of the past but because of what can be, because of what is possible. In this conception, things continually face a plenum of possibilities, something limits the plenum, and only a few possibilities or only one of them is available for each thing. As the thing acts it incorporates and specifies the possibilities that constrain what things can do and be.

The contrasting notion in this essay is that the past is definite and that individuals come to their ways of acting not through possibilities that have been portioned out to them but by forming themselves on those portions of their own being that are passing and are finally past. Where the grand alternative is defined by the principle that "nothing can come to be that is not a possibility," the principle in the notion of a real and effective past is that "nothing can come to be that cannot become past."

Like the principle of possibility this principle can seem to be an empty or easy one that restricts nothing. What comes to be must become past; it must pass away. It cannot do anything else. The limitation, however, is simply that what comes to be does not remain unformed; it comes to be formed within individuals in ways of acting that are themselves conditioned by the past. There is no vagrant being in individuals that may or may not become past. What comes to be is formed in a way that allows it to become past. The forms that it will have are derived from the prior and the past. The past, then, is effective in *controlling* what occurs, in having what is occurring give to itself the only kind of definiteness that it can have: the definiteness of the past. The past's effectiveness is solely in its reality. Nothing need take it up or act on its behalf. Individuals are the centers of activity, and the past does not affect them by being a cause, whether formal, material, or final. Of the Aristotelian causes it is perhaps most like a final cause in reverse, meaning that individuals form their final definiteness on it, yet its causality goes not as a final cause would go, from the future to the present, but from the past to what is active in a present time.

PART III

THE FUTURE

CHAPTER NINE

THE REALITY OF THE FUTURE

THINGS WILL continue to happen. We know that the world will not stop or cease to exist, but how is this great fact to be understood? Most philosophers think that it is understood by explaining what things are, what they can do, or what is possible for them. They do not think that to explain why things continue to go on we must suppose the future to be real and to have something in it. In this chapter I argue for just the opposite: even in accounts that seem to leave aside the future, something of real futurity is presupposed, and to understand anything about how and why things go on we must think the future to be real. Unless the future is real we will not understand what things are, what they can do, or how anything is possible for them.

The Going On of Things: Three Important Views

The Greek atomists suppose that atoms are the final, real, and simplest things, that they are everlasting, and that everything else is made up of them. Atoms stick to one another because of irregularities on their surfaces, or they combine with one another because of their shapes, or they simply may come to adjoin one another. Their weight may have caused them to combine, or their combinations may be the results of earlier impacts, or some force may drive them together or pull them apart. Whatever the causes of their combination, atoms and their combinations are all that exist, though because of impacts and forces, new combinations of them will occur from time to time. There are no future atoms or future combinations of atoms; there are only the atoms there are. Future combinations of atoms are only what we imagine or predict. Atoms and their motions, the atomists believe, are all we must suppose to understand and explain the going on of things. The future is not real, though we can imagine the configurations that will come about.

Aristotle has a very different view of the going on of things. Though he thinks that something like atoms is the most basic of formed matters, his main idea is that there are substances, *large* formed matters that are capable of moving and, perhaps, changing themselves. It is mainly their motions and other changes that Aristotle thinks we must understand. Changes are continually going on in them because, in part at least, there is a continuous activity in a substance of a very different kind.

The changes in a substance are changes *to* its matter, changes in the forms that it takes on. A substance has potentialities to become this or that, though there is a limit to the changes that a substance can undergo and still remain the same. The most intimate limitation in a substance is in its developing, in a seedling's becoming a tree or a child's coming to maturity. The form of a substance is a cause of its development, or the form and the matter together are the cause, and the direction of the development is toward as much self-containment and independence from other things as the form and matter or nature of the substance will allow.

Development and other sorts of changes in substances occur continually because their form and matter must continually be adjusted to each other. There is a constant unsettlement of the matter in any substance, perhaps most of all at the lowest level of organization. Even a substance that seems to remain unchanged has some activity within it, some new or renewed hold by its form on its matter. Its other changes are the development or degeneration of its essential characters or alteration in its modifying, incidental qualities. For Aristotle, to understand the continuing going on of things, we need only to understand their natures and their aspiration to be as much like the unmoved mover as they can be. We can measure the time of their changes as they occur; we need not, Aristotle thinks, refer to anything apart from what is actual to understand them.

Plato disagrees with this last note. He does not think that substances exist, and to explain why different states of flux continue to come about he appeals to realities that are not in time, namely, the forms, which many other philosophers call "possibilities." Possibilities seem to be forms relevant to the field in which they might be exhibited. Forms or possibilities are not in the future. Their manifestations have yet to occur—they will occur in some future present time—but the forms themselves are not temporal at all: they did not come to be, they are not in a "now," and they never will be, even when they are manifest. To have the forms exhibited is not to move them into time; it is not to incorporate them into temporal things. Nothing happens to the forms. Still, whatever makes for the definiteness in the ongoing, temporal world makes the world definite by reference to the forms. This process of making for definiteness, which seems so difficult to understand, is also not in time. It does not occur *in* the present, nor is it in any obvious way a process that begins in the future. Because for Plato there is no real future, it is not even a process by which what is future comes about. The ongoing of things is to be understood by the being, or near nonbeing, of the flux, by the forms, and by these forms serving somehow in having something definite come about.

Here, then, are three accounts of what things continue to go on and how and why they do. Every other philosophical account of ongoing seems to be a variant of one of them. There are philosophies that provide no account of ongoing, but they do not deny that it is real; they simply assert that the causes for it cannot be known. If, however, we *can* understand the going on of things, it is implausible that the three classical accounts should be entirely unsound in their ways of explaining it. It is not implausible, however, that an even sounder account will be a modification of one or all of them.

It would be an easy criticism of the classical accounts to note again that it is difficult to understand what forces are, what participation is, and how the development of substances is to be explained; these notes have already been brought out several times. In what follows I will take account of these familiar criticisms but not by arguing that these accounts must be replaced because there is something inexplicable in them—though that is also true. I will argue instead that in each of them there is an implicit reference to a kind of being beyond atoms, forces, substances, and forms or that there is an implicit reference to a time beyond the present. The argument is not that incorporating these references into the classical accounts would strengthen them—it is doubtful that the references could be simply added to them; instead, the argument is that the implicit references in all three classical accounts of going on are references to a real future and to what is real in it. All three accounts of going on suppose that there is a real, full future or something very like it, and since the classical accounts are models for all our accounts of going on, we should conclude that all, or almost all, accounts of it take something to be real and future, even if they do not explicitly acknowledge it. I want to show that this is so.

References to the Future

Whether and how things go on depends on what they are and on there being something else as well. No one has ever maintained that singular things go on of themselves; even the eventfulness of events must be explained, for we think of singular things as being actual, as already being what they are, and therefore not requiring change. They certainly do not need to change to be what they already are, so that when they are changed or change themselves, it is because something else unsettles them, pushing, moving, or luring them. These causes are themselves always in some kind of activity—the flux flows, forces force, the unmoved mover is in the motion of its own thought—but then these are great principles and not singular things. If singular things must be made to go on, what ultimately causes them to go on is not itself made to go on.

So it is with atoms, substances, and the entities that are patterned after forms. Something forces atoms to move; perhaps they are always being forced to move. Substances are capable of changing, and something is always luring them to change. The flux that always sloughs its forms is always formed again. Each of the classical accounts obviously involves something that is present but not wholly or merely so, and the question is how this something stands to time. Is it, while present, partly in some other time as well, or is it not in time at all?

The alternative that the classical accounts explicitly address is between actual and not actual, where the actual is a starting point for change (which can therefore be said to be present or to be in time), and what is not actual is then not in the present or not in time at all. This choice between actual or not actual, in time or not in time, seems not to be sheer or sharp, yet each of the three classical accounts is strained by citing something besides atoms, substances, and forms that does not quite fit the alternative but, since the alternative seems binding, is nevertheless put on one side or the other. On the classical accounts, then, there can seem to be a moving that causes either something in time or at the present that is more or less than actual or something that mediates between the actual and what is not in time but that is itself not quite outside of time. The alternative, actual or not, in time or not, has only two places in which to locate the things that go on *and* the realities that explain their going on, and it is the attempt to locate all these in just those two places that makes for deep unclarity in the classical explanations of going on.

In atomism, the unclarity is the ambiguous notion of "always" in the claim that atoms (or some of them) are always in motion. The ambiguity is between being in motion at each moment and being in "motion" continuously, and it depends finally on a difference in what atoms and forces *always* do. Atomism says that something always goes on, but the issue is whether that going on can be explained by what is and is not actual, by what is and is not in time. If one or the other side of the alternative must be thickened in the explanation, then the alternative should be redrawn so that we think of something that is real but neither actual nor apart from time.

Even the earliest formulations of atomism acknowledge that there are forces of different kinds because there seem to be motions of different kinds. Later, more sophisticated versions of atomism distinguish curvilinear and rectilinear motions. The most fundamental rectilinear motions were initially thought to be falling; later on, however, all such motions were attributed to collisions, and, because of large collections of atoms, falling motions were considered to be more or less curved and explained by a different kind of force. The general notion became that there are local forces and forces that act at a distance; there are efficacies of at least two kinds. Currently, there are thought to be even more.

When atoms move in straight lines they are moved by other atoms that collided with them or by forces that were transmitted in a collision. Their straight-line motions are therefore owed to something else, and to explain both that a force causes the motion and that the motion occurs in the direction that it does, moving atoms are supposed to have some force that they transmit, wholly or partly, to the atoms with which they collide. It is difficult to understand how a moving atom transmits a force and how and when that force is efficacious. It seems that it should be efficacious all along or at least that it should be expended all along; it is implausible that a carried force should diminish or disappear and then increase or reappear when it is transmitted in a collision. Still, if a force is efficacious while it is carried in an atom, there is some question as to why it does not continuously accelerate the atom that carries it. When, where, and how impressed, latent, or potential forces are efficacious and why they are not dissipated is at best an obscure matter. We are uncertain, even now, what forces *do*.

There are also difficulties in understanding the nature of the force or forces that act over a distance. They, too, are somehow in atoms; they, too, are continually expended and not dissipated, but they have their efficacy in all directions, not only in the one direction along which an atom moves. It is not clear whether such forces are wholly contained within atoms—how could they be efficacious if they were?—or whether they somehow emanate or radiate from them. Were they to do so, the forces of different atoms would overlap. They might constitute a field in which different forces are resolved or even a space of different intensities, changing all the time. The notion of this kind of force also is somewhat obscure, particularly about the resolution of forces in a field and about their continued, undiminished efficacy.

There is, then, an "always" for the motion of atoms and an "always" for the action, efficacy, or expenditure of forces, but the two are not the same. Atoms move because of forces, but forces do not expend themselves because of anything else; they may expend themselves differently in different conditions, but they are always being expended. The "always" of an atom's motion has to do with its being in the same place or different places at different moments, with its moving or not moving. The time of its motion is measured, as usual, by a regular and continuous motion that serves as a clock. It is as though, for atoms, the time of their motions, the measure of their motions, is outside them.

The time for the expenditure of forces is different. Forces are carried by atoms: an atom may transmit some or all of the forces that are in it, but it can never be without some force, and that force is always being expended on or from inside it. Inside an atom, then, there is always a passing expenditure of force, and no clocks or other motions can measure it. There is only an indirect measure of an amount of force, calculated by inferring the force from the motions of atoms. Since force is not dissipated, the total force for all the atoms is thought to remain the same, though there has been recent speculation that the quantity of force in a closed system of particles might be reduced over a period of time. If that were so, one would have to say how force is lost. If the total amount of force is not reduced, there still might be dissipation, offset, however, by new force. If that were the case one would have to explain both the dissipation and how and from where the new force comes to be. There might, then, be slightly different meanings for the "always" of a force being expended, but all of them will be different from the "always" of the motion of atoms, which forces somehow cause.

Because of this difference, force does not fit easily into the alternative of actual or not, in or out of time. The alternative excludes a real future by requiring whatever is real to be in the present or not in time at all. Atoms always are, they are always present, but that is not strictly or simply true for force. The "always" of a force is that it is always being expended, whether dissipated or restored. The indestructibility of atoms ensures that there is always something that can be moved, but it is force and its inexhaustible expending of itself that ensures that motions will go on. A force, or its forcing, cannot be considered to be merely at a moment; although it expends itself in a moment, it is or has a real capability of continuously expending itself. It is not exhausted in a moment, but then it is not wholly in a moment, nor is its being altogether apart from time. The doctrine that forces are not dissipated enforces the strange nature of forces: they are effective now, and they will also expend themselves continuously. What is so striking about the notion that forces may be dissipated is not the prospect of slowed or stopped motions of atoms but that it involves a different conception of force with a different standing to time. It is not a factual matter whether forces can be dissipated: the classical notion of force precludes dissipation. A force that can be dissipated—whatever "dissipation" means—is a force differently construed: it is a kind of thing that can cease to be or cease being expended, and so construed it also would have to be the kind of thing that can come about.

Whether or not they allow dissipation of force, conceptions of force cannot readily or even with some slight change be fitted into either side of the actual-nonactual/temporal-atemporal alternative. Force strains against being actual and wholly in the present because its nature is to expend itself, and it is also partly actual and in time because it is expended or effective in every now. The alternative is too narrow, too limited, even for the classical conception of force. Most of the obscurities in the notion arise from its having been pressed into the wedge of the alternative. The alternative must be loosened somewhat or reconstituted, perhaps by allowing something to be real and not present yet not altogether apart from time. This allowance will require a reference to a real future, and perhaps a real past as well.

This strain against the alternative also occurs in Aristotle's conceptions of potentiality. Of the many sorts of change Aristotle describes with these conceptions the one he seems to have the most difficulty with is development or growth, though he also has difficulty explaining decay.

In Aristotle's usual account of the changes in a sensible substance, the matter of the substance remains the same, as does the essence, but an inessential form or character is replaced. What is so difficult to understand about the development of a substance is that its essence both remains the same but also changes; there is a change of or in the essence of a substance beyond the nonessential changes: an acorn becomes an oak; a child becomes more rational. The difficulty is that there is a change in a substance but not a change of its form or matter (or if there is a change of matter, the change is only incidental to the development)—but then, "form" and "matter" are the only terms Aristotle has for describing change. The change is perhaps in how the form and matter of a substance are together; then, however, using Aristotle's conceptions, it would be difficult to explain why form and matter must continually adjust to one another, how they do adjust, and how their doing so constitutes a substance's developing.

It is of no help in explaining development to note that a substance develops under certain conditions and that when it develops inessential changes always occur in it. It may even be that a substance must develop to make the kind of inessential changes that are required by the surrounding conditions; for example, they might confront a substance with new pairs of contraries. It is not the *when* of development that is so difficult, however, but the *how;* the difficulty is that there is something *going on* in development, but there seems to be no cause for it. The original efficient cause of the developing substance is no longer acting; a substance develops on its own. Still, its form cannot be the efficient cause of its development—a form is not substantial enough to act—and the final cause of a substance has no efficacy but is the fullest realization of the substance toward which, somehow, the substance aims.

Perhaps the most helpful resolution of this difficulty is simply that in Aristotle there is no separate cause for the development of a substance and that the form of the substance is itself its developing. The idea is that the form is naturally an embodied activity of development in the substance and that although there was an efficient cause for the becoming of the substance, there is no further cause for this activity itself. It is not certain that we can wrest this interpretation out of what we usually understand to be the meanings of Aristotle's terms; still, readings are often mixed, particularly in Aristotle. For example, a form has to be of and in a matter, and Aristotle's usual talk is of the imposition of a form on a matter, but development cannot be a form repeatedly imposing itself on its own matter, as if the matter must "take" the form "completely" in each moment. We have no notion in Aristotle of a form imposing itself on its own matter, and even if something like that were to occur, the repeated imposition of the same form would not make for development. For Aristotle, then, for a form to be the activity in development, there would have to be some other picture of both development and form.

We need a picture of a developing substance—any sensible substance—that has an activity arising from inside itself. The activity is the form of the substance or results from its form. There will also be incidental changes of the substance, partly due to the ways in which the substance acts on and with other substances; we refer to these when we say that the substance is still white or has changed its color. The direction or tendency of the activity is, again, the form of the substance or results from it; it is its desire or its thought, and just how the desire or thought is made manifest and at what pace the development becomes manifest depend both on the matter of the substance and the conditions under which development takes place. The form will continue its activity even after the substance matures, if it ever entirely matures. Then, its end will be to exercise and retain its mature form.

The form of a substance, however, is not the whole or the whole source of the activity that is natural to it. The form is a form of a matter, and the matter of a substance is not simply carried along in the activity of the substance's form. There is a *moving* in the matter, too, though it is not the becoming of anything. It is owed, through the tiers of formed matter in a substance, to the earth, air, water, or fire of which the substance is ultimately composed. It is not clear how the motion of the matter should be described—a kind of jiggling of the same matter, or a kind of passing, or both?—but it is clear that, even if the matter of a substance is not replaced, the development and other changes of a substance result from both its form and matter. Motions come from motions, changes from changes, and the motions and changes of a substance come from something like motions or changes of both its form and matter.

What we finally should see is that these notes about form and matter also bring out a tension in Aristotle's conception of actuality and potentiality. They make it easier to see that those conceptions also contain a sense of the being of a substance as not wholly or merely here and now, because an Aristotelian substance *is* what it is and also potentially what it can be. The substance *is* both. It is what it is because of its form, and it is what it can be because of its matter. It is what it is now, and when it becomes what it can be it will have actualized its potentiality. The clear difference between *is* and has in fact *become* is also a difference that can be measured; there is an interval in which the difference comes about. This is perhaps all that needs to be said about incidental changes, but for the inner changes of substances, changes of maturation and decay, changes related to a substance's time or age, there is no comparable distinction between potentiality and actuality.

If the form of a substance is an activity, then at any moment while the substance is what it is it is also active; it is in a kind of change. When Aristotle contrasts what a substance is with what it is potentially, the contrast is between two or more contrary characters, which the same substance cannot have at the same time. In the interval between its being first in one state and then in another, the substance is the same, and not only because its matter remains the same; it has the same essence all the while, but that essence is also continually maturing or decaying. Because this last activity is not a change between contraries, it has no measure or none that is direct. Therefore, "actuality" and "potentiality" do not directly apply to it. In their strict senses, "actuality" and "potentiality" describe a substance's development only when contraries associated with development come about; for example, when a small substance becomes larger or a weak one stronger. In the form of a substance itself, however, there are no contrary states, not even potentially; there is no matter in the form to which the potentiality could be referred. If we are not, then, to understand the development of substances by talking directly and strictly about the potentiality and actuality of their forms, how should we understand their forms?

The answer may be that in Aristotle's doctrine of development, we should understand "actuality" and "potentiality" metaphorically: by supposing that in the forms of substances there is, at every moment, both a kind of actuality and a kind of potentiality; by supposing that, at the same time, the form of a substance is both what it and the substance *is* and *was* and also, because of the form, what the substance will be; and by supposing that the principle of noncontradiction applies to a substance as a whole but not, in any moment, to its form. These suppositions are clearest for substances that develop and decay, but they apply equally to all substances; all substances decay, even if they are not the kinds of substances that develop and mature.

We must therefore look to a special actuality and potentiality in the form of a substance to understand the basis for even the simple incidental changes its matter may potentially sustain. We must look to the matter of a substance, too, for the matter of a substance has something to do both with how the form and matter of a substance are together and with their having continually to be together in somewhat different ways. The motions that are natural to the matter of a substance are, on their passive side, more or less accepting of the form of development, though there may, for example, be too much water or earth in a substance for it to develop well. The motions of the matter are then also part of the development of the substance itself; they provoke and resonate with the rhythm of development. As a form becomes less effective, they are also partly responsible for decay. Thus, for as long as a form is effective the natural motions of the matter are a condition for the continuous activity of a substance or of substances generally.

These interpretations of "form," "matter," "actuality," and "potentiality" in Aristotle are not extreme. They, or something like them, are needed to remove or press farther back the obscurities in Aristotle's discussions of development and change. These notions contain the idea that things must develop and change; they also contain an idea of what substances can become. Both ideas are about what a substance actually is at each moment.

We refer to the future in the most obvious way when we talk about *what* will come about tomorrow and next week; but the *what* that will come about is, strictly, neither now nor future. It is not in time at all. It will *be* when some future comes about. In the case of a developing substance, however, we could refer to the future as it *is* while it is future if (1) we think that an essence, a *what,* that is present is, even while it is present, the same essence that will come about (in a developed form) and (2) we also think that there is something present that, even while it is present, ensures that something will come about. These are the references we make when we talk about the form and matter of a substance. A substance is active even in a moment, partly stable and partly not, and the distinction between the two is vague. When a substance is present, it is now but not wholly now. Its very being is partly future and we cannot refer to what it is, or even think of what it is, without referring to its being a *what* that will also be. These *whats*

are aspects of the substance's form, and the form's activity is inseparable from the motions of its matter, one of whose directions must
therefore also be a passing. In the very notion of a substance, then,
there are references to the future, though they are not explicit in
Aristotle's rendition of "form" and "matter," notions that are especially obscure in connection with development. When we make them
clearer, we see that a developing substance has a *will be* in it; its
being is not wholly actual, as if the *will be* of the being were simply
to be a different configuration of the matter it already has. The *will
be* of a substance must somehow be in the substance itself but also
different from the being that is actual in it. It seems plain, then,
that we cannot think of substances as wholly actual or not, wholly
present and in time or not. They are too active to be that. We must say
instead that even while they are actual, substances are at least partly
future, too.

Finally, and more briefly, in Plato's account of change, there is also a
strain against the actual-nonactual/temporal-atemporal alternative, though
our first thought about Plato's view might be that it fits the alternative
exactly: the forms themselves are not in time; manifestations of them
are. The strain against the alternative becomes evident when we
think about how manifestations of forms occur. This is the obvious issue
about the forms, and the strain is that the demiurge and gods and souls
responsible for there being manifestations of the forms are not themselves manifestations of the forms, but neither is any of them apart
from time; their enduringness is not the same as the eternity of the
forms. Still, we look to them and to the flux for necessity in the
continuing of occurrences.

The great argument against the future's reality is that the continua-
tion of occurrences can be explained by referring only to what is
present or to what is not in time at all. The demiurge, the gods, and
souls are not quite either of these yet Plato clearly thinks that they are
the causes for forms continuing to be exhibited in a flux that restlessly
continues to unsettle whatever definiteness it comes to have. It is
unclear what kinds of causes they are, however. They are not efficient
causes, for there is no imposition of the forms, but if they were to
persuade the flux to form itself in certain ways they might somehow
provide for final ones. They are not themselves the future, nor does it
seem that the formativeness they cause goes from a future to a present
time, but they ensure that there will be occurrences in a flux that

cannot itself be said to be at a time, which is very nearly a reference to what will be before it comes about.

Here, then, are three grand and representative accounts of occurrence and change. Each gives its explanation by referring to the powers of things that are either at a present time or not in time at all. None even contemplates that there might be anything in the future that might bring the future or itself about. It never occurred to the Greeks who made these first formulations that the future might be real.

For them, the real is what can cause effects, and what can do that *is,* either now or, as the gods are, eternally. Its effects are what come about, and they are real only when they have come about, not before, when we can only think what they might be. Looked at the other way around, since the Greeks hold that nothing can come from nothing, what comes about must come from something real—real now or eternally—and the coming about itself must result from it. Yet each of the explanations goes beyond its proper references, either (1) giving more or different kinds of powers to things that are merely present than they ever could have or (2) giving to eternal things the capacity to be everlasting, involving them closely in having things continue to occur. These strainings in their accounts show that the ideas of things as they are at present and things as they are outside of time are not sufficient for the explanations—there must also be some verging toward the future in what is present and toward the present by what is outside present time. These vergings, these extensions of powers, seem to me implicit references to a real future. When they are made explicit and the notions in the original arguments are rearranged, if these last arguments have not been thoroughly contrived, the references should show that all three accounts take the future to be real.

It would be contrived, however, to say that each of the explanations implicitly refers to the same kind of thing as being future. The strain in each explanation is characteristic to it. In one case it is in the notion of an inexhaustible expenditure; in another, in an inner potentiality; and in a third, it is over the forming of definiteness in continuing processes. So, the obscure references in the explanations are not to some one clear thing that can simply be added on to them, nor could special references to different sorts of futures be added. My argument has been that the explanations are strained because more must be explained than their basic notions can provide. The remedy for this is not to add a notion about another reality but to change the basic notions of the explanations themselves, to come to new notions that encompass the future's reality. The explanations implicitly refer to a real future, and we refer to it as well, in the idea that there is a (not present) *what* that will come about, that there is a (not present) something in which a *what* will come about, or that there is a (not present) something that will assuredly bring a *what* to presentness. Forces, potentialities, forms, and the demiurge are strained ways of making these references. What would a less strained reference be? What coherent account can be given of the future's reality?

Future Time and the Future Being of Individuals

If the future is real, it must contain a future time; otherwise, the present and perhaps the past would be the only time, and anything apart from them would not be in time at all. We have, however, already seen the difficulties in supposing both that what is present or past is the whole cause of what comes about and that what is not in time can become present or even affect what is at a present time. What comes to be, then, or what mainly causes it to come about, is neither present nor outside time. It must be somewhere, though, and if it is neither present, past, nor out of time, the only place that it can be is the future. The future must therefore be real. Time is more than a measure of motions and changes—we cannot understand that motion and change occur without supposing that time is also real—and part of it must be a future time.

If the future is a part of a real time there must also be something in it, something that can and must come about. There is a *what* in the future or something in it that will become a *what* when it comes to be present. If there were nothing in the future there would be nothing to come about; were future time nevertheless to pass, it would pass of itself and all alone. It would pass through an unchanging world and its passing would be undetectable. All our explanations hold that what comes to be comes from something else. Because it cannot come from what is not in time and cannot come to be entirely from what is present, it must have its being in the future; it must also be something that will have to come about.

The upshot of these arguments, and the tendency of the earlier ones, is that the future is real: there is a future time and there is being that *is* but is neither present, past, nor altogether apart from time. It is the time that passes to become present and the being that, transformed, becomes actual in the present time. Once again, the present is not a place; each present moment is not the same moment with a different content. Each moment is new, and new moments, which are not nothing and which do not come from nothing, are new in being present but not new in being time; as time passes moments are transformed from being future to being present times. Time cannot be empty, and whatever is cannot but be in time. There is also something real in the future, and the way that it and time are together is the future's distinctive temporality. Time, in turn, gives to the being that is future the prospect of its actuality. What comes about is therefore not a whole new world but a transformation of something that already is but is future and not yet actual. The being and time that become present are a being and time transformed. This is very different from a change in the configuration of something that is always present or a change of the form of a permanent matter; it is different from creation, too.

The reality of the future is the reality of time and of something else that becomes singular when it becomes present but is not singular when it is future, namely, the being of individuals. The reality of the future is the reality of time and the being of individuals together in a certain way. Time dominates individuals in the past; in the present, the two are opposed, contending as time passes and singular individuals try to sustain themselves; in the future, the being of individuals domi- nates time. There are no singular individuals in the future. Their being is merged, and this provides the inexhaustible impendingness that is the unity of the two. In this essay I have claimed that individuals and time are basic realities. Each of them must therefore be and they must be together. Were there other realities as basic as these two, they might qualify the connections between them, but each basic reality makes an equal contribution to its being together with the others, and so it is with time and individuals. They are distinctive, however, in that they are or can be or must be together in different ways, and their distinctive ways of being together define the past, the present, and the future.

The idea that the future is dominated by the being of individuals is the idea that its unity is due to the being of individuals, not to time. Time unifies individuals in the past by overpowering them. It also unifies them in the present, though more loosely, as space and time. The being of individuals provides the structure of unity for the future. It is the being that all the individuals that are present will come to have.

The time and being that are future each have distinctive natures, and each qualifies the character of the other, but time can provide a unity only when many things are in it, as in the present, where there are singular individuals, and in the past, where different definitenesses have been achieved. In the future the being of individuals is merged, and time suffuses this merged being. The future as a whole is what will come to be, and what makes the future the *it* that will come to be is the being that is in it.

Future being is like Parmenidean being, only Parmenidean being does nothing and nothing happens to it. By contrast, the future being of individuals is addressed by the individuals that are present and is made to pass because of what they do and because of the time that is inseparable from it. The being that is in the future is a temporalized Parmenidean being that can come to pass and that does pass as time is provoked by those portions of it that are present and acting.

To compare the future being of individuals with another, familiar notion, the merged future being of individuals would be the same as the being of possibilities if possibilities were real, only it is merged and not divided—there are not many beings in the future—and it has none of the definiteness of possibilities. The doctrine of real possibilities supposes that definitenesses must be brought into a present; they are first future and then somehow brought into a present time. The notion here, however, is that what becomes present becomes definite only as it becomes present. It is not definite before it becomes present, and there are, therefore, no distinct units in the future, only the being that will come about or the *what* of what will come about. It is like the being that constitutes the possibility of real possibilities, apart from the definiteness that is thought to be specified in it. That being, as we have seen, is neither present nor altogether outside time. It is the being that is future, and it is continuous with the being of present individuals, whereas the time of the future is continuous with the time that is passing now.

It is as easy to be mistaken about the distinctive temporality of the future as it is to be mistaken about the past and for the same reason: we attribute to a time the characters that it had or will have when it is present and when presents occur successively. So it seems easy to think that the future contains what will come about next, and what will come about after that, and next after that, as if there were an endless sequence of *nexts* and that the ones that are far away will take longer to come about, either as they are moved into the place of the present time or as presence moves to light up what is future now. These notions of "near," "far," "earlier," and "later," these distributive and nearly spatialized notions, are not true of the future. They help us make predictions related to the regularity with which things will come about, but then predictions are about what something will be when it is present, not about what it *is* when it is future. The distinctive temporality of the future is that sense of time in which all that will come about is at the same time, and because we will not grasp this sense by imagining the future to contain the characters that presents do, we must think of it in another way.

The way to think about the temporality of the future is to think first that, as future, the being of individuals is merged and then that it will come about—that it will issue into new presents as the being of singular individuals. The future being of individuals is the being that will become present. It is more than what can become present: a "can be" is a tentative conjecture about what will come about. The future is *what will be*. The *what* is mainly due to the being of individuals; the *will be,* to time. The two are, however, inseparable. Together, they are the future.

The merged being of individuals does not move from the future to the present; it does not move from place to place but becomes present by being transformed. There are changes of it; it is divided and made definite, and its coming to have determinations will have to be described again. It is the determinability of the being that is future that gives to future time its impendingness. The *will be* of time is the character that time has because of its being together with the determinable being of individuals. The two suffuse each other; it is difficult to distinguish them. We would probably have no sense of their difference if they were not together in different ways in the present and the past.

Time and the being of individuals do not come together in the future to constitute futurity. They are together, and their being together is the future. The future is the inexhaustible maw of all coming to be. It is in the present, in coming to be and passing away, that time and the being of individuals tend to come apart. The being of individuals as future is continuous with the being of the individuals that are present, though it is also different from it in that the being of individuals in the future is merged. Similarly, the time of the future is continuous with but different from the time of the present: the difference is that future time is not divided, there are no singulars in the future, and time is not inside or outside single things. Both time and being in the future are continuous with what is present, and, as together, they qualify each other. The being that is in the future is determinable, and the certainty that it will be determined is secured by the time it is with. This time, in turn, is future; it is the time that will be present because of the determinability of the merged being of individuals. Each qualifies the other, and both are affected by the being and time of the present with which they are continuous.

The being that is future does not differ as being from the being of the individuals that are present. If it did, something would have to be added to it for it to become the being of what is in a present time. Were that true, however, the being would be not future being but just being—perhaps a *could be*—and whether it were made a *will be* would depend on the addition's being of a certain kind. The possibility of the addition would make the being future; the addition in fact would make it actual. This position is held by the Thomists, who think that when existence is added to essence the essence becomes actual. (They also think that an essence is discrete, that what is added to an essence is added by God, that adding it is not a temporal act, and indeed that time is not something real. There is no compelling reason to think that this understanding of being is true.)

Just as the being that is future does not differ from the being of present individuals, the time that is future does not differ as time from the time of the present. If it did, it would not be time or would not be real, and something would have to be taken away from it (from its eternity) for it to become the time of something that becomes present or is actual. It would then never have been future because there would not have been a coming to be. Time would not pass, the time of the present (without good cause) would be a passing away, and time would be very little like the present, as little like it as the present is like the past.

We are clearly strained in thinking and speaking of the future. Thought and speech are best suited to describing what is present or abstractions from what is present or for saying what the future becomes when it becomes present. We also want, however, to think of the future as future; we want to think of it literally or at least no more symbolically than we may have to speak of any other part of time. Of the literal claims that describe the future, the most general and surest claims are that the future is a common future for all the individuals that are present, that this one future is full, and that it is also inexhaustible. How should these claims be understood? What reasons are there for thinking that they are true? We must suppose that the future is real because we cannot describe any motion or change without supposing so. Its nature, however, must be described.

CHAPTER TEN

THE NATURE OF THE FUTURE

I T IS DIFFICULT to understand the future. We have intimations of its size and its bearing on us, but we come to know it most by thinking about what it must be before it is transformed and becomes a present time. The future must differ from the present, but not so much that the world's going on will be discontinuous. Some philosophers, therefore, minimize the differences between the two. They think that there are future events and that their only difference from the events of the present is their position in time, or they think that there are possibilities in the future and that the only difference between them and the characters that things already have is that they have not yet been brought about. Other philosophers think the differences between the present and the future are so great that we should not even talk about a natural transformation of the future into a present time; they think that the world must be created anew in each moment.

If the future and what is in it are real neither of these extremes is sound. The realities that are future are transformed in becoming present or become present by being transformed, not by being relocated in the place of a present time. Nor will it be sound to think that there is no transformation because there is nothing in the future that can be transformed and that instead something new is created at each moment. We need a notion of genuine transformation, and the notion we need supposes the being that is present and the being that is real in the future to be the same being—the being of individuals. I have already noted some features of this common being in arguing that the future is real. These should be explained more fully, and other features should also be described. Perhaps it will be best to begin by thinking why there is one future for present individuals common to them all.

Individuals and Their Common Future

Is there one future, or are there many, one for every individual? One reason that has been given for denying the former is that some of us are old and some are young; some of us will not live as long as others. There will, therefore, be a portion of the future that not all of us will share, and this will be true at any time.

This is the idea that the future is common to us only when we share the same extent of it, when we live the same length of time. There is obviously something right in it—though there are differences in how complex and simple individuals stand to time—but it is obscure about the notion of "extent," and its only sense of a common future is our continuing to be together in some same present times. This reveals little or nothing about the nature of the future. We might learn a little about the future if we suppose that we can not be together in a present unless we *face* the same future together, unless *our* next moment will be the same, but even this is finally a picture of us in a present, of a next moment and then another with some of us in those moments even after others have ceased to be. There are no differences in the picture between "having a common future" and "existing at the same time," so the picture gives us no sense of the commonness of the future while it is future and no sense of how our being is in time. It might be better, then, to look for a fuller meaning for "common future" by setting aside these notions and turning for a moment to an opposite notion, namely, the idea that present individuals do not have a common future. Instead, you have yours, I have mine, and they are of different lengths, as if for each of us there were a channel extending forward and the channels of some were short and of others, long. Is this a feasible idea?

Some complex individuals will live or last longer than others, but we will not understand even this fact if we think of our futures as being in separate channels of different lengths. Except for the matter of length, this is how Leibniz pictures individuals, but there are anomalies in this picture at almost every point. For example, are the channels empty or not? If they are empty, what are we to make of an extent of time with nothing in it? What could measure the extent? There are no unit parts of empty time. Then too, an empty future, however long, will be long or short depending on the pace at which it is filled. One could live through it like a miser or a profligate, so that the notion of an empty channel of time does not help us explain even the fact that some of us will live or last longer than others.

The picture of channels of futurity is little improved by supposing the channels to be full. This is Leibniz's wonderful idea: the future states of monads are definite; their "future" being is already real. In making this claim, however, Leibniz must deny that monads have a capacity to act and that there are contingencies in the actions that will occur. These consequences come about for him, as they will for any "full" channel view, because the parts of the separate channels must be coordinated: what will occur to me or in my actions will be coordinated with what occurs in the actions of other individuals. You cannot take the car "when" I do, and the car must be there for the taking as its future and mine each separately come about. This extraordinary coordination must somehow be ensured; it would be too massively coincidental for individuals, each acting on its own and inside its own time, to do what fits with what others also do. The forces that could arrange for such coordination would be so powerful that it is they who would be acting, not us. We would have been made to be in the arrangements they had previsioned, and we could not unsettle or rearrange them.

There is another awkward consequence: on this view of things, there is no difference between the past, the present, and the future, however long. Every state or stage of things will have been "prearranged." It is not clear whether the stages must be played out, whether there will be any difference in them if they are, or even whether they can successively occur, for their being enacted one after another would require a still further time in which all that had already been made definite would come about in fact. We will, therefore, not understand the notion that one individual lives or lasts longer than another by thinking that our actions, short or long, lie in channels extending into the future and that moments of the future encompass the same singularity and privacy that there seems to be in a present time.

So we come back to the notion that there is a single future, and we must say that there is something in it. We also must say that all individuals not only face a single future but also transform what is in it into their singular selves. The single future is indefinite, which is why it can be common to all individuals. There are no definite parts of it, some of which belong to one individual, some to another. Still, we must be uneasy about a single common future. Certainly some "portions" of the future will not become present for us; we will not live forever, so some "portions" of the future are so far beyond us that they are not *our* future at all. Does this mean that we must give up the notion of a single common future after all? Does it mean that we must think of many common futures, one after another, each less than an instant long? Or should we look for a new formulation of the notion that there are different futures for different individuals?

We need do none of these. We can consistently hold there to be a single future common to all the individuals that are present if we set aside the view that the future is *ours* only so far as it becomes a present in which we exist as singulars. This is near to the old idea that we are wholly present, that our whole being is singular, and that we can persist for a time as new presents come about. We have already seen the power and importance of this idea, but we have also seen that it cannot explain what it itself supposes—that new presents come about, that individuals continue to be in them, and that they change even while they remain the same. The ideas we should have instead are as follows:

- The being of an individual is not wholly present.
- Individuals interplay with time in one way to define it as present and in another way to define it as future.
- We individuate our own being as time passes and new presents come to be.
- Our being as future is not ours alone, and we cannot even mark out a part of it as ours or ours alone.
- We no longer exist when we are no longer able, as the composite individuals we are, to individuate the being we share with others.
- Our future being, never ours alone, is the being of other individuals as well.
- Even after we have perished, other individuals and new complex individuals continue themselves by individuating future being.

It might help in thinking of these ideas to see them as a modification of Leibniz's view. The themes I have set out are ones that Leibniz would have argued for if he had supposed monads to really act, to be singular only in the present, and to be not yet definite in the future. Still, the notion of future being remains obscure. I want to try some suggestions to make the idea of future being more accessible and then return to the issue of the future's being common to us all.

The Future Being of Individuals

That our being is not wholly present but also future is the most unfamiliar notion in this account of going on. The difficulty with it is over *what* future being is and how, if it is not definite, it really *is* something and not nothing at all.

The question "what is it?" is never simple. It is always "what is it that . . . ?" and it always calls for a connection between the "it" and something else; the *what* explains the connection between the two. Something is a something that does something to something else, that affects it in some way or is affected by it. What something *is* is in its connection with something else, or at least that is what we can explain and understand about what it is.

If we are to understand what the future being of individuals is, then, we need to understand its connection with something else, but what? It was itself introduced in connection with an answer to a "what is it" question about present individuals, and that introduction remains the only intellectual access we have to the idea of "the future being of individuals." It is not as though we understand that there are individuals in the present and then go on to make a separate factual discovery that those individuals have part of their being in the future. We would not understand that individuals are present without seeing that their being is also future even then. The present being and future being of individuals are connected, and to understand future being we need not and perhaps cannot ask how it is connected to some still further reality. What would our question be? What would the further reality be? If what things are is in their connection with other realities there must be an end to asking what things are, otherwise nothing would ever be explained. Our only course, then, is to stay with the connection between future being and individuals as they are present and to try to understand more about it. This will not be circular: though their being is the same, their relation to time differs enough for each to reveal something of the other's nature. We can see much about the nature of future being by thinking about the most fundamental change to occur in the being of present individuals.

The most fundamental changes in individuals are not incidental to them. It is not as if, whatever they are, they have their unchanging natures and their only changes are in what can be added on to the natures they already have. The fundamental changes of individuals are changes of their very being and are more fundamental than changes of their natures. The natures of individuals also change; they are modified but remain the same. These natures are the general ways in which individuals change and act. They are in the being that is passing in individuals, and they are continually formed in the being that comes into them. The most fundamental change in individuals is that the very being of individuals itself passes. This is a change *of* them, and as that change occurs there are changes *in* them as well. Future being comes into individuals; it becomes the being of singular individuals, and it becomes definite as it comes into them. It has no definiteness before it comes into them. If it did, the future would consist of separate channels filled by strands of characters, as in Leibniz. There would be no passing and no action, only different states before and after one another, and no one of them would be really new.

If future being is indefinite, though, why should anyone say that there *is* something in the future? Why not say that there is no future or that the future is nothing at all? What is the difference between a future being that has no definiteness and a future that has no being at all or is not real? The difference is that one *is* and the other is not, and there is no *what* to this difference. It is a difference but not between things, not the difference that future being has some character and nothing does not. Having and lacking a character is the kind of difference there can be between things that already are, but the difference between something and nothing cannot be the same in kind as any of the differences that could hold between things that are: it is not a difference in what one thing has and another does not or in what one thing does and the other does not do. We therefore cannot say that future being has a certain *what* that nothing lacks. That would attribute a definite character to future being and both being and character to nothing, but the first attribution is mistaken and the second, contradictory and senseless. Future being has no *what* and nothing is nothing at all. It is as if, almost paradoxically, there is no difference between them because there are not two of them and the two of them are not the same. There is no other to being; there is nothing outside it because there is no limitation in it that would allow for an outside. There is nothing beyond the future. We feel the fullness of being from inside.

If the being in which singular individuals continue themselves is new in being in them, the future must be real. The alternative concep tion for such new being is sheer creation, creation from nothing, not even the being of a creator. This is the ultimate position to which one is driven, as Whitehead is, when one is driven to think that what we can understand depends finally on something we can only acknowledge but not understand. It is, therefore, not an effective refutation for an ultimate principle to say that it cannot be understood, for a philosophy that allows such a principle or such a turn of mind supposes that not everything can be understood. Though we can not refute such a position, however, we can turn away from it.

The opposite principle in philosophy is that everything can be understood, and this is not only a difference in a principle but also in the attitudes, judgments, and dedications we have in philosophical thought. There is a reconciled despair in the notion that we know not everything can be understood. There is, on the other hand, a presumption in the notion that everything can be understood and that we can have no conception of what cannot be understood, but the presumption is softened by supposing that everything need not or cannot be altogether understood at once; we are never to know whether we are done with understanding. This is the attitude I want to take toward the ideas of time and individuals. When it seems that our understanding is not sound or full enough our practice should be to correct our ideas; we should not suppose that they are really right and that they need only a final completing supplement. I think that the conceptions of time and individuals provide as much understanding of change as it is sensible to look for and that no final, closing principle is needed to explain why there is always something new in individuals as they last and act. The being that comes to be new in them had been future; it is not created in each moment. It is carried into them by time, and as it comes into them it comes for the first time to have definite characters. This is the idea to be tested, and the condition for testing it is that it first be at least understandable. Arguments can then be given either to enlarge our understanding or to show that what we understand is true.

One of the great arguments bearing on understanding indefinite being—or not understanding it—is given in Book 12 of Aristotle's *Metaphysics,* namely, that last matter and form can not come to be. Aristotle's argument is simply that "everything that changes is something and is changed by something and into something. . . . The process, then, will go on to infinity, if not only the bronze comes to be round but also the round or the bronze comes to be; therefore there must be a stop." The stop for Aristotle is the claim that the final real things are substances of natural kinds. There can be no last matter and form because every substance comes to be "out of something that shares its name." If last matter or form could come to be, if there could be a last matter or form, there could have been no efficient cause to found the natural kinds of things. For Aristotle, then, indeterminate matter or formless forms are not real, and they could not have been real in the past. The notions cannot even be understood because there is nothing in them that we can grasp, and we cannot connect them with what we know to be real and with the processes by which substances come about.

Aristotle's argument is very strong. Should an argument like it, then, also be made for the future? Should we also say that from an entirely indeterminate future nothing definite can ever come? I think not, for neither Aristotle's argument nor analogues of it apply to the future being of individuals. What carries Aristotle's argument is the idea that one substance acts on another as an efficient cause and that it is the cause of a new definiteness in the matter of the other substance. The future, however, is neither a singular substance nor made definite by an efficient cause. It becomes definite as it becomes present and then for the first time. It could not have been definite before because if it were, it could not have become definite in and as the individuals it continues. This is because of the way that the future is made to be present.

As Aristotle more or less says, when future being becomes definite, it is made definite by what preceded it, but again, the question is whether what comes to be changed is definite before it is changed, whether the change is a replacement of a definiteness it already has. Aristotle thinks so because he thinks that what is changed is the already formed matter of a sensible substance. The change in future being, however, is a change of the very being of singular individuals. The being that comes into singular individuals comes to have definite characters, but not, as Aristotle might think, because its matter has first one form and then another; all the definiteness that future being comes to have, all its characters, are new to it. The future's first definiteness is due to neither an efficient cause nor the imposition of forms. The future being of individuals becomes definite when, in becoming present, it forms itself on what is passing and what is past.

Aristotle is right to think that if matter and form had ever been indeterminate, substances could never have come to be. By contrast, it is only because the future is indefinite that individuals can continue to be and to achieve definite characters. Aristotle's thesis about last matter and form, therefore, cannot be turned around to argue that the necessity of definiteness in the world of substance implies that the being of the future cannot be completely indefinite. The comparison does not hold; the beings and the causalities are different. Even if we were to agree with Aristotle on the general point that there could never have been a completely indefinite being in the past, the future would still have to be indefinite.

Is it understandable, then, that the future being of individuals is indefinite and without any character and that this is what allows it to be common to all individuals? The idea meets Aristotle's tests—it has a place in a comprehensible account of how individuals come to change—but it is not obvious how we can justify an answer to a question about something's being understandable. The question presupposes a profound issue that involves the very nature of philosophy, namely, whether understanding a philosophical thesis requires that we know that it is true and if not, whether we can construct arguments for or against theses we understand but do not know to be true. We need not argue this issue, though, because understanding must be achieved in either case; it must proceed from something we already understand, and each of the steps in the procession is a kind of argument. What we must do, then, is argue, asking questions about the indefiniteness of the future, answering them, and giving reasons for thinking that the answers are correct.

Perhaps the most direct question about the future is whether the characters of singular individuals become definite only as the future becomes present. Plato, Aristotle, and others admit that some addition or further determination is made to a form or property when it is exhibited or actualized—red becomes this red, for example—but they would not allow that the whole definiteness of an individual's character originates in the present. They would not think that it could come about because the accounts of change that they think are sound are about the "relocation" or modification of characters that are already definite.

For example, take Plato's view that becoming is what occurs and is present but that the basis in a becoming is too indefinite to be the whole cause of what comes about. What most makes for transience in becoming is the flux—in Whitehead it is creativity—and for some definiteness to come about, items of definiteness (forms, or eternal objects whose home is not the flux) must model it or be introduced into it through participation or prehension. What is sheerly present—which of itself has no *what*—cannot cause itself to become definite; what is not in time must somehow enter it to give to what is unsettled such definiteness or intelligibility as it can come to have.

This is a profound view of process and of the way in which, and the depth to which, a form makes a process intelligible, more or less and for shorter or longer periods of time. It is, however, a view only of moments of process and of nothing else in time, and even so, it can offer us no explanation for why such moments must occur continually. The reason for this is that forms and flux exist apart and separately. Each is a separate world; neither, of itself, contributes to the being of the other. The two are never really joined, though something else, a demiurge or a divine, is said to do something like joining them. Once so informed, however, the flux does not sustain the form it has been made to have and, for some cause or reason, the demiurge or divine fashions it again. Even when it is formed, the flux does nothing except agitate itself and lose its form. Forms do not sustain themselves in the flux, nor do they affect which forms will follow them. Neither flux nor form, nor the two together, does anything. All that happens is that a flux, which by its nature resists having a definite nature, is formed in a certain way or forms itself around a form that has been given to or imposed on it; it is only in such ways that Plato thinks a flux can become a process. The definiteness in process must be brought into the flux; as it is apart from it, apart from the present in which process occurs, it is not at all indefinite.

The idea that the activities of individuals are the fundamental processes is very different from Platonic views. The differences are over what realities are fundamental, how they are related, and the nature of processes or activities themselves. In this idea, the fundamental realities are time and individuals, not flux and form, though time passes and individuals form themselves. This is a real difference because a process is not, as Platonists think, only a moment of forming, even complete forming. The activity of an individual in the present is rather a continuing to be present and a coming to be past. There is no becoming past for Platonic forms; they are never really present, and the vestiges of them that are present do not become past but cease to be. If a process has duration, however, there must be both a coming to be and a becoming past inside of it, and what comes to be is coming to be what it is because of what is already becoming past. What is passing in the present is definite, or almost completely definite, and it affects what is coming to be, but not by changing its direction or by imposing itself on what is becoming singular.

What becomes present becomes definite as it becomes present. The being that becomes present must therefore be thought to be indefinite when it is future. There is enough definiteness in the present, in what is becoming past even while it is still present, to have the unformed being that is becoming present take on form or character. If we were to think that the stuff of the present is indefinite and that the present is the moment in which it is formed, we would have to suppose, as Platonists do, that forms or characters must be imposed. On the other hand, we can think of the present as a becoming past as well as a coming to be, and then the present will not be wholly indefinite. We can also think of what is coming to be as continuing what is becoming past and thus see new definiteness as introduced not by imposition but by conformation. This permits us to conclude that the future being of individuals is indefinite and that all the definiteness individuals come to have arises wholly in the present. A generous Platonist might say that this notion of activity is like supposing Platonic forms to be in the past and individuals to form themselves by taking account of them—and perhaps it is.

Can we now confidently conclude that the future being of individuals is indefinite and that it comes to be definite in the present? Are we sure that these conceptions of individuals and their future being are sound? Perhaps not, for one other theme about possibility might be thought to oppose the conceptions: the notion that what comes about must first have been possible and the associated argument that, if there are real possibilities, then the future cannot be entirely indefinite. This is a strong argument, but I think the first part of it should be reinterpreted and the second part should simply be strongly opposed. Thus, I want to (1) acknowledge that possibility is real—it can be thought of as the future being of individuals—but (2) show that what is really possible is indefinite. There is a little complication in these two responses.

(1) It is almost empty to say that what comes about must first have been possible. Those who talk about possibilities suppose that for everything, it is either possible or impossible for it to come about. If it has come about, it was not impossible for it to have come about, and the possibility is therefore something real and not nothing; what comes

about cannot have come to be from nothing. So it is supposed that there are possibilities. They *are* before they come about, and it is they that come about. Some of them get actualized, and for some reason, cause, or other obstacle, some do not. The near emptiness in this is simply that the argument does not say what possibilities are or how they come about; it does not say what it is in possibilities that makes them all possibilities or what makes for there being different possibilities. Something is at least possible if we do not know that it will not come about, but that "something," that "it," might have to do with any sort of thing—it is possible for atoms to be configured in a certain way, for a matter to be given a certain shape, or for a form to be instantiated. Every account of motion and change defines some notion of possibility, real or not, but the formal argument about possibility tells us virtually nothing about the reality and nature of possibilities or about the specific account of motion and change that we should have. It only says that motion and change must continue.

The more specific notions of possibility that bear on the definiteness and indefiniteness of what has not yet become present are about the entities that are present or actual and that will come to have different properties or relations. A thing is now short or smiling; it can become tall or frowning. Tall or frowning are possibilities for it, and it may actualize these possibilities. The possibilities for an entity are the properties or relations that it can actualize, whatever properties and relations are and whatever "actualization" means. What it is most important to note about such a notion is that there is not much difference between a property's being a possibility and its being actualized because all that a thing can do to a possibility is actualize it—make it part of itself or give it a point or place of attachment—and that only makes it the property of that thing—its frowning, say, or *this* frowning. Actualization doesn't deeply affect a possibility. What comes about is almost completely definite before it comes about; it is only incidentally indefinite, it is missing a *this,* and this indefiniteness has nothing to do with it being the property or relation it is. This is very different from the idea that the whole present being of an individual becomes newly definite as it continues to exist.

There is no need to repeat the long argument about whether it is better to conceive of the singular things that are present as remaining the same and unchanged in their being or nature or as individuals and activities. The notion of definite possibilities goes with the first conception; the idea that the future being of individuals is indefinite goes with the second. However, it is worth considering an argument that is critical of the first view and almost transforms it into the second. The argument begins by acknowledging that properties or relations or possibilities are real but goes on to show that real possibilities cannot be sharply discrete. The idea is that possibilities are very general—so general, in fact, that there is really only one possibility that must continually become definite. This will be the same, or nearly the same, as showing my second claim, that what is finally or really possible, the being of the possible, is the future and is indefinite.

(2) We start, easily enough, by acknowledging that things change. It seems simple to describe the possibility of their changing: at one time, things have certain properties and relations, and then they come to have different ones. The ones they come to have were possible for them before they came to have them or were among their possibilities.

The matter is not so simple, though. For a property a thing comes to have will have been a possibility for it only if it also could have come to have a different property. A possibility need not come about. If a thing changes it is possible for it to become this or that, but neither outcome is necessary. So, red will be a possibility for a thing only if the thing could also become green or some other color. If red were the only color a thing could come to have, it would be necessary that it become red, not merely possible.

Our small complication, then, is that when we represent what it is possible for a thing to become we must consider several properties as being together. They are possibilities only as they are together: a possibility is one of a collection of properties, each one of which could be brought about. Because of being the properties they are, however, or because of their being connected as they are, to instantiate one is to exclude the others. A thing that actualizes a possibility has a place for only one of the properties that are its possibilities.

How shall we represent the collection of possibilities? Should we picture there being several properties of one kind, say, $P_1, P_2, P_3 \ldots P_n$? Or, to suggest that the actualization of one is the exclusion of the others, should our picture be $(P_1 \lor P_2 \lor P_3 \lor \ldots P_n)$, where each P is an entirely definite property? Or should we represent or understand the grouping of possibilities in some other way? The answer depends on how "actualization" is to be understood. We should not simply suppose there to be properties that somehow are actualized but also consider what actualization is and think of possibilities as being what gets actualized.

Is actualization a process of freely selecting and then bringing about what has been chosen, thereby eliminating the rest of the collection? This is what it would have to be if possibilities were discrete and definite properties, no one of which necessarily has to come about. We choose the one we want and cause it to occur. Some actualizations seem plainly to occur in this way, but this is also a process of very high mentality not found prominently in nature; indeed, some say that it does not occur at all.

Flowers, for example, do not choose their colors. Something in them is the nonchoosing cause of their coming to have the colors they do. This is usually taken to show that of all the properties that are mistakenly thought to be possible only one is really possible, and there is no possibility of its not coming about. In this way, the notion that possibilities are discrete and definite properties leads readily to the view that, except for the cases of really choosing what to bring about—if such cases are real—there are no possibilities at all: certain properties are simply sure to come about. This view is then either taken comprehensively, holding for all kinds of things, or unusual exceptions are claimed for some humans and some animals at some times, or there are the extravagant exceptions that everything that comes about has been chosen for manifestation by God or by the demiurge but not by us.

An understanding of possibility that so readily leads us to think that there may be no possibilities is so awkward—though there is other ungainliness in the idea, as we will see—that *if* we need a notion of genuine possibility we should try to develop a different conception of it, one that will not make choosing an exception among processes but will regard it as an intensified or specialized version of all coming to be.

What will this different conception be? Above all, it must construe possible properties as not definite or discrete when they are possible. If we think that $(P_1 \text{ v } P_2 \text{ v } P_3 \ldots P_n)$ represents what might come about in a thing through its own agency, we shall mean that there is a possibility P but that when it is actualized it is made more definite, becoming either P_1 or P_2 or $P_3 \ldots$ or P_n. P_1 or P_2 or $P_3 \ldots$ or P_n will be understood to be either the definite, discrete properties that we know have come about already and that we think can, under certain conditions, come about again or the definite and discrete properties that we imagine can come about. The important point is that, on this conception, a possibility is not an entirely definite property while it is a possibility. As a possibility, it is in some respects indefinite; it is, perhaps, a kind of property—color, say, rather than red or green—and "the" property or the "stuff" of properties becomes definite when the possibility is actualized. Actualization will be a process in which some propertylike possibility is made definite. It is a natural process; in intelligent beings, it may be deliberately guided and directed by thoughts of what we want and choose to have come about.

On this conception, then, possibilities will be real. Their being will be like the being of properties, only they will be somewhat indefinite. They will not be definite or even discrete while they are possibilities and will come to be definite only when they are actualized. Were this conception sound, the argument that what is not yet present cannot be indefinite because possibilities are definite would be very deeply qualified. Possibilities are real but not entirely definite. Can we go further and show that they are not definite at all? That would be the same as showing that the future is real and full but not definite (though still speaking of possibilities). Except for one small part, this step can indeed be made by making two changes in our far-too-simple picture of definite possibilities.

(1) In the very simple picture of the possible future properties of things, possibilities are represented as if their being possible depends only on the thing itself: because of its nature, an acorn may become an oak. Although the potentiality of a thing may depend only on its nature, its potentiality is not the same as the properties it is possible for it to have. A potentiality has to do with the limits or range or kinds of properties a thing can come to have and with those that would most fulfill it, but what the possible properties are depends not only on the nature of the thing that actualizes them but also on the other things that can and do affect them. Whether it is possible for a particular acorn to grow depends on whether there are squirrels nearby, and whether it is possible for some particular squirrels to become fat depends on whether there are acorns for them to eat. The specific properties that things may possibly come to have depend on their own natures and the things around them, not on their natures alone.

How shall we take account of the possibilities of things when we think of things affecting one another? I have already said that for a single thing it is possible for it to have a certain kind of property but that the specific property it comes to have is not completely definite until it comes to have it. Even so, it will not be right to represent the possibilities for an acorn and a squirrel by supposing that the next change for the acorn will be some definiteness in an appropriate A possibility and the next change for the squirrel will be some definiteness in an appropriate S possibility. The oversight is in not showing that what is possible for one depends on what is possible for the other, and there is no hint in the representation that the next change for each of them will occur at the same time. The next changes for each must be represented together, both as next and as dependent on each other.

These two changes (even if the next change is "staying the same") must be braced together so that our representation should at least look like this:

$$\left.\begin{array}{l} \text{Acorn} \\ \text{Squirrel} \end{array}\right\} \begin{array}{l} \text{A} \\ \text{S} \end{array}$$

Even this, however, is not yet fine enough. It does not show or even suggest that the possibilities for the acorn may or do depend on the possibilities open to the squirrel and vice versa. We must therefore suppose that the presence of the squirrel affects the kinds of changes that can occur in the acorn and that the acorn affects the kinds of changes that can occur for the squirrel, with the kinds of changes for each being within the limits of its nature.

This, too, is not as fine as we should like, but it opens a further and important point. The possibility that is open to a single thing when it is considered by itself is indefinite, and the property it actualizes is also indefinite until it is actualized. Considered together with possibilities for other things the possibility that is open to a thing is even more indefinite, because other things affect what it will be. Not only is the property that a thing will actualize indefinite but also the kind of property.

This indefiniteness is not a matter of our inability to plot what kinds of properties and particular properties a thing will have. It is simply that there is very little definite in possibilities. They are not definite and then chosen and actualized; "they" come to have their full definiteness as they are actualized, and although there is a little definiteness in the possibility of coming to have a property of a certain kind—a color, for example—there is far less definiteness in the possibility of a thing coming to have a property of one or another of certain kinds of properties. It is, no doubt, not subtle enough to talk about kinds of properties or kinds of relations, still, the point remains: the possibilities open to things are especially indefinite when we see that the possibilities open to one thing are affected by other things and the possibilities that are open to them.

We can go further and can consider not just the possibilities of one thing or another but the possibilities of all the things that can affect one another at any moment. The consequence is plain: if the possibilities for things considered together are much more indefinite than the possibilities that are open (though only abstractly) to a single thing, the possibilities open at any moment to all the things that affect one another are vastly more indefinite. There are possibilities for changes of even the kinds of changes that things might undergo: a child's way of affecting what can happen to acorns differs from a squirrel's, and so on for other sorts of things. The next moment in a world of many things, then, is almost entirely indefinite. The only shred of definiteness of which we can be assured is owed to the notion that things have natures, that what can come about in them must be within the limits of their natures, and that the changes come about in a certain way. The definiteness of the future may be even thinner than this, however. It will be evanescent if there are possibilities not only for the next change or the next moment but for the further changes that can occur in things.

(2) One reason the simple picture of definite possibilities is so simple is that it is a picture of the next change in a thing. It is made fuller when we take it to represent what can be true of a thing in "the" next moment and if we also think of things affecting one another's possibilities. We can make it even fuller by thinking of possibilities beyond the next moment.

Our notions of possibilities are dominated by the idea of a *moment* if we think of possibilities as definite: a thing cannot have, or cannot come to have, both a property and one of its contraries at the same time in the same respect. A thing must now be or next become either this or that, not both. The definiteness of possibilities holds us to the moment, for a thing *can* have opposing properties in different moments. On this view of things and possibilities, then, we think of things as stuttering along in the actualization of properties, being basically the same over a period of time because of their unchanging essences and altogether the same if they continue to actualize the same properties.

Even so, on this now not-so-simple view of things, there are either possibilities beyond the next moment or there will be further possibilities when the next moment comes about. We sometimes think that this or that will come about: if it is this, then there are or will be other possibilities; if it is that, there are or will be still others, and for each of these there will be still others and, in turn, others afterward. The lines, the branches, go on indefinitely. The only reason to think of not continuing them infinitely is that the thing for which they are the possibilities might die or be destroyed, so that after awhile there is nothing for which they are the possibilities. Still, we should also think that, in the plentitude of properties, "possible" lines and branches are still there, "possibly" pertinent for new things and really possible for others that still survive. The pertinence of properties to things is what constitutes their being possibilities, not the connectedness of properties among themselves. Such connectednesses, though, are "possible" possibilities or "possible" pertinences; they can go on and on, and as they go on, there is less and less definiteness in them. The *next* moment for everything is hardly definite; the farther future is much less so. There is something real in the future, namely, the properties as they are pertinent to things, but they are ever more indefinite the more future they are, and because they are indefinite, they are hardly separable from one another.

In summary, my argument is against the notion that what is not yet present cannot be indefinite because things are of certain kinds and because they confront definite possibilities. It presses the issue of (1) whether, in changing, things incorporate definite possibilities or (2) whether what they incorporate becomes definite only when they come into the things themselves, whether or not we can anticipate what those properties will be. The first view, if sound at all, is sound only in special cases; it could not be true of nature generally. The second view is generally sounder and allows for the special cases in which we think, choose, and act deliberately, so that what comes about comes to have the definite properties we anticipated. The consequence of the second view is either that there are no possibilities or that possibilities are indefinite, and more and more so as we acknowledge that things affect one another's possibilities and that possibility extends farther and farther into the future.

Such definiteness as is left by the argument is due to the ideas that there are things and that they have definite natures limiting the changes and kinds of changes that can occur. There are limits to what individuals can become, but they are not imposed by unchanging natures; indeed, the supposition of such natures should not be sustained. The idea that because of their natures things incorporate new properties by reaching out to them and actualizing some of them is inexplicable, as is the idea that things are always actualizing possibilities; we do not even know why they must always do this. The root of these difficulties probably is that *things* and *properties* or *possibilities* are conceived to be too different in kind really to be connected, so that answers to questions about why and how things actualize possibilities and why they must actualize them will be too vague and metaphorical.

The notions of time and individuals used in this essay do not involve these difficulties, and the consequence of referring to them instead of to substances that have essential natures is that the being of the future is characterized as entirely indefinite. The whole being of a singular individual is in process at each moment; the change within an individual is not just a change of incidental properties. The whole being of a present individual changes, and though there is always something definite in an individual, a new definiteness in every moment, that definiteness is what makes for the definiteness of what comes about. For individuals, then, we should say that their futures, their "possibilities," are indefinite. They need not be definite so that individuals know which ones to "reach out" for, which they can incorporate in themselves. Individuals do not reach out for their futures. Instead, (1) the future being of individuals is entirely indefinite, (2) it is forced on and into them as the time that is together with them is made continually to pass, and (3) the being that is forced on or carried into individuals is made definite in the present by forming itself on the already definite portions of the individual that are becoming past.

The final stage of the argument, then, is that even the remnant of definiteness remaining in doctrines of things and possibilities should be set aside. The difficulties in these conceptions cannot be overcome. What we can say, though, is that some of the same reasons that have led people to think properties or possibilities to be real also suggest that the being of individuals that has not yet become present is real. It is as if it were made of the same stuff as properties, as if it were the being that all possibilities have in common. The future being of individuals is what properties would be if they were indefinite, merged together, indistinct from one another, and future rather than timeless, always impending because of the time that is also future.

The notions of properties and possibilities are therefore to be set aside. We are to speak instead of individuals and their future being; this is the one "possibility" for all individuals that are present, the one being in which they all share. It is then a further and important note in these conceptions that the future being of individuals is the same being that individuals have in the present time. Substances and their unactualized properties are of such different kinds that there is no understanding why things must acquire them, how they reach out for them, and how they change them from being possible to being actually theirs. There is no such difference between individuals in the present and that being of theirs that constitutes the future. There is some difference between them, but it is not in their being; it is in their being together with time in different ways.

The being of individuals is not wholly present. It is also future, and as singular individuals become past some of their future being comes into them. Individuals are continuing activities. The being that comes into them when they are present is their own being, not some different kind of being that is added on to them. It does not become present by having what is present reach out of time to take hold of it or by having a powerful entity place it within the present's reach, nor does it come to the *place* of the present, the point from which measurement begins or ends. It becomes present in an individual's activity of becoming past while it is also coming to be: this is its continuing to exist.

This is also time's passing. Time does not pass of itself or all alone. It passes because of the provocation of the individuals that are present, and it brings into individuals that being of theirs that is inseparable from them. Time and individuals are never apart from each other, though they are together in different ways. I have already argued that in the future time is dominated by the being of individuals but that in the present individuals contend with time. Individuals are singular in the present, but their being is not divided in the future. The future being of individuals is, because time is also future, "a comprehensive possibility," the "possibility" of being made definite as the being of continuing singular individuals.

The difference between the being of a singular individual and its future being is not a difference between two ontological kinds. It is not like the differences between "substances" and "properties" or between "actualities" and "possibilities" but is rather the difference between singular and merged, many and one, contending and dominated, and active and potent. These are differences in the ways that the being of individuals is together with time. When the future being of individuals is made to be present it does not change its kind but comes to stand differently to time. Because of the ways in which indefinite being is formed when it is brought into singular individuals, individuals in the present continue to be singular; they are empowered anew in each moment and enabled to continue in activity. If they are complex and not able to form their new being as they had in the past, they do not continue to be the complex singulars they were. Their future being is then made definite by other, simpler individuals or by new, complex individuals.

This last observation about complex and simpler individuals settles the question that remained in one of the themes considered earlier—how all individuals can have the same future though some of us will continue to exist longer than others. The answer is that we, and perhaps everything else, are complex individuals and that some of us will continue to exist longer in our form of organization than others. This does not mean that there is no common future, that there are separate futures of different lengths, or that, if there is a common future, some individuals extend further into it than others. There is one future, it has no length, and the being that is future is shared by all individuals. To say that some individuals last longer than others means that some complex individuals are able to continue their complex organizations for a longer period of time than are others. Even so, the future remains common to all individuals, however they are organized and for however long.

As complex individuals we last only for a time. We come to be and we will cease to be. We are formed in activity, and we will cease to be when we can no longer make certain forms of activity our own. We are episodes in the world's going on. Because we provoke and shape activity, however, we are not merely configurations of the being that constitutes us, nor are we entities of a different make that ride astride temporal being for a time. We are, so far as we are singulars, singulars empowered in activity. The future we face, the being and time that is future, is full and inexhaustible, but not, as we shall see, because it is infinitely long.

The Inexhaustibility of the Future

For most philosophers there is no question of the future's being inexhaustible. It simply is not real. Their analogue of its being inexhaustible is that there must always be activities, happenings, or events. These are not in the future before they occur but exist or come to exist only when they do occur. The present is the time of these occurrences, and they must always be happening because there are permanent and indestructible entities that for some reason must always change. Instead of talking about an inexhaustible future, then, these philosophers think it sounder to posit things that were never created and cannot be destroyed—they always are—and when we think of them as changing, we think of them as being in the present time. Atomists, materialists, and Aristotelians take this sort of view; for them, time is not fully real but only a derivative, a measure or attribute of motion or other change.

There are other ways of thinking that, even though the future is not real, things will have always to go on. Instead of supposing the things that must move or change to be fundamentally real, some philosophers think that the deepest reality is the flow or flux itself and that configurations made or marked on it are what we think of as changing things. There are various accounts of the ways that these configurations are thought to occur, but the ongoing is ensured in any case. It is the moving "stuff" of things; it neither comes to be nor ceases to be, and there is nothing that could make it do either. It always is; there is no past or future in it. This sort of view is shared by Heraclitus, Plato and Platonists, some Kantians, Schopenhauer, Bergson, and some pragmatists. For them, too, time is not a fundamental reality, though that is because they think of it not as the flux but as the form or measure of the transient.

I have already considered these sorts of views several times and given arguments to show that they are not true. The arguments have been about the necessity for there being changes and about the possibility and the sense of notions of a flux or flow somehow so wholly in the present that there is no past and no futurity in its being or its becoming. As another way of testing these arguments I want to suppose for a moment that they are sound and that the future is real. That will not end all our problems; it would be no test if it did, for we have to consider whether the future, both time and being, is inexhaustible. It may be that there is a real future now and that individuals must act so long as there is a future for them, but what if there need not always be one? If the future were exhaustible, there would at some time be only a present or a past, individuals would no longer act, and there would be some fault in my arguments for time and the being of individuals. And it is not easy to show that the future is inexhaustible.

If some of the being of individuals is in the future, if it comes to be present, if it is really transported in becoming present, what ensures that there will continue to be occurrences? Why could it not happen that the future being of individuals is exhausted and that the *last* of it becomes present and remains so, with no future to be provoked into passing to make what is finally present finally past? Time and individuals are together as the past, the present, and the future. Must they be together in these ways, or could they, as if time were itself in time, come to be together in only one or two of them? There are some *little* arguments that show they cannot.

If there is or must be a present, a real present that includes passing, there must be a past and a future, too. There would otherwise be no passing in the present time, for there would be no time and no being from which the present arose and that transforms it as it passes. Could it come about, though, that time and individuals are together only as a past because either the future never was or because it will be exhausted? Or could not time and individuals be together only as a future, in which case the world would not have (yet) begun?

These options are extreme and they are not finally possible. For everything to be past it would have to be made so—things don't become past of themselves—but then what makes the last of things past could not itself be made past: it would have to be present. It would also have to be effective enough while it is present to make things past, and it could have this effectiveness only if there is also a future making its contribution to the passage that occurs as a present time. The world could, therefore, never be or become entirely past.

At the other extreme, if there were only the future, the future could not be the future of anything, nor could it ever come about. It could not come about of itself—or if it did, there could be no explanation for why it came about when it did—and the supposition is that there is nothing present, so there would be nothing to instigate the future's activity. Even if the world was or could be created, it could not be created from "the world's futurity" by having the future pass into presentness because there would be nothing present to shape the passing into definite form.

The future, or what is in it, is not definite, and it doesn't become definite just by passing. Real, present individuals must make it definite. The world could not be created by having a future world pass or begin to pass into actuality but only in some other way, perhaps from the discrete forms of things. If it were created so, however, there would be no explanation for why what was created would have any necessary connection with a real future or how it could have come to have one. The being of the future would be gratuitous.

These *little* arguments are of some weight in establishing the necessity of transience, that time and the being of individuals cannot be all past or all future. There is no sense in the notions of everything as past or everything as future. Were we to say that everything past was once present we might have to think that there would have been a present and a future without a past. Likewise, if everything that is or was ever present had first been future we might have to think that there could have been a future without a present or a past. What makes for these anomalies is thinking of the parts of time as if they were set in another kind of time—a kind of eternal *present* for which there is no contrasting past and future—and thinking that something could happen to them *there*. The anomalies, to put the point another way, stem from our neglecting to see that the different togethernesses of time and individuals do not themselves come about in time. Time and individuals do not come to be connected, they are not connected merely now, and they cannot be separated, so there is no question that they might come to be connected in only one or two ways in some unusual future time.

Our final assurance, then, that there must always be transience is based not on the little arguments about what would have to be true if there were only one or two parts of time but, as the arguments suggest, on the ways in which time and individuals, as being basic and being the realities they are, must be together. The past, present, and future are their being together in different ways, and their being together in these ways neither comes about nor ceases to be in any one or all of them. Time and individuals are equally basic. The one is no more real than the other, and though they are different realities, they do not differ as being real. How can time and the being of individuals be together? There is no common "space" for them in which they could exist separately, so they must each make a contribution to their being together. That is how they are both real. Because of what they are, however, they must unify each other in different ways. There is no alternative for them; their unities are as necessary as they are. Their unities are the futurity of time and individuals, their passing in the present, and their being as past.

The future cannot be exhausted but not because it is of infinite length. The future has no length. There is nothing definite in it that could be arranged or set out on a line; there is nothing in it that even has extent. The future cannot be exhausted because time and individuals are both fundamentally real; because they are together in different ways that make for there being a past, a present, and a future; and because they cannot be together in only two or even one of these. Time and the being of individuals cannot not be together as a future; they must *always* constitute a future; something must always be. The future is therefore inexhaustible—at least we may say so if we are careful that our image of inexhaustibility does not misguide our other thoughts of time.

It still may seem that everything or even time itself somehow must be in time, however, because this conception of the future is not clear enough about time and the notion of the whole of things. We want some notion of the whole of things. Perhaps we are driven to want one, as Kant thinks, or perhaps we are led or misled toward one by our logic or our language. The task, then, is to conceive of a boundary or a limit to things that makes them a whole and then to set off the whole against something outside of it—otherwise, we would not think of it as a whole. Many of us have supposed that time provides the limits on things by establishing a first and a last and an order in between, or we have supposed that, whatever this limit is, the whole of things is a whole *inside* of time but that outside of it there is a further kind of time in which the whole of things is to be thought, and this, the realest kind of time, is the only reality that can either bind things into a whole or contain them if they are otherwise unified. The urgent sense that even the parts of time must be in time is an expression of the sense that there must be a unified whole of everything that is real, even the parts of time, and this idea makes it seem possible that time and individuals are themselves in time and that they might not *always* be together in the ways in which they are together *now*.

The irremovable difficulty in thinking that, as a whole, things are set off against something else—it would be poignant for us if we were not able to think in any other way—is that we cannot complete our understanding. Our thought becomes regressive: the whole of things and its background themselves must be in another whole, and that new whole must have a background, too. There is no end to further backgrounds. We never come to a conception of the whole of things in this mode of thought but instead fall into contradictions trying to construct the conception we think that we must have.

We can make sense of the whole of things only if we conceive it as self-contained, with the several kinds of realities affecting one another so as to be together as a whole of things. This is how time and individuals are together. They are together in different ways as past, present, and future, but they can never be apart from one another, nothing else has to hold them together—there is no further time before, after, or otherwise outside them—and there is, therefore, no possibility of their being together in any other way.

The future is not inexhaustible because there is an inexhaustible amount of it. To think there is will lead to the contradiction that there is no whole of things or that there could be one only if the future were not inexhaustible. The future is inexhaustible because time and individuals are a whole together, a certain kind of whole. The parts of time constitute the whole; changes occur within it, or the parts are the changes, the future becoming presents and presents becoming past. The future is endless because of the ways in which time and individuals are together. They are not inside something else. If they were, they might not fill it all; it might seem that they could be just present or be past. Time and individuals are a whole themselves, however, and there is no possibility of there not being a past, a present, and a future time.

The most general notion about the future of which we can in some measure be sure is that it consists of time and the being of individuals and of their being together in a certain way different from the ways in which they are together as the present and the past. The most general truths about the future are that its reality consists of the reality of time and individuals, that there is one future for all individuals, that it is filled and not empty, that it is entirely indefinite, and that it is inexhaustible. These are obviously so closely connected that they should probably not be taken as separate claims—but then, either singly or together, they are also very general. We should know more specifically about there being one future and about the extent of its determinability. There should also be some less austere reflections about the values we find in the future and the other parts of time.

CHAPTER ELEVEN

THE DETERMINATION OF THE FUTURE

W E OFTEN have intimations of what will come about, and we can often predict what will occur, either in the next moment, tomorrow, or years from now. Some of our expectations are based on fears or hopes, but the most reliable are based on past experience, our own or others'. Things always or nearly always have come about in certain ways in certain conditions, and we expect or think that they will continue to do so. The sun rises and sets every day; we have been able to see some order or regularity in almost everything that has occurred, and we believe that it will continue. Even if we believe that the future is not real or that it is real but what is in it is indefinite, as I believe, we still believe that we can predict some of the kinds of things that will become present and even predict when that will be. We cannot see into the future, however; it does not lie before us filled with events that will become present, so our thought about what will come to be—whatever kind of thought it is—is based on the regularities that have been impressive or that have impressed themselves on us in past experience.

There are two kinds of theories about how our thought of the future is based on the regularities of the past. One of them is that our experience causes us to expect what has always or usually happened in certain kinds of circumstances to happen again if conditions of those kinds reoccur. Past experiences are past; the regularly associated events that we experienced are past. We can summarize the facts of their occurrence, but those facts are about past events only and are not a reason for believing that events like them will occur again. Hume says that there is no reasoning about matters of fact that goes beyond what we remember or what we experience in a present time; our thought about the future consists only of the expectations we come to have. These expectations are caused to occur naturally because of the kinds of minds we have, and there is no question of whether they are justified. Experience itself will change our expectations if they are not borne out often enough.

The second sort of theory is that the regularities we have experienced do provide a reason for believing that in certain conditions things of certain kinds will come about. The reason derives from our seeing in what occurs the cause for occurrences of that kind or from our understanding either the natures of the things whose actions produce changes or the processes of change themselves. Such sight and understanding is a premise from which we reason that there will be certain results in or after circumstances of a certain kind, always or for the most part. There are general facts to be seen or understood in our past experience of regularities, though we may require a great deal of experience before we can make them out, and even then we may not understand them exactly or be sure just what they are. Such general facts take us beyond any new particular circumstances in which they are seen. We can, therefore, have a reason based on a fact for believing that something of a certain kind will come about. Occurrences are not all independent of one another; there is some connection between present events and those that will occur.

Expecting something to come about and having a reason for thinking that it will occur may seem not to differ much. Having an expectation and having a reason are both, after all, states of mind that arise naturally in us after some experience. We do not reason to establish our reason that something will come about, or we don't reason out our reasons endlessly, and expectations and reasons can both be reliable guides to what will occur. When we think of what explains what *expectations* and *reasons* are, however, the difference is very great. The notion of an expectation that is not based on a reason goes with a special view of mind, the view that we cannot reason about matters of fact, that we are capable only of seeing similarities and differences, and that we are hardly, if ever, able to control the associations by which one idea follows another. On the other hand, the notion that we can reason about such things is the notion of a mind that can act, control, and criticize its own actions, that can develop meanings and fashion its beliefs, often about matters far from its experience; such a mind can also direct action in the world about which it has beliefs. These are very large differences.

There are also large differences in what these different kinds of minds can know or in what they can think the world to be. A mind that lives only in expectations, in the convictions that occur naturally in it and in the memory of those convictions, is a mind in which there is no notion of anything's being true. There is only expectation and belief. Such a mind has no reason to believe its beliefs are true, so that it cannot even ask itself whether the world really is what it believes it to be or understand that it is or should be skeptical. The confidence that such a mind has in itself seems to be simply the conviction that minds work well enough in the affairs of common life, where experience will change our expectations if they are not borne out; there is also the conviction that we should stay to those affairs. Were we to allow mind to associate ideas apart from the immediate effects of new experience we might lose sight of the experiences from which the components of the ideas were originally derived. Mind should not be trusted to go its way alone apart from new experience, for in doing so it readily falls into rhetoric and sophistry.

The conception of a mind that can reason about events is much more ample. Its confidence is not that mind always reasons well but that if it reasons badly, the beliefs it comes to have eventually will be found false, if not by it then by another mind. Reasoning thus can be corrected continually to more closely approximate the truth. What is true is true of what is real, and therefore we can know what the world is: it is what we believe it is when our beliefs are true, and those truths cannot elude us forever.

A great deal in our understanding of ourselves and the world thus turns on whether we believe that we can expect certain things to come about only because of the regularities we have experienced or that we have real reasons for believing they will come about. The issues on which these views differ are difficult; still, I think we can decide between them. The most important difference between them is in their account of regularities. Both views grant a role to regularity in our coming to believe or to have a reason for thinking that certain things will come about. Which view provides a sounder account of regularity?

Regularity

Regularities are reoccurrences of events of certain kinds in certain kinds of circumstances and at certain intervals. Our apprehension of them depends on our ability to remember what has occurred and to recognize important kinds of similarities. Some regularities have been so prominent that they have always stood out for us, for example, the cycles of the sun, the planets, the tides, and the seasons. These are reoccurrences at regular intervals, and such cycles seem to many the very model of lawfulness. We look for cycles everywhere, in the large and the small, in the motions of the galaxies, and in the changes in even the smallest entities. The great cycles stand out for us because most events do not come about according to the same kind of rule.

Some of them do occur in cycles, but either the interval between the occurrences is not always the same, being sometimes short and sometimes long, or the occurrences themselves are not quite the same, or both: for instance, spring is both late and unusually warm this year. Then too, some reoccurrences are not cyclical at all but come about only now and then. They come about regularly in certain circumstances, but the circumstances themselves occur irregularly, perhaps even infrequently. Sometimes we produce the circumstances: for instance, I have trouble sleeping when I drink coffee late at night. Regularities like these are also a model for us: whenever certain circumstances occur, we expect or know what will follow them. Finally, the occurrence of some events does not seem to be part of any pattern; they may never be repeated, like a single balloon ride. Still, the occurrence of even singular events should be understood. They were caused to occur, and if we can come to know the cause, even without its having occurred often and without having the occurrence impress us, we think we will understand the occurrence as an instance of a regularity that would be obvious if the cause were to reoccur. We might say that a one-time occurrence is an instance of a possible regularity or that it is the only instance so far of an actual regularity, or perhaps it would be better, as I think we will see, to regard it as illustrating an actual law about deeper and continual reoccurrences, as every other occurrence also does.

There are, then, varieties or degrees of regularity, and we must wonder why. Why are there reoccurrences at regular and irregular intervals? Why are there other reoccurrences only under certain circumstances? Why are there sometimes no repetitions along certain causal lines? Is it because our limited capacities do not let us see the same order all the time and everywhere, perhaps because we are able to recognize only a few kinds of similarities? Or is it because of the kinds of things there are in the world or their different natures or groupings, so that some act the same way all the time, some only now and then, and still others are often unpredictable?

The obvious answer to these questions—unless we suppose that the world might be very different from what we could ever know it to be—is that such differences as there finally are in the order or regularity of things reflect what is in the world itself. This is something that we can come to see through experience or that we must think to make sense of our experience. We may even have to think that there must be a basic order in the world and that other regularities derive from it but do not have its necessity.

Ideas of grades of order culminating in a highest or perfect order dominate the imagination of the classical Greek philosophers. Their notion is that the lesser orders are sullied versions of the higher ones, that they are lesser because the higher, purer ones cannot be preserved in certain materials, and that the least order is to be found in the least formed or most inferior of materials. They think that the ensured order is in the alternations between love and hate; that there is justice in due season; that there are forces that are expended uniformly; and that the world is continually being formed through an aspiration for the Good. Aristotle's explanation for the lesser and imperfect orders is that substances have their own natures that limit the degree to which they can imitate the continuous contemplative activity of the unmoved mover. It is important in Greek thought that the fullest order is either the regular alternation between opposites or otherwise a continual doing of the same thing. Even in the human endeavors where order seems to grow—in learning, the arts, and forming and administering political states—it grows from our increasing sight and imitation of the fullest, finest, and eternal order. No Greek supposes that more order and more intelligibility could develop from processes that are not as well organized.

The notion that order or regularity (or more successful adaptation) can arise from the less-ordered or less-adapted through thoroughly natural processes has, however, become prominent in the last two centuries. We have supposed that, to a point at least, order can evolve. There have been many reasons for this dramatic change of view, but it grew mainly from criticism of Greek ideas of causality: even were higher orders to exist they could not impose themselves on the matter of the world to enhance its regularity, nor does the matter change out of an aspiration for a finer, more independent regularity. The higher orders are neither the efficient nor the final causes of all the other orders of the world. Those who made this criticism therefore had to think of other causes for variations of order or the seeming changes in the natures of things.

Though there have been many conceptions of evolution, the most popular is that it proceeds mechanically, by efficient causes, so that no natural thing itself evolves and there is no unusual cause for evolutionary change. Instead, slight variations in the members of a species are preserved in procreation, and there can come to be circumstances in the surrounding world in which even these small differences among members of a species make a difference in which of them stay alive. The characters of the species thereby come to change more or less slowly, and it seems also to happen that species members whose characters favor their survival can no longer reproduce with those who do not have the favored characters but that have nevertheless managed to survive. Statistically, then, a new species originates, whether or not the older one survives, and the whole process proceeds by mechanical or efficient causation, which is how adjustment and procreation are thought to come about. There are no exceptional causes in biology. The same kinds of causes explain changes in both animate and inanimate objects; a single conception of causality supposedly suffices for the description and explanation of all the kinds of changes in the world.

Even if this were true it would not address the question whether, as the Greeks thought, there is a perfect, basic, or final law according to which all change takes place but only where and what such a law might be. Perhaps, as modern critics of the Greeks suppose, what makes for nature's regularities is not something eternal or otherwise apart from time, but then, if there were or had to be a basic law, we would have to think of it as being wholly within nature and of its order as not being owed to anything apart from time. Does what we know of nature suggest that there must be such a law? What must it be?

Our strongest sense about the world, though it is very vague, is that it must go on, that there must always be things that constitute it, and that these things must always move and change. This sense is far stronger than any specific expectation that this or that kind of event will reoccur, and it is perhaps difficult to account for our having it. It seems to be very different from expectation, for it is presupposed by the notion of experiences that sometimes lead to our having expectations and sometimes not. Perhaps the explanation for our having this sense is a consciousness of what Hume calls a principle of association, or perhaps, if we think that minds themselves come to be formed through a course of *experience* with things, our sense of the ongoingness of the world is an insight into the things that we *experience* or into the nature of the experience itself. In either case, our sense is that there is more continuousness in the world than occasional regularities.

A regularity concerns only our expecting or knowing that a Y will occur if an X occurs, but our sense of continued ongoing is that something will occur between the occasional occurrences of Xs and Ys and that something will occur even if X never occurs again. Things must happen all the time, and our sense of that's being so is not, in Hume's terms, a relation between the ideas of "happening" and "time" or otherwise analytic. Still, it seems, though vaguely, to be necessarily true of the world. And if it is, then there must be a basic law that is exhibited in all occurrences and that the occasional regularities of the world illustrate and specify. It will be unconditional—that is, not a matter of what will occur *if* something else occurs—and it will result from realities that are not themselves derived or in any other way dependent for their being on something else; derivations must come to an end. We may have to consider what such a law would be. This much, however, is already clear: the form of the basic law is that some final realities must always do the same thing.

It is interesting to note that many Greek philosophers came to this same conclusion, namely, that the basic order of the world results from the necessary and uniform activity of some fundamental reality. Plato explains his meaning by referring to the Good and the demiurge; Aristotle, by referring to the unmoved mover. Philosophers of more modern times who have explicitly held such a view—for example, Peirce and James, Bergson and Whitehead, and some modern idealists—have supposed that the basic order of the world consists of different basic realities or of their activities. We will have to find our own way. We have at least some idea of what we are looking for, namely, fundamental and necessary realities that explain the ongoingness of the world and that are basic in all that has, does, and will contingently occur.

Regularity and Law

There is more order in the world than is represented by our knowledge of its regularities. This knowledge is about the kinds of events that have occurred whenever circumstances of a certain kind have occurred, and we anticipate that if the circumstances occur again, events of the companion kind will also reoccur. Such regularities encompass what occurs now and then, either at regular or irregular intervals or only occasionally, but there is obviously some order in the world in the intervals. There is some order all the time.

How should we construe the order in these intervals? Should we suppose that on a single plane, as it were, and through a single course of events there is an instance of a regularity and then, in the subsequent interval, there is some other fill-in order, perhaps followed by another instance of our regularity and then another fill-in order and on and on?

There is no sense to this. It is artificial even to suppose that as things go on and on their procession is to be understood as taking place along a single line, as if nothing that occurs on any other line could have a bearing on them. What we should suppose instead is that our representations of a regularity are made at a certain level of generality and that the regularity we have represented is a special case of a more basic regularity; there might be other cases, too.

Regularities do not stand alone; each is a version of a more basic regularity, and each might itself become or be made more specialized. There is, for example, a regularity about smoking and disease, and there can be more specialized regularities about smoking and age and smoking and diet. Our notion, then, should not be that between the occasional instances of a regularity there is some other order of the same level of generality; it should be that for any instance of a regularity there is a more basic regularity beneath it that may reveal something about what order there must be between instances of our regularity. This line of thought leads to the conclusion that there must be a basic law, a basic order underlying all other regularities and that if there were no basic order, there could be no orders at all. Any order, then, should testify to there being a basic one.

The principle in this argument is that whenever there is an instance of a regularity that shows itself only now and then there is a deeper law that includes occurrences before and after the instances. If this is true, there will be deeper laws and still deeper ones, and we come finally to think of a different kind of law, one whose instances do not occur only now and then but that instead embraces every occurrence and all the times of the occurrences: we go from what occurs only now and then and here and there to what occurs always and everywhere. The form of this law is, therefore, that the most basic of realities are always doing the same thing. The next questions are what the basic realities are and what their activity is.

Our notion of their activity will not be full enough if we suppose that their actions and effects lie only on a single line of occurrences. There are distinguishable lines of occurrences: apples grow in Maine while salmon swim up Alaskan streams. Nevertheless, it is also clear that what occurs in one line goes with, or is coordinated with, what occurs in another; neither would have occurred if the other had not also occurred, though neither is the cause of the other.

This is virtually acknowledged in the cautious and protective remark that only in certain conditions is an X the cause of a Y. The condition is not a cause of either X or Y, but X would not cause Y without it. Because the world does not divide into separate worlds with altogether independent strands of causes and effects, our soundest supposition on this point is that what occurs along one line of actions is coordinated with what occurs in other lines of action—indeed, in all of them. At any and every time all the parts of the world are coordinated, more or less loosely. They are more or less clearly mated because of the ways that the occurrences affect one another then and there, or because of their relation to one another through their common past, or through their having become present together. There are something like Leibnizian windows in all occurrences.

In understanding the activities of the most basic realities, therefore, we should not imagine them to be additional occurrences along single strands considered separately, as if there were some same basic activity along or under each of the distinguished strands. It is convenient and practical to separate occurrences into strands, but they are not the ultimate order of realities. There is only a moment when individuals are singular, and even then there is some connection between them that is concerned with occurrences being at the same time. Everything that occurs does so at the same time as everything else that occurs; everything that occurs, as it occurs, becomes definite at the same time; and no occurring ceases to be present until it and every other occurring has become as fully definite as it can have become. There is some vast coordination between everything that occurs. What accounts for it?

Most philosophers who have thought about all occurrences being coordinated—not many have—have supposed that it cannot be explained by anything that causes or enters into the occurrences themselves. Whatever does that has been thought to be effective along only a single strand of occurrences and therefore too specifically located and too limited in power to produce the harmony that suffuses all the strands. Thus it seemed to these philosophers that there must be an additional and very powerful reality apart from what seem to be the causes of individual occurrences. Plato thinks of it as a demiurge that contemplates a single Good; all that it forms is coordinated accordingly. Aristotle thinks of an unmoved mover that is the final, but not efficient, cause of change and that in a way coordinates all changes in that substances try to imitate it. Descartes, Leibniz, and very many other philosophers (Whitehead in recent times) think there is a God who either creates the world or harmonizes the strands of its ongoing.

No such suppositions need be made, however, if we think that time and individuals are the basic realities and that their continuous activity is to have individuals continue themselves while time passes through and around them, continually making them past. The philosophers who suppose that a powerful reality coordinates the actions of entities make their suppositions because they think that, of themselves, the entities that act are wholly here and now and that they are not able to affect or be affected by many other entities, if any at all. It is not that individuals have the extraordinary powers that philosophers have imagined in their powerful realities; but then, those realities were imagined to have extraordinary powers just because the entities they governed were thought to be so isolated and so limited that they could not affect one another much.

This is not true of individuals. They are singular only in the present. They share their being in the future and the past, and when they become newly singular in the present they form themselves not only against one another but also on both their own and their common past. The past is massively effective in their self-formation. Individuals, therefore, need not be coordinated by a powerful reality apart from themselves. They coordinate themselves as they form themselves on their own and common past. Then too, individuals are made to be present and to become past by a time that comes into each of them as they are becoming present and that then spreads between them as well. These notes about the nature of time and individuals outline an explanation of such coordination and harmony as there is between them, despite their singularity.

Individuals are not substances, monads, or actual occasions; time is not a demiurge. If such entities rather than individuals were realities, there would have to be something in addition to them to explain how and when they are together. Nothing in addition to individuals and time need be supposed to explain how they are together. There might have to be a reference to a reality beyond them to explain something else—the good of the world, for example, if there is such a good—but not to explain (1) the coordination of the time and actions of individuals or (2) the fact that, in a present, each individual becomes fully definite. The outlines of the explanations of these themes should be familiar by now.

First, individuals have a common future when they are singular and present. The future time that passes to become a new present comes into singular individuals but is also common to them all. Inside them it dimensions them; outside, it exists as a space as well. The temporality of individuals or individual occurrences is a being together of time and individuals. It is because individuals penetrate time together and time as a single reality penetrates each of them that the times of occurrences are coordinated. Individuals resist and oppose one another only in the present. They constitute a contemporary world. Together, they cause time to pass both as far and for as long as it does. They remain contemporary as it passes; they are present for the moment and then become past together.

But why is it that each individual, as it becomes present and verges toward becoming past, becomes fully, completely, and equally definite? The answer depends, again, on the ways in which time and individuals are together. Time brings individualness into a new present, and it carries the individuals that are present into the past. It is part of their future, part of their past, and it is the passage in the process in which they form themselves. It is in the process from future to past that individuals have to become fully definite.

The future being of individuals is indefinite; their being in the past is fully definite. The present is the time in which that being of theirs that is future portions itself among singular individuals and the individuals make themselves more definite by acting out of the definiteness they already have. They take hold of their indefinite future being and make it definite; they form it on the more definite being in them that is becoming past. It is not true, as Whitehead supposes, that elements of definiteness must be introduced into occurrences to reduce the indefiniteness that is in them—just the opposite. Indefinite future being becomes present, and individuals make it definite through what is already definite in them.

Thus, the following four familiar themes explain the thorough and coordinated definiteness of individuals in and through the present: (1) Individuals are already partly definite in the present; they could not be present if they were not. (2) The future being that all individuals share becomes the being in each one of them; it is portioned among individuals as they continue to be singular. It is forced on them and passes through them, even while it is taken up by them. (3) The definiteness that individuals achieve as they form themselves on their past and on their opposition to one another is enough to render the being that comes into them entirely definite. What comes into the present in individuals is indefinite. However, it can remain neither present nor indefinite. (4) Time carries the indefinite being that comes into individuals onto the more definite passing portions of those same individuals; individuals make themselves singular against other individuals in definite ways, and they make themselves continuous with what they have been doing and what they have already done—they make themselves and are made to be continuous with what is passing in them and with their common past. I may not shape and fulfill my indefinite being in the way I want to, but it will be made full and definite nonetheless by what I and what others do.

Time continues to pass and individuals continue to act because of the way that time and individuals are together. They do the same kind of thing again and again, and their doing it is the most basic order of the world. The most obvious facts about the world are that the world goes on and that there is great variety in what occurs. The world must go on and there must be variety, though we can imagine that there may be more or less variety at one time than at another. The ongoing of things is necessary; there must be a world and it must go on. The variety in it, however, need not be the variety it is. There are contingencies in all occurrences. Why there is both necessity and contingency has to be understood, as do the connections between them.

Necessity and Contingency

The necessity for the world's going on is explained, I think, by there being time and individuals and by their having to be together in a way that leads both of them to act continually. Time and individuals could not be and be apart. Nothing stands between them or separates them;

they cannot even succeed in holding themselves off from each other, though this is what they try to do. Individuals act to continue themselves and time passes, and each does what it does because of the other. Individuals must reconstitute themselves and time must pass. Their acting to do the same thing again and again is the necessity in the world's going on; nevertheless, although individuals must continue themselves, there is no complete necessity in their continuing themselves as they do. There is some contingency in what individuals will do or how they will continue themselves, and all the other contingencies in the world, all the lesser regularities, derive from them.

It is difficult to understand both what a contingency is and if and why there is contingency in the world. The usual idea is that a thing or character is contingent if it need not have occurred, if something else could have come to be or could have occurred instead of it. In opposition to this idea, however, or almost in opposition, many philosophers have thought that whatever occurs is completely caused to occur by something that preceded it and that this cause is caused in turn, so that there is no place in a chain of causes where something different might have occurred; consequently, there is no possibility that things might have been different from what they in fact are. Many philosophers, perhaps most, think either that everything is necessitated or that nothing is, and in either case, it is impossible to understand why anything must occur at all.

For those who think that there are or must be both necessities and contingencies, that one does not preclude the other, the most common reconciliation is not that this or that particular occurrence could have been different, with everything else staying the same, but that, although everything in the world is necessitated, the world itself could have been different. Everything in it could have been different; its laws could have been different, there could have been different lines of causation, and so on; there are different possible worlds. Contingency, on this account, is about what is possible *before* the world begins.

This is not a credible reconciliation because it does not allow for contingency *in* the world. Where we think that this or that might have been different, the reconciliation says that, indeed, it might have been but only if everything else had been different, too. It is perhaps unclear just what we mean or should mean by "contingency," but it is very clear that we cannot mean what the reconciliation says. It supposes possibilities without giving an account of what makes it possible for there to be possibilities. It also supposes that possibilities are discrete, though this does not seem to be the case, and it gives no account of why or how any possible world is made actual or how, whatever the necessity for its creation or the contingency in it, it could have been made actual without being made actual all at once. The reconciliation tangles the modalities and multiplies them: there are possible and actual possibilities, a necessity for actualizing one of them, and then the one that is actualized contains a part that is not actualized as yet but is not longer merely a possibility. The modalities, in this reconciliation, are not soundly arranged.

It would be better to hold that there must be contingencies and that necessity is the basic modality. If possibility were basic, nothing would have to be, not even possibilities. How, though, can what need not come about be based on or derived from something that must be? How is contingency related to necessity?

The difficulties we have with these questions are insurmountable if we suppose that the contingent derives ultimately from some single basic reality. If that reality must be there can be no contingency in it or in what, because of its nature, it must do. We already know the difficulties in doctrines of creation and emanation and of other unfoldings of being—the difficulties, for example, in the doctrine that although human beings are free everything else that God created is not free. There are ingenuities in some of the doctrines, like supposing that the basic reality has to choose among possibilities or that there is a good in having something freely achieved. These ingenuities are useless. There is nothing real apart from a necessary being that could make for its having to make a choice, nothing that could stand in the way of its creating something or exfoliating itself, and nothing that could distinguish the being itself from what derives from it—indeed, there is no difference between the two and therefore no difference in their modality. If there is to be a contingency in the world, though, there must be a difference between what is of necessity and what depends on a necessary being but need not of necessity have become what it actually is. We also need to understand how this difference itself could have come to be.

We will, I think, come to this understanding by seeing that although nothing contingent can be derived from a single basic reality, contingencies can be derived from two of them, in particular, from time and individualness. How these basic realities are together explains why there are occurrences, why those occurrences are just what they are, and why some of the characters in those occurrences are contingent.

When we think of time and individualness as being real we should not think of them as being apart from what occurs. They are not removed realities, like distant gods who create what comes about in fact. They are what occurs, and they are the future and the past as well. Contingencies occur along with necessities. They occur because, although the basic realities are inseparably together, they also are and remain distinct. There is contention between them, or there is in the present, which is the only time at which there are occurrences. This contention within occurrences necessarily occurs and must be resolved, but the details of how it is to be resolved are not settled by necessity.

Time and individuals wrest with one another as occurrences, which is why there is an ongoing in them. Then and there, for the moment anyway, neither overcomes the other. One dominates in the future; the other, in the past. In the present there is contention between them that is being settled in and as there are occurrences. What is going on, or the outcome of it, is not exactly what it is until it is settled. The exact nature of an occurrence is therefore not derived from anything outside of it. What is apart from an occurrence—time and individualness—comes to be in occurrence, but how the two are together in an occurrence is settled by them only when they are there. It is the contention then and there, or the settlement of it, that makes for the contingent character in what occurs.

The usual notion that no occurrence contains a character contingently is the notion that its every detail is fixed to be just what it will become before the occurrence is actual; it is determined by something that is apart from the occurrence itself. The notion is usually that occurrences are only rearrangements of things that never change, which shows the roots of modern forms of determinism in classical mechanics. However, if we think that an occurrence consists of time and individuals being together in a new way, changing as they are present, then it is not merely a rearrangement of what they had always been but rather a transformation of the future being of time and the future being of individuals that yields something new. It is, or is the outcome of, exactly how time and an individual are together then and there, and although there must be an outcome, what it will be is not altogether fixed by what time or an individual or anything else has been before. It is fixed by time and an individual in the occurrence itself. The ways in which individuals act, the ways they form themselves on their pasts, the implacable passing of time—these make for as much predictability as there can be, yet something more is needed to constitute an occurrence, namely, the contention between time and an individual. The resolution of the contention is an occurrence's having fully determinate detail. An individual's becoming fully definite is not, as it were, simply a matter of having all of the properties that it could have and having each of them be made as specific as a property of that kind can be—as if the properties filled the *space* of an individual, breadth, width, and height. *Individuation* is not a matter of an individual's becoming or even being present, however, it is a matter of an individual's becoming past. As an individual becomes fully definite or is fully definite it possesses its properties, it has come really to possess them, so that it is part of the past of everything that has not yet come to be present. The so-called problem of individuation cannot be solved if we think of individuals as coming to be or as being only in a present time. For its resolution we must consider what it is that individuals come to be, and what they come to be is past.

There is, then, a basic order in the world; there must be one. It is that individuals act to continue themselves again and again and do not simply last, as atoms were thought to do. They change and act, they reconstitute themselves, and in the course of doing so they settle for themselves at each moment just what they are. The past has a bearing on what they will be, but they do not entirely determine themselves on it. Other contemporary individuals also affect what an individual does, but it is in their own acting that individuals make themselves singular and determine what they are. Determinists never allow that things can really act, but individuals must act because of time's passing into them, although they must act in certain ways and with other individuals, and they must conform themselves to the past. What they are or what they in fact become depends on their acting then and there, so although they must act and although their continuing themselves is the basic order of the world, there must always be some contingency in just how individuals come to have their characters and to make their characters their own.

There is even more contingency in the world's other orders or regularities. Individuals never act entirely alone; they also act together in groups, and the groups do not always do the same thing. The order or regularity of groups is not the same as the simple order of their constituents. It is more complicated, and there may be different degrees of order in it. The general form of such orders is that "things act in the same way, but only under certain conditions." The difference between the basic order and the other orders is the difference between "acting to do the same thing all the time in all conditions" and "acting to do the same thing some of the time in certain conditions." In some conditions, groups will always act in the same way, and in others they will act in a different way. It seems plain that, whether groups act in one way or another, their regularity and all grades and levels of regularity beyond the basic order somehow result from the basic one. Groups of individuals, however, whatever kinds of groups there are, aspire neither to imitate the basic order more closely nor to escape it entirely. The individuals in a group act only to continue themselves fittingly. Together, as á group, they do more than that. Their actions are the actions of a complex of individuals, and their order is a complication of the simple order of their parts. The basic order may not be prominent in the complex, but it is never without effect.

Our understanding of groups is very limited. We have only a little understanding of why there are groups, groups of groups, and other kinds of groups and of how these come to be and what causes them to lose their connectedness. The internal connections of only some sorts of groups have been mapped out. We seem to know more about medium-size groups than about very small or very large ones, and more about inanimate groups than animate ones. We seem to know more about electrons than cells and more about both of them than about bodies, minds, and societies. What is most obvious is that any group can do things that individuals separately cannot do. Our questions, then, are what they do and how, why, and when they do them. These questions are mainly about the agencies of groups, and there are special questions for those groups whose actions seem to be directed toward ends and that modify their ways of acting to achieve them. There is little overt repetitiveness in actions of these kinds, and we must therefore think that their regularity is not that they conform themselves to their past but that they follow certain principles, now in one way and now in another.

There is a basic order for individuals, then, and there are other orders for groups of individuals. There are continual and occasional reoccurrences, and perhaps the least obvious regularity is in always acting on the same principle but always doing different things. The only necessary regularity is the basic one: all the others depend on it. There are contingencies even in the actions of individuals, however, and these contingencies compound as individuals combine with one another to form groups, groups of groups, and, at last, the totality of things. What all the orders are cannot be deduced from the basic one, but not because of lack of sight. There is contingency in the basic lawfulness of individuals, and that contingency is compounded in contingent ways in groups and their actions. Their orders therefore must be found out, and it is likely that they are of different kinds. It is also likely, because there are contingencies in even the basic order, that all the other orders will change in time, though it is not certain whether those changes will be in the direction of more order or less.

Laws of Nature

The major regularities of the world or in our experience are often called "laws of nature." There are many philosophical questions about them, for example, what kinds of things they are, what they answer to if they are true, why things behave according to them, and whether the laws that govern now will hold in the future. Most philosophers, however, seem to think that there is little we can understand about laws of nature and little to understand, because a law seems to them only an obvious regularity in our experience and they think we cannot know what causes it.

In general, this is their view: in the same circumstances, things of a certain kind always or for the most part behave in the same way; we see how they behave, we remember how they behaved in the past, and we summarize our experience in such formulas as "the sun rises every day," "water freezes when it is very cold," "good bread is good nourishment," and "if something is an X then it will always or for the most part be followed by a Y." We can refine our sight and our formulations, and we may even search for regularities and force them into sight, but however refined our formulations, there is nothing more to laws than this, that among past occurrences certain ones are in certain ways similar, as are the conditions of the occurrences. The statement of such a past regularity is a law of nature. The philosophers who take this view usually add that no one can know why there have been regularities and, indeed, why anything occurs. Hume, for example, says that we have no experience of the secret springs that *really* cause our experience. Our experience is only of what is manifest to us, and it can tell us far less, Hume says, than speculative philosophers suppose. Still, our experience affects us; ample amounts of it lead us to have the expectations that Hume says become the great guide to life.

According to Hume, our expectations that certain things will come about are not reasons for thinking that they will occur; this observation was made earlier. A formula about Xs being followed by Ys summarizes some of our past experience. That cumulative experience somehow causes us to expect a Y whenever an X occurs, but it does not give us a reason for believing that a Y will come about, though we do believe that it will. It does not give us a conclusive reason or a reason of any other kind. There can be no conclusive reason for thinking that what we expect will come about because, Hume thinks, the contrary of such a state of things is conceivable, what is conceivable could occur, and what could occur cannot be proved to be impossible. There can be no other reason because experience has discovered no connection between what has already occurred and what will come about. Even if "All Xs have been followed by Ys" is true, a new X is not an instance of the formula about past Xs. According to Hume, nothing that happened to be true of those past Xs need be true of what will follow the new X; what was true of the other Xs might turn out to be true of the new X, but then again, it might not. Our past experience produces our expectations about what will occur, but because experience discloses only what is then and there it provides us with nothing like a reason for thinking that one thing rather than another will come about. Our expectations or our beliefs about the future are not the conclusions of any kind of reasoning. For Hume, there really is no reasoning—none about matters of fact and none even about the relations of ideas; in such so-called reasoning we simply arrange ideas so that we can see whether they are the same or not.

Some important parts of this account of experience are true, but some very important points about the nature of ideas and our experience of passing, transition, and activity are not sound. Hume thinks he has shown the base of our experience to be simple impressions, which are so clearly what they are that the simple ideas that copy them can never be confused with any other simple ideas. Except in some few and very special cases, however, experience does not show very plainly that there are simple impressions, and reflection does not testify to there being simple ideas—but then, perhaps impressions and ideas do not really answer directly to experience but have a place only in an analysis of experience and ideas that supposes there must be simples into which experience and ideas can be analyzed. Perhaps the insistence that there are such simples is based on the notion that without simple and altogether clear ideas there could be no clear compound ideas and this unclarity would preclude our making saving distinctions between the ideas that arise in a sound sense of experience and the confused ideas that lead to extravagant philosophical theory, theology, and sophistry. Hume thinks the latter lead to disabling skepticism and an unsettlement of the affairs of common life. It is almost as if Hume were telling us that we should understand ourselves and our experience so that we can see why there is sense and surety in the great routines of life.

But what is one to make of such ideas as a thing's lasting and changing and of one event's causing another? They are not simple, nor do they seem to be compound, and Hume has no notion of a simple complex idea. According to traditional empiricists, it is a mistake to think that these ideas arise directly from an experience of change or of an event's being caused. What we are said to see when ideas of lasting, changing, and causing are made really clear is that their origin is not in the experience of things but in our having certain ideas and expectations. So, for example, we may have had an experience of a thing's having a certain quality and a later experience of its having a different quality; we have different experiences, and so far as we can compare the ideas that derive from them, we simply note the difference. What we mean by a thing's changing is that, at different times, our experiences of *it* differ in some important way. We remember what something was; we see what it is; and our idea of change is an idea of something's being different at different times. There is no experience of change itself.

Something like this, as we have seen, is said to be true of causation, too. One event follows another, and if we experience like events occurring after one another over a period of time we come to expect that events like them will continue to occur one after another. To say that Xs cause Ys or that this X will cause a Y means only that those who have experienced Xs being followed by Ys expect that in certain circumstances a Y will occur whenever an X occurs. The word "cause" does not name anything that we have or could have experienced in our experience of Xs and Ys. We experience no connection between adjoining events, so the idea of one event's causing another is about events and an expectation or a habit of expectation in our minds. It is not about a transition between events themselves. One takes this view, very largely, because of notions about what seem to be the *contents* of experience.

There is a very different view in modern pragmatism. William James, for example, thinks that we really do experience the transition between successive states of the same thing and between one event and its successor. James calls this amendment to traditional empiricism a *radical empiricism* because of the other additions or changes that it requires in the earlier empiricisms, especially in the nature of the meaning of ideas. The basis for James's claim, and Peirce's, is not simply contentious: do we experience transitions or certain kinds of relations or not? One of the observations on which this claim depends is that traditional empiricism deals not with experiencing but with what we have experienced, with experience that has been completed, and there is no transition in a completed experience or occurrence as it is remembered. Content is what is remembered. It is then organized—first this, then that—and because there is no content to a transition, there is no idea of a transition in a completed experience. Such transition as there was in the occurring has passed. James, however, thinks that in the experience of one event's leading into its successor there is a transition, though it produces no impression of sensuous content. There is, perhaps, a point in a transition when it is unclear what the sensuous content is, but if all we can remember is the content of what we have experienced, if all our ideas are derived from simple impressions of distinct qualitative characters, then obviously we will think that we have not experienced a transition and that our experience has been only that there were different contents at different times.

This last notion—that there is a difference between experiencing something and having completed an experience of it—is very important in thinking about causation. There is a firm distinction in traditional empiricism between successive events, and it is thought that there is nothing between them because there is no room for anything to be between them. If one holds instead with James that we do experience a transition between events, then it is unclear just when one event is through and the other has begun; contents are smudged at their edges, and one cannot confidently say just when the two events are two. The distinction between there being one event and then another seems to be made both after their occurrence and for reasons that perhaps have little to do with what is in fact occurring. The transition itself is not plainly divided; it is not even, in itself, readily divisible, and because of this we can say that our experience of a transition is an experience of a cause or that the transition is a causal one. We might then represent our experience loosely as having been that "an X causes a Y," and the word "causes" would stand for something in what we experienced, something different from the content we had experienced and without sensuous content of its own. If we experience transitions, then, "cause" may stand for the transitioning that occurs in what we experience and in our experience itself. It is not just the name for a feeling that develops in our minds after we have had certain experiences.

There is thus a very important difference between the traditional empiricist's interpretation of, say, "Xs causing Ys" and a more radical empiricist's interpretation of that phrase. Hume and many other philosophers think the phrase should be understood to mean that "Xs have been followed by Ys and those who have experienced first an X and then a Y usually expect a Y to occur when an X occurs." The word "cause" does not appear in their analysis, and thus is said not to stand for anything in what we experience; it is a confused or shorthand reference to something else.

On the other hand, if we experience transitions, "X causes Y" (though the expression is perhaps somewhat loose) means that X causes Y: the word "cause" is not removed. Though complex, the phrase cannot be represented as a conjunction of phrases about only Xs and only Ys and the expectations that occur in the minds of those who experience them. "X causes Y" or "X will cause Y" is a simple though complex phrase, not a compound one, and if it is true, then just as the "X" and "Y" are taken to stand for something, "cause" must be taken to stand for something, too. It is not merely a grammatical feature of the phrase or an indirect reference to the expectations that persons of experience have been caused to have. What is true of the world points to what is real in the world, and if "X causes Y" is true as stated, then causes are themselves real. Of course, it is also true that persons who have experienced Xs being followed by Ys will have expectations about a Y occurring when an X occurs and will believe that it will occur, but there also will have been something that they experienced, some processiveness in things, that makes for a distinctive conviction in their expectation. Though this processiveness is not a distinct thing or quality separate from the X and Y as they are in the transition, it is real and furnishes for those who have had the experience a reason for their believing what they do.

This processiveness is something different from both the qualitative characters that are given in experience and the givenness of those characters. It is, however, not something that is ever apart from them, as if there were a processiveness but not of or in something. It is therefore something that takes its distinctive definiteness from the things, characters, and resistances in and through which it is the transition. C. S. Peirce characterized it, or something like it, as an active generality or an active general principle or cause, and that seems to me right. It is active in being a passing and general in being specified by the characters that are in the transition. The processive strand in our experience of things or in those things themselves is the ongoing in them. It takes its distinctive character from the entities in which and through which it is the ongoing, so that although it is distinct from them—though never apart from them—it affects and is affected by their characters. It should, I think, also be said to be the reconstitution of individuals and the passing of time.

The special importance of experiencing transitions is that what we experience becomes a reason for believing that certain things will come about: it is the basis for our thoughts. The most severe difficulty in Hume's philosophy is that Hume cannot explain how what we experience becomes an idea *of* anything. He thinks that a simple idea arises from an impression or a sensuous consciousness, but because he also thinks that an idea is no more than an impression preserved or copied, it is not significant; it is just what it is and not a sign of anything. Were content the whole of our experience we would need to do something more than preserve it to make it significant. We would need to do something to it or with it; we would need to make it be *about* something. Hume seems not to see this point; he certainly does not deal with it explicitly. The strongest doctrine he could have would be that merely in preserving what we can of our experience we establish an idea of it; from a quality of feeling we go to an idea of a quality. This is a very special and difficult account of consciousness, however, and there is nothing in Hume's writing that could be used in defense of it. Indeed, there is little or nothing in his writing to suggest that he even thought of it. For Hume and for traditional empiricism, ideas do not mean anything.

Kant's contribution on this point is of the greatest importance, and something like it is developed in radical empiricism and pragmatism. Kant's view is that ideas are not merely sensuous materials preserved or reproduced but rather that conceptions are constructed; sensuous materials are made to be significant by being combined in certain ways, by being taken up imaginatively and according to certain rules. Because of these rules or categories, the sensuous contents of one moment's experience are significant not of something beyond or underneath experience but of other contents that might or will appear to us in other of our experiences.

The critical issues in this view are about the construction of conceptions, the rules or categories for constructing them, and our using the conceptions to formulate judgments or beliefs. Kant deals carefully with all these issues, but the one I especially want to note is that in constructing the conceptions by applying the rules, the fundamental condition for combining imagined sensuous contents is that they be seen to have their preliminary organization in time or in space and time. Thus, the categories apply only to what is in time, so that we can form conceptions of what is the same over a period of time, of what will be the same at different times, and of what will be conjoined at the same or at different times.

What strains against this extraordinary condition is its ambiguous construal of time. Time is both the preeminent order of the content of our experience and also the formal condition for applying the rules in the construction of conceptions. In one of these, however, time is the time of a changing content, a time of before and after and now and then; in the other, it is purely a form for the representation of all times at once. It is as if time is both too close to the content of experience and too far away from it. The standard criticism of Kant—and a valid one—is that conceptions cannot be constructed as Kant thinks they can; his account is not even a reconstruction of how we come to our ideas.

The major alterations that Peirce makes of Kant's view, and that James follows in his own way, are (1) to view the categories not as rules for the organization of sensuous content but instead as the kinds of content we experience through the kinds of consciousness that disclose contents of different kinds (for Kant, it is as if all contents are simply sensuous and as if differences in "kind" are formal differences introduced by the use of the categories) and (2) to argue that time is itself something experienced not as a sensuous content but as the transitions of things. Peirce says that this transiency "pours in on us."

The most absorbing consequence of these themes is the view that ideas arise naturally for us. This is what Hume wanted to say about simple ideas, but he could not explain their meaning anything. Must we say, as Kant does, that the sensuous is not significant but is made so when we use it in constructing ideas? Peirce argues against this. His suggestion on this point is not that ideas occur to us because we have the kinds of minds that can construct them but that we have the kinds of minds we have because we have been able to discern something like ideas in experience. The narrowing supposition of much of modern philosophy is that ideas are only in our minds and there is nothing anywhere in the world that is at all like them, which makes it impossible to understand how thoughts could ever occur to us or where we could have ever gotten the idea of constructing them. Peirce's view, however, and James's, too, is that there is something in our experience that is in the nature of a thought, and once we come to have such thought we can develop it critically.

This something in our experience that is in the nature of a thought is that there is a "will be" and then a "could be" for all the sensuous content we experience, a sense that something is impending and, I think, that something has also been. No content is experienced without transiency—though when we are accomplished we can abstract the content and consider it by itself—and our apprehension of this transiency is the vague thought that something else will occur. It then may become the finer thought of what that something else could or will be. On this view, our experience contains a thought, and our own first thoughts are our experience of it. Thought, then, is not wholly constructed out of the sensuous materials of experience but is in its most basic forms experience itself. As experience of similar thoughts continues, it is as if, of itself, our thought gains clarity and becomes a kind of inference whose conclusion is that things like this are always or for the most part followed by these other sorts of things. Peirce thinks that for all the force or irrationality there is in nature, nature has its thoughts and reasons and that our experience is our first thought of them.

On these notions, then, our beliefs about how things are caused to come about are not simply our coming somehow to have expectations about occurrences, as they are in Hume's account. We do come to have expectations, but there is another explanation for their occurrence. They are grown; they grow from our ideas that something is impending, and they grow into ideas about what is impending while our belief in these ideas also grows with our clearer sight of how the things that come about form themselves on what precedes them. The generality and the conviction in our beliefs that things will come about or that Xs are the cause of Ys are not mysteriously produced by mind. They are the conclusions of a kind of reasoning, and they come about for reasons, too.

These pragmatic notions provide an account of causality very different from traditional empiricism's account. They also provide a different account of the laws of nature. The older empirical accounts characterize laws as summaries of previously observed like occurrences under like conditions. Regularities are interpreted differently if we think of ourselves as experiencing transitions between occurrences and if our experience convinces us of what the transitions are. "All Xs are Ys" does not merely summarize the past occurrences of the Xs and Ys we have experienced but expresses the belief that there is a bond or a transition or a continuous process between occurrences like X and occurrences like Y. Our experience is a reason for believing that there really is a bond or transition or continuous process between them, that this is how nature works, and we have no reason to think that it will change or change very much in the future.

Of course, we can imagine that, though Ys have followed Xs in the past, they will not or may not follow them in the future; there could be other sorts of occurrences instead, regularly or not. Hume says that because we do not know the secret springs that really cause the occurrences we do not know that this could not occur, and he also says that we would not contradict ourselves in supposing that it could; in other words, the occurrences of Xs and Ys are independent of each other.

Such imagining does not show much, I think, or it shows something too fabulous to be true: if Xs were regularly followed by Ys, if it had been observed regularly over a long while and in many places and were not a conjunction that showed itself, say, only in Edinburgh on the occasional rainy Thursday afternoons, then if a Y did not occur after an X had occurred, if something else occurred, as Hume says it could, its occurrence would be miraculous or nearly so. There would be no accounting for its occurrence—not that there could have been an accounting of the regular occurrences of Ys.

Hume himself discusses the possibility of miracles. His view is that, were there to be convincing evidence for a miracle, it would be more miraculous for the evidence to be false than for the miracle itself to have occurred. Hume's exercise in the logic of evidence, however one measures the more or less miraculous, shows the extent to which he thinks that we believe in regularities and what sort of experience would be required to unsettle our belief. Oddly enough, it is a consequence of Hume's own account that regularities themselves are miraculous and that, if we were really reasonable and not creatures of habit, the occurrence of fortuitous events would be just what we would expect.

Why so? How so? For Hume, the occurrence of every event is fortuitous. A Y might or might not occur after an X, whatever has occurred in the past, and the occurrences of Xs are likewise fortuitous. When there is a regularity of Xs and Ys, then, it is fabulous that Xs, which might not have occurred, and Ys, which might not have occurred, occur together and do so many times. If an occurrence that is a departure from a regularity is a miracle, how many more times a miracle is it that, of all the kinds of things that could have occurred, Xs and Ys should have occurred regularly. Any reflective person who shares Hume's view and who could control his mind (which is not something Hume thought we could do) should have no expectations about the future: anything can come about at any time.

Hume does not believe that anything we can imagine will occur, but not because he has a reason for not believing it. There is, Hume says, no refuting "academic skepticism," but our human nature sets aside the notion that the future might be loose. We are, Hume says, active as well as reasoning beings—indeed, in his view, we are more fundamentally active than reasoning beings—and where we are active in the affairs of common life our beliefs about there continuing to be regularities are firm and stable. They are modified, if at all, by the course of experience itself, not by possibilities that are only imagined; imagined possibilities are not sturdy enough to affect the customs and habits that guide our lives. We do not believe that what we have imagined might be so, but Hume still thinks that our imaginings might turn out to be true.

More than any other, the notion that enables Hume to imagine an exception to a regularity is the idea that successive events are independent of one another, or at least that our ideas of successive events are conceptually independent of one another: one billiard ball hits another, and we can imagine either that the second moves or that it remains in place. There is no logical contradiction in either thought.

If one event is continuous with an event that succeeds it, however, if there must be a transition between what we come to regard as two events, then not just any event can succeed the first. What can occur is what will fit with the first event, what will be continuous with it and can complete the transition. We can imagine events and think of any one of them as being located after an event that has in fact occurred, but events do not come about by being relocated, by being moved from an imagined or a possible world into an actual one. They grow out of prior events, or they are formed on them, or they result from the further actions of the agents in the first events.

Our experience does not consist only of little dots of qualitative consciousness and momentary givenness, as Hume supposes it does. Transition and continuity are themselves experienced, though not in separate, simple sensuosities. Our experience of them is our experience of things being this and our thinking of their changing, then their being not quite this and not yet something else, and finally being something else. It is of these being one after another, without a sharp distinction between any two, and arises from separate apprehensions of simple qualities or from separate impacts in which the impressions of those qualities are given.

Our experience is spread in time; it is not momentary. There can be no experience that takes no time at all. The only feasible distinction we can make in experience so we can think of ourselves as having had different experiences is in what we experience. Thus, we can say that we had the experience of this and then the experience of something else, but we can make such a distinction only when we have a sense that our experience is no longer of this quality but is or is beginning to be an experience of another. Unless experience occurs in blinks, unless there are distinct experiences because there are distinct units of consciousness—and there is no reason to think that either of these is true—then our experience must include transitions between qualities, and transitions require a spread of time. Our present consciousness, like everything present, contains a coming to be and a becoming past.

How are we to understand the transitions in things? How are we to understand what things are so that we can understand that what we experience are transitions in their states or qualities? Three sorts of answers have already been considered several times:

1. There are enduring things, and changes in their states or quali-
    ties result from the things themselves or from other things and
    other kinds of things that act on them.
2. Changes of state or quality arise from the actualizations of
    already definite possibilities. The actualizations are units or
    moments of process. Appropriately provided possibilities coa-
    lesce around a definiteness that has been inherited from past
    actualizations.
3. The transitions are the processes in which individuals continue
    to become singular, as the future being they share with other indi-
    viduals comes into them and is made definite in those individuals
    while they form themselves on those portions of themselves
    that are becoming past and on the other individuals that are
    contemporary with them.

We must ask which of these constructions provides the fullest sense
of our experience of the transitions in or between things or events.
Neither the atomic nor the Aristotelian form of the first construction
seems to suffice. Neither classical atoms nor what are thought today to
be the truly elementary particles change in themselves, and the only
change of them is in their place and, therefore, their configuration.
Moreover, these changes must be calculated, and we have little notion
of how the sensuosities of our experience are related to them. Our
experience is of secondary qualities. Even if there were transitions in
the experiences of which those qualities are constituents, we could not
reliably infer anything about the motions of the real atoms of the
world.

Aristotelian substances, on the other hand, are thought to change in
themselves, so there is a kind of transition in them, but Aristotle
provides no notion of how transitions come about. The potentialities
of substances do not change or change a substance; the substances
are passive, and it is difficult to see how the forms of substances can
be thought to be active and a cause for change. I suggested earlier
that if entities thought to be wholly actual cannot also be thought
to contain a quiescent power, then we should think that their power
is not a part of them when they are present; instead, the effectiveness of a power is exhibited in them as they change—but then this suggestion is not appropriate for substances; it is about entities of another
kind.

The second conception is also insufficient. The process it characterizes is not a transition within an occasion but the formation of an occasion itself, and there is no transition, no continuity, between one occasion and another. In "each moment," Hartshorne says, speaking for himself and Whitehead, "there is a new determinate actuality." These new occasions take account of their predecessors, but they do not continue them; one follows the other, but there is no transition between the two.

The conception of an object necessary to account for there being transitions in or between things or events seems, then, to be that objects change not only in their positions and their qualities but in their very being. Such an object is called an "individual." In being and continuing to be singular an individual continually changes itself. It is continually in transition; it forms on its past that new being of its own that comes into it, and it also forms itself against its contemporaries. The time that passes through it is the cause and measure of its process, but what an individual specifically is and becomes depends on it alone.

It seems, then, that we must suppose the conception of individuals and of a time that passes through them to account for the transitions in our experience of things. Because our experience of things can also be a true judgment about the things themselves, the things themselves must also be individuals. They are entities that continually form themselves, and their being or their becoming accounts for the most basic lawfulness in the world and for all of its genuine regularities.

The most basic lawfulness of the world is that things go on and go on together. There may be different rates at which they move or change, but we can think of them as having different rates only if we think of them as being together. The way to think of them as being together is not to see them moving against an unmoving, endlessly present background time but to think of the finally real individuals as being activities when they are present and as being constituted by a future time that comes into them and that then becomes spatial as well. The entities that constitute the world could not continue to exist if there were not a real future, nor could they have come to be what they are unless there were a real past, and this is true of individuals at any present time.

What things are, what groups of things there are, and what both will become depends on how individuals form themselves. Their basic regularity is that they form themselves, so far as they can, in the ways in which they formed themselves in their own immediate past; the world does not begin anew in every moment. Individuals may not be able to do just this, however; their pasts may themselves be changed as their contemporaries become past, their contemporaries may change, and they may otherwise have to change the ways in which they form themselves. Our experience may assure us that some individuals and some groups of individuals do not change their ways of forming themselves or do not change them much or often or radically. Some sciences suppose that the entities and groups they study never change, at least in certain ways, and that they can confidently predict what will occur for as many years ahead as they care to calculate. Our predictions for those groups that do change are short-term and less secure. The laws of nature, or laws of any kind—economic, political, psychological, and social—may take different forms. Not all need be expressed in the form of recurring pairs of occurrences; for example, some may provide for the calculation of quantities. All regularities and all laws, however, depend finally on individuals continually forming themselves as closely as they can to the ways they formed themselves before. This is the fundamental constancy in all the changes of things. It is how the future is determined when it becomes present, and it will continue throughout the future, even if the laws of nature change in ways that we cannot foresee.

CHAPTER TWELVE

EPILOGUE: TIME AND VALUE

E VEN THOUGH everything is always changing, many philosophers
think that anything we know to be true is true not only for a time
but forever. Truth does not change; what is true is always true. Some
philosophers even say about a truth that it was and will always be true,
even though there was a time when it was not known and there may
come a time when no one will think of it. The things that it is a truth
about may themselves change or even cease to be, but what was true of
them as they were at a certain date is true of them forever. Philosophical idealists as well as others think it sound to suppose that truths are
permanent. Many of them also think that we should have the same
view of the value of our actions.

They think that if an action of ours is good or better than anything
else we might do, then its goodness will be a fact both before and after
we perform it. An action, they think, does not change its value. If it
was good in prospect it will be good in the doing, and it will always
remain good that we did it. Likewise, the bad, the trivial, and the
worthless have those same values at every time. Our judgments of such
values may change over time, but that will be simply because we were
mistaken about what the values really are: we may think that something
is good in prospect but then discover when we are doing it or when it is
done that it was not good after all. Or something may appear to us bad
but we come later on to think that it was really good. Theologians
often say to those who are perplexed by the great evils God permits
that, in the whole of God's plan, what now seems an evil will be seen
to be what it already is—good, necessary for the perfection of the world.
They believe that without faith we do not know enough to see the
real value in what occurs. Our sight of the values of actions, then,
and our judgments of them may waver, but in the opinion of many
philosophers, the values of actions, like truths about the world, are
fixed and firm. They must be so because actions are only at one place

in time and cannot have one value at one time and another at another time.

Two pictures of where actions are in time support the idea that actions have only a single value. One of them is that actions exist only when they occur, when they are present, when we and the things around us use our powers to form the kind of intentional configuration that is both an action and a fact. Forming the configuration is the action, and the action has its value then and there. We may anticipate what the action and its value will be, and we may remember it, but the action has its value only when it occurs. It is really at only one time, so there is obviously no question of its having different values at different times.

The second picture—the idealist's picture—is very much the same, only it supposes an action to be not just something then and there but a manifestation of something even more real than the action itself. The argument on behalf of this picture is that there is something artificial and even unintelligible about the idea of a single action. Actions are inseparably connected with other actions; indeed, there are no single actions at all. Actions seem to be actions and seem to be single only as they occur; how we experience them is how they seem to us to be. It is the same way, Royce says, with a note or a phrase in a piece of music: the composition itself is, as it were, all there, all at once; we hear it part by part, but we can even then comprehend the whole of it. The second picture says that we should understand actions similarly to have a place in the whole of a series of actions, a series that is all at once but that appears to us sequentially. The real value of an action, then—like the real value of a musical phrase—depends on its place in and contribution to the whole of which it is a part. Because it has its place once and for all there is no question of its value ever being changed, nor can the value of the whole ever change.

Both these pictures of action are deeply unsound, and their notions of the kinds of values that actions may have are insensitive. We have already seen that neither of the pictures can explain why or how anything occurs: the first cannot explain what things are and how and why they must act; the second cannot explain why there are occurrences, why the real appears to us as a sequence, or even why—if the real is real—there should be anything to whom its can appear. Both pictures have to be set aside and such insights into values as they have should be changed somewhat.

Their insensitivity about values is that they fix too firmly on the value that actions have when they occur or on their part in a series of actions that has a value of its own. They come then to slight, disregard, or misinterpret the other values that are implied in their own views. For example, if we think that an action would be good to do, what is the value of *what* we think to do? It is not the same as the value of the action itself, but it is not valueless. Even if only as something imagined, the *what* has a value, as does the act of imagining. If we suppose, as the second picture does, that actions or occurrences are manifestations of something both more real than themselves and really valuable, the manifestations still have a value, and we will want to understand what kind of value it is. Is it the same as the value of the reality it manifests, only diminished somewhat? Or does a manifestation transform the most real value into a value of another kind? In both pictures there are more values, perhaps more kinds of values, than the pictures themselves represent, and those values are slighted in the pictures. We should like to have a balanced account of them, but this account should also reflect the theme on which both pictures seem so clear—namely, that an action has its value and can never come to have a different value of the same kind.

This more balanced view must first, I think, have a changed account of action. For example, it must set aside the notion that acting things have their whole being in the present time. Entities that have their whole being in a present time cannot act at all, as Descartes showed. The balanced view must also set aside the notion that an action is wholly a manifestation of a reality outside time, for we cannot understand how and why such manifestations could come about. What one should say instead, I think, and what I have argued in this essay, is that though individuals change and act only in the present, they are also partly past and partly future and that it is because of their being so that they can and must change and act. I think we should also say that something whose being is really apart from the present becomes manifest in action—on this point the idealists are right, in general—yet the reality that becomes manifest in the present is not something apart from time; it is rather that being of individuals that is in the future and that becomes manifest in the present when it is made to become present by passing time. In this view of time and individuals, then, important points in two important pictures of action are preserved. In my opinion, only those parts of the pictures that cannot be understood have been replaced.

What changes should be made in what the two pictures have to say about values? They are right that the value of an action *as an action* does not change and that we can change our minds about what its value is, but the pictures are otherwise wooden about values. They seem to represent them as if the same kind of value were always in question—namely, the value of an action—and they are insensitive to what we judge when we judge whether an action is, was, or will be good.

The change that should be made in these views, I think, is to see that there are three parts of time matched to three kinds of value: there is the future, the present, and the past, and there is aesthetic, moral, and historical value, the kind of value that something has in being historically significant. So the view I suggest is that what is future, or what we can imagine might be brought about, has aesthetic value; that our actions in the present have a moral value; and that when those actions become past, they have a historical value. It is thus true that an action does not have one value at one time and a different value of the same kind at another time, but it is also true, I think, that over time there are changes in the *kinds* of values that actions have.

As we think of what we might do, *what* we think of has aesthetic value, good or not. When we do what we imagined and then thought to do, *what* we do, or our doing it, has moral value; we transform something that had aesthetic value into a doing that has moral value, good or not, though there will remain an aesthetic strand in it. When *what* we do is done and our action has become past it comes to have historical value or significance, good or not, colored with some of the moral and aesthetic values it previously had. The kinds of values that things have depend on where they are in time and change as time passes. What is imagined is aesthetically good or not; if and when we enact it, it becomes morally good or not—and it can be a lesser or a greater good morally than it was aesthetically. When it becomes past, it has historical significance, good or not, and it can be a lesser or greater historical good than it was a moral good when it was going on.

This adjustment to the notion that the values of action never change is, I think, sensitive to the variety in our judgments of value, to there being kinds of value and to what seems to be the change over time in the kinds of value an action has. It enables us to reinterpret the harsh cruelties in some of our judgments—for example, that what is really terrible when it occurs shall be seen to have been really good all along—and it enables us to reinterpret the blundering calls for redeeming action and the stiff-necked claims that redemption is impossible. Above all, it calls for us to aim not for this or that kind of value alone but for all the kinds of goods there are. This is the Good at which we are to aim; it also seems to be the good with which, by nature, we are concerned, however dimly we may see it and however often it is changed in its specific nature. The questions are whether this view of time and values is true and whether it has other values, too.

The future is real but indefinite. When we think about what we might do we first imagine it, and what we imagine has in itself an aesthetic quality. Though we may have many interests in what we imagine, in our aesthetic apprehension we consider it without any further interest at all. Aesthetically, as everyone notes, we consider what we imagine as it is by itself, apart from even a possible relation to anything else. Doing this is considering the quality it has as a whole. It may not be a quality that engages us, but whether it does is not part of the nature of the quality itself. When such qualities are considered in themselves there are differences between them in the measure of unity they have, for example, material differences and formal differences, but there is no question of rank or grade in qualities. There is no sense in one quality, considered aesthetically, being more valuable than any other. There are just different qualities.

When we rank or judge aesthetic qualities we think of something besides the qualities themselves. We think not only of whether we are pleased or repelled by them but also of whether we would like to have them incorporated in objects and actions. A judgment is the conclusion of an imaginative experiment on the qualities we imagine and on the objects that might be made to exhibit them. As far as we are able to, we imagine the feelings, moods, and interests in which we might turn to consider the qualities, and we ask ourselves whether the qualities would affect us so that we would be thoughtfully and appreciatively absorbed in them. The conclusion is a judgment of the qualities' power to engender and sustain a consciousness of feelings that we feel would contribute to the fullness of our experience.

Our first judgment about what we might do is thus an aesthetic one: what we imagine is admirable or not. If it is admirable and we cannot feel ourselves sustained in only the thought of it, we resolve to act on it. This is our sense of having to enact what we have imagined, though it is usually our sense of something's having to be done that leads us to imagine what it might be. Our aesthetic judgment is not itself an impulse to action. Indeed, there is no special impulse to action; we are always acting and are always concerned to act, and the question of what specific action we shall perform depends on the fittingness of our concern to act with what we imagine we might do. When we are young and there is almost no consistency in our conception of what we are concerned to do we do almost anything we imagine. When we are more consistent and can deliberate on our concern and on how things can be brought about, we are willing to do only some of the things we have imagined—though our concern often becomes so stiffened that it would be good for us if we were unsettled by a flush of imaginings. In either case, our action gives what we have imagined and valued aesthetically a place in an action that we value morally. The transformation of an aesthetic value into a moral one is a deep change in it.

An aesthetic value is transformed into a moral one when we approve of as an end something that we have imagined and appreciated and when we act to bring about that end. The value is not transformed until we act. Nothing has happened to it when we judge only that it would be good to do what we have imagined; something has happened to it, however, when we judge that it was good to have done what we did. Such judgments express our moral approval of an action. They take note of moral value, and making such judgments is perhaps itself a moral act, but the moral value of the acts they approve is in the acts themselves. It is the valuing of means as means and ends as ends. The transformation, then, is that in enacting what we have imagined we thicken our valuing of it by embedding it in a *doing* that is also of value because it has an end; two values are joined. It is nevertheless not true that the moral value of an action is always greater than the value of its end considered aesthetically. It may or may not be, depending on its end and what happens in enacting it. We all remember the importance of this theme in Plato, where it is not clear that we should try to construct the ideal state because we know that we cannot do it ideally. It is also very important in those theologies that reflect on God's nature, his creation of the world, and the value of the world itself.

The valuing that occurs in an action, the approving and disapproving that guides the action, appeals not only to the end of the action itself but also to something that enables us to approve or not approve of ends and of the ways in which we enact them. This is often and rightly thought to be our ultimate and final aim in action: it is an aim in the sense that we aim in all our actions to approve of the end of our actions and to judge any changes in those ends because of the ways in which we enact them. We want finally a consistency in our judgments and ourselves, in what we think and do, and we come to it within a final aim.

Such an aim seems beyond imagining, though our apprehension of it may proceed through images and be stabilized by them. It is something we think of, and our thought of it, it seems, can never be wholly wrong—our thought would not be a thought of *it* if the thought were wholly wrong. Our final aim is also something with which we judge, and our judgments are never wholly wrong. From time to time we change our judgment of the value of what we have done—approving of something at the time we did it, say, but later on not approving of our having done it. In changing and correcting our judgments, though, we do not change our final aim; we had some sight of it even in doing what we came to disapprove, and there was something in what we did about which we were surely right. Our disapproval of an earlier action is never a thorough disapproval; we cannot be thoroughly out of touch with our final aim. Not even Leibniz's God could have imagined a world there would be no good in creating. We think of our final aim, we imagine something like it, we use it in approving what we do, and because we are always acting, we are always acting on it, too.

Many philosophers believe that what we ultimately aim to do is to be very like or be in accord with a final reality; because it is timeless, this reality can be a final end for all of us, and its nature is so beyond our own that none of our devotions can ever be fully fitting to it, which is why it is endlessly demanding.

This is an exquisite and inspired conception of the object at which we finally aim. It is not clear, however, whether it is a conception of the human good or whether it is not too far removed or inaccessible. Nor is it clear whether, if there were such a reality, anything else could in any sense be good. It seems to me that although we should think of ourselves as ultimately aiming at a reality, our final reality is not something apart from time but is instead the whole of the past, the present, and the future and all the value there is and can be in them.

This object of our final aim is not something we can become clear about once and for all time. In each era, even in each moment, what we must do is make definite and effective for ourselves new versions of the good. This is the kind of thing we do in seeing that we have lived too much in the values of the past, too much in the present, or too much in the hope that our failures will be redeemed. There are different kinds of values, not just one, and our conception of our final aim should include them all and take account of how they change.

The good at which we finally aim is not any one of the kinds of values but all the kinds made to be beautifully and morally together, with each enhancing the values of the other kinds—aesthetic values contributing to moral values and high moral values contributing to a historical significance that in turn prompts fresh verges of imagination, and on and on. We have a sense for the quality and fittingness of values, one kind with another, and this sense can guide us, though we must always make it definite. Times and values change, but there is no change in there having to be a sense for the fullness of values in the fullness of time. Our own value is diminished if we do not always allow this sense to guide us. Leibniz did not tell us whether it was difficult for God to think of the best of all possible worlds, but however difficult it was God had to do it only once. It seems to me that we must think of a different best possible world every day.

The moral value of an action is in the action itself. We intentionally bring different kinds of things together in an action, and as together, the value they have is the aesthetic quality we had imagined, qualified by the value of their being made to fit with one another in the way we think it best for them to be combined. It is very difficult to construct an action in which there is a great deal of value; doing so depends on our insight, our imagination, and our skill and virtue in dealing with the elements. These can be extreme and intractable; each can seem to have an end of its own. Most of our actions are so habitual that we do not pay attention to the value in them, which is why we think that genuine moral value is so unusual. All actions, however, have moral worth. They all have ends about which we can be circumspect and responsible; they all can show our care and craft. There is also some value produced and undergone in each.

The value produced in an action is judged from outside it; the value undergone in an action is undergone inside it. From the outside, the moral value of an action is judged by comparing and combining two judgments, a judgment of *the action* first as it was when it was prospective and then as it is when it has been done. These tell us how good the action could have been and how good it was. The judgments bracket the action and render its moral value indirectly, which is why we learn so little about the nature of moral value from them.

Moral value is formed inside an action. There is deliberation and control as well as thoughtful looking forward and back, but the thoughtfulness is about the doing, not merely about a prospect or the accomplished outcome of enacting it; thoughtful doing is always between a prospect and an outcome. A person who acts feels the fittingness of the action as it is going on; this feeling is the person's undergoing its value. There is a two-sidedness in action, and the actor feels for the action's going well or not. Outside judges have only an intimation of this value.

Matters are much as Plato and Aristotle say they are on these issues, for example, in Plato's discussion of the training of physicians and judges and in Aristotle's discussion of the development of virtue: young persons are nurtured to courage by imitating courageous actions, for instance, but they are not courageous unless they do the actions *as* the courageous do. In acting, the courageous are thinking about the most extreme and demanding mean and enacting it. The young are straining for a mean that is beyond and not really relative to them, but they are acting as morally as young warriors are able. The courageous are truly acting morally, perhaps all the more—this is the aesthetic note in moral action—if they are doing the actions well.

Moral and aesthetic values stand differently to time. The aesthetic is always prospective and has to do with a quality, or a quality of qualities, that might be brought about. The moral has to do with bringing it about. There is also a third kind of value, namely, historical value or significance which concerns the value of things that is worked out in time. Many philosophers, however, seem to think that it is either not real or not different from values of the aesthetic or moral kind.

Many philosophers deny historical value because they suppose that the past is not real. They think that the value of an action that has been done is the value it had when it was present, and they enjoin us to remember it, as if there were some further good in doing that. We are besieged with such enjoinders: museums, memorials, holidays, anniversaries, and rituals all aim to bring to mind what things were at the time that they occurred, though there are other purposes to them as well. The usual notion is simply that what occurred was good or not when it occurred and that there is a good in remembering or knowing about it, even if it was bad.

But if, as I think, the past is real, then there is also a value in our relation to what is in it. There is a distinction between what something was when it was present and what something is as it is in being past. One kind of value is found in the first and another kind in the second: the first is moral value; the second, historical value or significance. In becoming past, something that had moral value comes to have a value of a different kind.

For example, consider the past horrors in past wars. What are we to make of them? They were horrible of course, but what more? We should always acknowledge that they were horrors and should not forget them, but what more? We should—and do—resolve that such horrors shall never occur again, but what does such a resolution come to? It can be paltry and trivial, a matter only of words that leaves most losses to be borne in vain. The resolution will have body, though, if we see that our actions in the present are formed on what is past and that our resolution really has to do not with the airy business of not enacting certain possibilities but with the muscular business of precluding powerful influences, with continually forming the actions that grow out of a past we in part still despise.

The value of the past consists in how we can affect how it affects us while yet having to submit to it. In our concern for all that can be brought about we are concerned for all that has become past, and we can change the way in which it has its effectiveness. It is this to which real resolution directed. We cannot change the past or undo anything that has happened, nor can we make up for it. Neither are we to do nothing about the past because, as some theologians think, it is and was good even when it was present, a part required in a divinely perfected world.

The notion I am suggesting is that there can be no assurance of the perfection of the world and no assurance of any balancing or redemption for the imperfections or even the evils that have occurred. An evil is an evil and not an unavoidable means in the perfection of the world. The malicious is malicious and nothing else; the unconscionable is unconscionable. But things move on and time passes. What we have been right to approve and right to condemn becomes past and changes in doing so. The kind of value things have changes, too. To think of what is past as it was when it was present is to fail to understand both what it is and its bearing on what we might and perhaps should still do.

There is no making up for what has become past and no erasing it. What we can do, though it may not come to much, is adjust the way in which what is past has its effect on what we do. The past has mighty effects in the present, not by acting on it—the past has no agency—but in the way in which we shape and form ourselves on it. It is the basis of all the definiteness in what comes about. We may not know much about the past, we may forget what occurred, we may lie and falsify our histories—still, the implacable past always has its way with us, one way or another. In the agency of our own making and doing, however, we can affect the way in which it affects us, and we should, depending on the value we think it has.

For many of us, there are dark notions about the past and about the prospect of our own becoming past. It can seem to us that nothing we have done has really come to anything. It can seem to us that except for memories of us in our children and friends it will be as if we had never lived at all. The mood I mean is not the mood in which we think of what we have done and think that it would have been better to have done other things instead; the darker thought is that nothing we have done really comes to anything. Everything, we think, will pass away, and all our value will be lost.

Much of what we see in this mood is, I think, sound, but its abysmal and terrifying darkness stems from our not understanding how we stand to time, especially our not understanding that the past is real and that the value of what we have done is preserved in the past, though as a value of a different kind.

It can be deeply disheartening to sense the difference between what something is in prospect and what it becomes in fact; I mentioned previously how Plato felt about the imperfection of the objects that participate in pure and perfect forms. It is nearly the same when our actions become past, even the most worthwhile of them. The actions are transformed, their values are transformed, and then, in the massiveness of the past, our actions are very small and they contribute very little to the past's effectiveness. We may have thought of ourselves as mighty, though that is vanity, of course. The terrible issue is whether what we have done has any value at all. What good was it to have been concerned for the moral and the aesthetic good?

We know how the issue is usually discussed: doing the good is good itself, and we should be content with that—besides, our having acted well may, some think, have a bearing on our immortality. My answer is that what is morally good is good but that it also becomes a value historically, in some measure or degree. It will not be a mighty good, it might not even be a good at all, but it will be a part of something that will have some value for the future. If we also understand, as I think we should, that we, too, are singular only in the present but that our being is future and past as well, we may, even while we are present, have some patience with what we really are.

The singularities that occur in the present are not of incomparable value. What is of incomparable value is value in the whole of things or the changing value in the whole of things. What is of incomparable value is what can be, what is produced, and what is effective as a past. In our concern for the whole of things and for the ceaseless changing of value within it we can for a time have the measure of the different values that have their places in the different parts of time. We should measure our own value in that light, too.

There is a way, then, in which the timeless is a measure of the value of what is in time. Time is a reality, and all that is, was, and can be valued by individuals is a part of it. We have a sense at each moment of how full that value is, of whether we are too dull, too much given to imaginations, too careless and unartful, or too routinely dominated by the past. The fullest good is the good for all of time, but time passes, the fullest good changes in its composition, and what we do changes in its kind of value. There is in each moment a conception of the fullest good for the world, which never changes in being the fullest good. It is as staid as the sameness of a truth, only it must always be filled in by the actions of individuals. Something like that should be true for truths, too. Being merely true is not as valuable as truths can and ought to be.

ACKNOWLEDGMENTS

THE MOST general idea in this essay is that what is real is an unchanging totality; there can be no additions to it, and nothing can be taken from it. This does not mean, however, that things do not change and that there are no novelties. It means that all processes and the passage of time itself take place inside the otherwise unchanging totality. For some time, I saw but had not collected the parts of this idea. My colleague Thomas Seung helped me to a fuller sight of it. He also once said that though I thought there were many individuals, there was a Spinozistic strain in my ideas. I had not studied Spinoza's thought then, but I turned to it because of Seung, and it was a pleasure to learn from it. The other philosophers who most influenced the ideas in this essay are Aristotle, Descartes, Leibniz, Kant, Peirce, Whitehead, Paul Weiss, and, most of all, Plato. Indeed, it might be said that the only thing I have done is set the forms, the flux, and the demiurge in time. I do not think this is true, but I can understand someone's saying so. Because of the ways in which I have thought of Plato's idea and the ideas of the other philosophers I have mentioned, here and there criticizing them and adapting them, I hope it will be plain on what points I have learned from them. I have also learned a great deal from Sally Colbert, Timothy Ferris, Susan Foster, Joyce Goldstein, Paul Ilie, Novella and Albert McKinney, A. J. Langguth, Franklin Mitchell, Nancy Negley, Lynn O'Leary-Archer, James Stramel, and Alan Yamahata. They helped me to see which parts of this work were most unclear, which were too labored, and which most needed support and argument. I was also given special help by Bruce Bethell, who edited the manuscript with great care. I want finally to mention my indebtedness to the late David L. Miller. He and I often talked about time. We were close colleagues for many years in the University of Texas at Austin.

INDEX